STORYTIMES
for Two-Year-Olds

Second Edition

Judy Nichols

Illustrated by Lori D. Sears

AMERICAN LIBRARY ASSOCIATION
Chicago and London   1998

While extensive effort has gone into ensuring the reliability of information appearing in this book, the publisher makes no warranty, express or implied, on the accuracy or reliability of the information, and does not assume and hereby disclaims any liability to any person for any loss or damage caused by errors or omissions in this publication.

Project editor, Joan A. Grygel

Cover by Baugher Design

Composition by the dotted i in Bookman and Tekton on QuarkXpress v 3.32

Printed on 60-pound Finch Opaque, a pH-neutral stock, and bound in 10-point coated cover stock by Edwards Brothers

The paper used in this publication meets the minimum requirements of American National Standard for Information Sciences—Permanence of Paper for Printed Library Materials, ANSI Z39.48–1992 ⊗

Library of Congress Cataloging-in-Publication Data

Nichols, Judy.
    Storytimes for two-year-olds / by Judy Nichols : illustrated by Lori D. Sears. — 2nd ed.
        p.   cm.
    Includes bibliographical references and index.
    ISBN 0-8389-0719-9
    1. Storytelling—United States.   2. Children's libraries—Activity programs—United States.   I. Sears, Lori D.   II. Title.
Z718.3.N5   1998
027.62′51—dc21   97-44295

Printed in the United States of America.

For Jim . . . for his love and support . . . forever.

In honor of Lucy Gallup, who shaped me into a librarian
and never once doubted the choices I made.

In loving memory of Nancy Renfro,
whose inspiration and *joie de vivre* are missed.

Contents

Preface

Sixteen years ago I faced my first toddler storytime armed with a few journal articles, three months' research into the characteristics of toddlers, and ten years' experience with preschool storytimes. During preparation I felt confident and prepared, thinking, "How different from preschool storytime can it be?" Then I faced the room full of wiggling, distracted tots whose parents were frantically trying to get them to sit for that first program, and I realized I was in uncharted waters. I was scared stiff!

Two-year-olds (the core of the toddler group that ranges from 18 to 36 months of age) had terrible reputations. Everyone had heard of the *terrible twos.* Is there a more challenging, more confusing time of life for children and parents? Toddlers have strong moods and preferences, yet they enjoy watching, following, and copying others. They will eagerly share discoveries or show off what they've learned when they feel safe, but they do not like to participate in group activities. They understand far more than they can communicate using simple two-word sentences, but their vocabulary expands every day. Toddlers like to repeat simple tasks and activities, and they are developing listening skills, self-control, and the ability to follow directions. But this process is a slow one.

Coworkers and parents reacted alike when I first proposed a toddler storytime: "Great idea! But it'll never work here." Toddlers were viewed as unpredictable, undisciplined, and too flighty to participate in any group activity. Parents told us they were reluctant to bring them into the library, fearing they would be disruptive. Some staff members agreed.

Still, the number of toddlers in our community had increased noticeably, and parents were looking for "meaningful" activities for them. Few preschools included them in their programs, and publishers had just begun to target this age group. In our branch library we had purchased materials aimed at toddlers and had added titles concerning this age level to our parenting collection, but these items were not circulating well. Few parents even knew we had materials for and about their tots. Thus Two Times, a storytime for toddlers, was created in 1981.

Advertising only with a library poster, we plunged into the program. We took ten registra-

Toddlers and parents listening to stories

Father and toddler waiting for storytime to begin

tions for the first six-week session. After the first program, three more parents called to enroll their children. After the second week, we had ten names on the waiting list, and after the third week, there were more than fifty names of those waiting for the second session to begin. All of this was from "word-of-mouth" advertising.

As the program continued we discovered how important the sessions had become to families: fathers took days off from work to bring their toddlers when mothers could not. Grandparents came with grandchildren; neighbors, baby-sitters, and nannies attended with their toddler friends. Vacation plans, weekly schedules, and out-of-town visitors were coordinated around the toddler-storytime calendar. After the first two sessions, we eagerly anticipated the next in the series . . . encouraged weekly by parents and toddlers!

The results were immediate and gratifying. Circulation of picture books and parenting materials increased. We noticed more families coming to the library together, which was reflected in increasing circulation statistics in all categories. Awareness of the toddler program, because of its uniqueness and "cute-appeal," created more interest in the library than any other activity.

Along with this came some unexpected benefits: Within a year our toddler "graduates" began

entering the preschool storytime, and we discovered that they were much calmer, more eager to attend, and more willing to participate than other three-year-olds. They knew what to expect and what would be expected of them in a library program. Instances of crying children clinging to parents and too frightened to enter the story space dropped dramatically. Preschool storytimes became less stressful and more focused for both the storyteller and the children.

We had not anticipated the fierce loyalty so characteristic of toddlers. Parents told stories of taking elaborate detours to avoid the library if it was closed, because a toddler would "demand" that they stop as soon as the building appeared. Relatives, friends, and family visitors were brought to the library by proud youngsters as part of their sight-seeing tour of the city. It was the type of community support all librarians dream of.

As the program progressed, we discovered that Two Times had become as important for the parents as it was for their toddlers. Some parents had never before participated in structured learning experiences with their children and were amazed how much their toddlers knew and the level of skills they displayed. Following the role model of a storytime leader, parents remarked that they were "playing" more with their children at home. Adults were introduced to appropriate materials to help their children develop intellectually and socially. First-time parents even viewed Two Times as a support group, taking the opportunity before or after the program to talk with other parents, share ideas and problems, and even form playgroups.

And they kept coming! Preschool storytime enrollment increased, and families visited the library regularly even during program hiatuses. Habits learned early in life can be powerful, and parents will generally return to places where their experiences with their children have been positive.

As children's librarians gathered at conferences or informally over coffee, we talked about the programs we were doing. Those of us who offered programs for toddlers discovered we had all gone through the same research and trial-and-error process because there was no source to turn to for ideas and information. We were each reinventing the wheel. Other librarians expressed a desire to do toddler programs, but they didn't know where to begin.

With these factors in mind, *Storytimes for Two-Year-Olds* was first published in 1987. It was designed to introduce the special considerations and materials needed for a toddler storytime program. Divided into thirty-three thematic programs with examples of appropriate books, storytime props, fingerplays, and activities, the book also included follow-up ideas and crafts for parents and children to do at home. Notes to librarians were provided, giving practical tips and descriptions of how certain materials were used in storytimes. The work was directed at librarians wanting to create or enhance storytime programs for toddlers. It was hoped the resources and activities would be helpful to others working or living with young children: parents, caregivers, and early-childhood educators.

What Have We Learned?

In the ten years since this work was first published, toddler storytimes have grown and spread in libraries throughout the world. Long-standing programs continue to be offered and are considered the most popular children's storytimes in some locations. Programming for toddlers in libraries has been proven to be not only "do-able" but enjoyable as well.

Children's librarians have battled the "shhh" stereotype for years, an image that does not reconcile itself well with the presence of young children in libraries. Toddler programs have encouraged more families to bring children of all ages to visit libraries, a trend seen in changing youth collections that include more board and cloth books, toys and puzzles to entertain children in libraries, and picture book materials featuring simple illustrations and stories appropriate for the youngest children.

A decade ago Head Start, preschools, and day-care centers did not include toddlers in their programs. Children had to be three years old before they could be enrolled. Now, early-childhood educators and caregivers include not only toddlers but infants as well. Preschool program staff and librarians have discovered that very young children can and should be targeted for special programming.

Parents were not always the adults who accompanied toddlers attending daytime programs. Grandparents, baby-sitters, nannies, or friends often brought the child to the library while the parents worked. Evening programs were far more successful at attracting parents, sometimes attending together or alternating as the other parent watched older or younger siblings. With that in mind, the word *parent* is used in this edition to signify any accompanying adult.

Social and scientific studies have confirmed that learning begins much earlier than previously thought. Taking these findings into account, several excellent resources have been published, including *Books, Babies, and Libraries* by Ellin Greene, *Literate Beginnings* by Debbie Jeffrey, and *Beginning with Books* by Nancy DeSalvo. (These and other professional books are listed in the bibliography at the end of this book.) The *need* toddlers have to learn cannot be overemphasized. Absorbing information like sponges soaking up water, toddlers' learning is fast-paced and multileveled. And as librarians and parents realized the importance of introducing children to literature at the earliest opportunity, lap-sit programs for even younger children (babies 3 to 15 months old) have been introduced in libraries.

What Has Changed in This Second Edition?

Ten years ago it was a struggle to find appropriate titles for the thirty-three themes, using several of the materials more than once for lack of alternatives. Some titles were included with suggestions to adapt them for use with toddlers because the illustrations were not appropriate or the stories were too long. Many were out of print, due to their older copyright dates and changing laws regarding publishers' inventories.

This second edition of *Storytimes for Two-Year-Olds* has fifty themes, and the biggest challenge was narrowing the selections for each, using no title more than once. It seems publishers have responded to the demand for toddler materials with abandon, and most of the offerings targeted for this age group were appropriate. In this edition every consideration has been given to titles currently in print, although some older choices were too good not to include. Furthermore, in this era of publishing conglomerates, it's difficult to know what will be in print from one day to the next. Titles that have been in print for decades are suddenly gone; still others reappear under new imprints every day. Luckily there is much from which to choose, and programmers are encouraged to select titles based on their own preferences using the guidelines outlined.

This edition includes new action rhymes and songs for each theme that can be sung to familiar tunes. Parent's Follow-Up Ideas have been expanded, and Program Notes are now less structured to encourage creativity on the part of programmers.

In addition, every effort has been made to reflect the increased awareness and understanding of the multicultural world in which we live.

Books, rhymes, or crafts representing different cultural perspectives are included when possible for each theme. The same consideration has been given to varying abilities, including sign language words, materials appropriate for use with children with visual impairments, and titles in which characters who have disabilities are prominent.

A Few Words of Thanks

No program is solely one person's creation. I wish to thank all the librarians who have shared their ideas and materials at workshops and through correspondence. Many thanks also to library administrators who understand the need for and give support to toddler programs. I am especially grateful to Becky Arnold, Linda Bogusch, Mary Lou Dwyer, Theresa Overwaul, and the late Nancy Renfro, who made the first edition possible. My thanks also to Debbie Lewis, Gwen Harris, Terri Hubbard, Jane Dean, Jean Hatfield, Pat Rogers, Nina Hand, Lisa Hattrup, Fran Stallings, and Hiroko Fujita, without whom the second edition would have been impossible. A special thank you goes to my editor, Joan Grygel.

Acknowledgments

"The Little Turtle," reprinted with permission of Macmillan Publishing Company from *Collected Poems of Vachel Lindsay*. New York: Macmillan, 1925.

"Creeping Indians," "I Shut the Door," "Pound Goes the Hammer," and "Make a Valentine," reprinted from *Let's Do Fingerplays* by Marion F. Grayson. Copyright 1962 by Robert B. Luce, Inc.

"Eskimo Clothes Pin Birds" adapted from *Look At Me: Creative Activities for Babies and Toddlers*, by Carolyn Haas. Copyright 1987 by Carolyn Buhai Haas. Published by Chicago Review Press, Inc., 814 North Franklin Street, Chicago, IL 60610. Permission granted by the author.

"Busy Windshield Wipers" from *Preschool Story Hour* by Vardine Moore. Copyright 1972 by Scarecrow Press, Inc. Permission granted by the publisher.

"Rainbow," "Turn-Around Faces," "I Know An Old Lady Sack Puppet," and "Caterpillar/Butterfly Sock Puppet," adapted from *Puppetry in Early Childhood Education* by Tamara Hunt and Nancy Renfro. Copyright 1982 by Nancy Renfro Studios.

"Bears Everywhere," "Doughnut," "I Dig, Dig, Dig," "Houses," "Monkey See, Monkey Do," "Where are the Baby Mice?," "Sometimes I Am Tall," "Boom! Bang!," "Wind Tricks," and "Five Winds," reprinted from *Ring a Ring o' Roses: Stories, Games, and Fingerplays for Preschool Children*. Copyright 1981, Flint, Michigan, Public Library.

"Finger Circle Puppets," "Ping-Pong Family," and "Zipping Bag Book," adapted from *Toddler Theme-A-Saurus*, by Jean Warren and Judy Shimono. Copyright 1991 by Totline Publications, a division of Frank Schaffer Publications. Permission granted by Jan Warren and the publisher.

1
Planning Considerations

Many considerations go into planning any kind of program, and the same holds true for toddler storytimes. Understanding of the characteristics of this age group, careful audience preparation, the physical location, time of day, and program format are the most vital considerations.

The most immediate concern when programming for toddlers is the length of their attention spans. They are easily distracted—the slightest noise or action may rob you of their attention. Don't panic! Keep in mind that a longer attention span does not just occur on the child's next birthday, as some parents think. Attention is a *learned* behavior as toddlers focus and refocus their attention on words, objects, pictures, and actions for increasingly longer periods of time. Toddler storytimes are created around this primary consideration.

Other important considerations include the following:

1. Toddlers have not yet mastered the motor skills necessary for small hand movements used in most preschool fingerplays.
2. They have limited group experience and social skills, which means they are shy and do not readily share.
3. They have a lot of energy that needs to be channeled often into large movements such as hopping, marching, etc.
4. They react strongly to changes in their routines or environment.
5. They are at the crossroads between dependence and independence, needing an adult near them for security, yet wanting to do things for themselves.
6. Abstract concepts and sketchy illustrations do not hold their interest.
7. They like to touch things, learning by physical contact with objects.

This curious mixture of insecurity, independence, and limited skills requires careful planning and preparation. Toddler storytimes use more visual aids and repetition than do preschool storytimes. They also involve the parents as active participants and role models, helping their toddlers concentrate, stay focused, and feel secure. A variety of programming materials should be used in the program to capture interest, encourage cooperation, and promote retention.

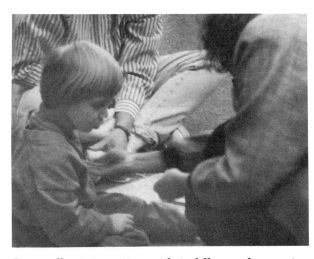

Storyteller interacting with toddler and parent

1

Preparation of Participants

Parents are not observers at toddler storytimes. From the beginning enlist their support in preparing their toddlers for the program. Keep in mind that many of these parents may have little experience with storytimes themselves and may not understand what the program entails.

Registration is essential for a successful toddler program. Limit the size of the group to ten to fifteen children and their parents, since larger groups overstimulate young children. Registering in advance helps parents view the program and their participation in it more seriously, especially when it is popular and there is a waiting list. Information to gather during registration includes the child's name and any nicknames, parent's name (name of the adult who will accompany the child, if different from parent), address, phone number, and child's birth date. Begin registration four to six weeks before the first program. Some libraries hold an orientation session the week before the first storytime, introducing parents and children to the story space and the storyteller and making certain everyone has library cards.

Upon registration present the parent with a letter or program brochure describing the program and emphasizing the cooperation among parent, child, and storyteller necessary to make it a quality experience for all. Putting this information in writing lets parents and children know what to expect and what is expected of them and reinforces their role as participants in the program. It also lessens the complaint, "I was never told that," common to all children's programming. (See figure 1 for a sample registration letter.)

Giving directions, clarifying program elements, and outlining your expectations will become a verbal part of the beginning of each session. Reinforcing the information delivered in the registration letter keeps everyone aware and focused on what is happening and why. For example, as children line up to enter the story space, tell them what to expect: "We are lining up to go into storytime together. See the rug spots on the floor. You pick the one you and Mom or Dad will sit on. You and Mom or Dad can sit together on a rug spot." Always give your directions to the child; the parent will listen and follow your directions. This makes both of them feel at ease and encourages them to be good listeners.

Physical Location

The Library

Libraries offer programming to bring people into their facilities and to encourage them to check out materials and use the services. Storytimes for toddlers work in all types of libraries: from large, well-staffed branches with ample materials budgets and separate programming rooms to tiny, one-person facilities housed in a couple of rooms and relying on volunteers and donations. You can program for families with toddlers in your community, but there are a few issues that should first be examined.

Before offering any programming, look at the materials collections that target the programming group. For toddler storytimes, a well-defined picture book collection with materials appropriate for infants and toddlers is essential. There should also be books on child development and raising toddlers in the adult section. Display the parenting materials during registration and the beginning programs of each session to familiarize patrons with them.

Examine the hours of operation to find the best time for a toddler program. Ideal times are mornings or early evening. Afternoon programs have not been as successful since most toddlers need afternoon naps. Evening programs encourage working parents to participate, and pairing a toddler storytime with a preschool program (back to back) works very well. For very small libraries, toddler storytime can be scheduled one half hour before the library opens to keep distractions to a minimum.

Encourage parents to arrive early so that children have time to get settled before the program begins. If possible provide a place other than the story space where the program will be held for parents and toddlers to wait until storytime begins. This gives them the opportunity

FIGURE 1   Sample Registration Letter

Storytimes for Two-Year-Olds

(name) _____ is scheduled for storytime on

(day) _____ at (time) _____ AM/PM for 20–30 minutes. Programs begin

(date) _____ and continue for six consecutive weeks.

For many children this will be their first group experience. Your cooperation and assistance in the following ways will make it more successful for your child.

1. Visit the library with your child and talk about the storytime before the first program. Explain that there will be stories, fingerplays, puppets, songs, and games, and that you will enjoy them together. If you would like to see the story room, we will be happy to make arrangements.

2. Bring only the toddler who is enrolled in the program. Older or younger children should not be part of this activity. If child care is a problem, ask the librarian for suggestions that have worked for others in the past.

3. Attendance is important! Activities of one week are often dependent upon those shared the week before. Please call (phone #) _____ if you cannot attend.

4. Once the program has begun, no one will be admitted to the story space. Two-year-olds are easily distracted, and latecomers become the focus of attention. Please plan to arrive early. Parking notes: _____.

5. Name tags will be provided for your child and yourself. They will help everyone get to know each other and feel at ease. Please talk about wearing name tags with your child and practice pinning something to your child's shirt so he or she will feel more comfortable with this process.

6. We will hold each storytime in the story room and will enter together when it is time to begin. There will be rug spots on the floor for seating. Let your child choose the place you will sit together, with your child on your lap or in front of you. Dress comfortably to sit on the floor. If you have physical restrictions that prohibit sitting on the floor, please call the library so other arrangements can be made.

7. If your child becomes restless or uncooperative, please step outside for a few moments. This helps everyone else to concentrate and your child to focus on your wishes. When your child is ready, you may quietly rejoin the group.

8. This is a time for adults and children to fully participate in planned activities together. If you want to chat with a friend, please do so before or after the program.

9. Toddlers enjoy watching others rather than participating themselves, especially in situations new to them. Please do not insist that your child join in any activity. If you participate and have fun, your child will soon join you.

10. A storytime handout will be provided each week, listing books, fingerplays, songs, and rhymes used in the program along with a craft idea and follow-up activities for you to do at home.

11. Plan to check out books for your child to take the storytime experience home with you. Some books will be in the story room for you and your child to choose. The librarian can show you where to find others. To apply for a library card, ask at the checkout desk.

Our goal is for everyone to have a good time. With your help, we can develop and nurture your child's love of books and the library. Library staff will be happy to assist you before or after storytime with the selection of books or other library services.

Toddler computer in use

to choose books, greet friends, chat, and play. Keep simple puzzles or toys on hand for little hands to stay busy and to direct excess energy before the program begins. Be certain there are enough materials for each child to have one. Toddlers do not share.

In this age of libraries going online, toddlers are naturally drawn to computer monitors and keyboards. Providing a toddler computer lets them copy what they see others doing safely and prevents them from banging on active computer keyboards, damaging equipment and nerves. Set an obsolete monitor and keyboard on a low table that toddlers can easily reach without climbing. Do not plug in the unit, and cover the blank monitor screen with a large colorful picture of some kind. Toddlers can punch keys and turn knobs to their hearts' content. Put a sign nearby to alert parents that this is a "toy," and it is acceptable for young children to play all they want with it.

Story Space

The ideal toddler storytime is held in a small room with a door. It should be free from distractions such as ringing telephones, squeaky doors, book drops, etc. However, libraries can host successful toddler programs without having special rooms. If a small story space is not available, cordon off a smaller area in a large room by arranging chairs, book carts, or tables around it. For libraries without separate meeting rooms, the storytime program can be held in a space as far as possible from the door and telephone.

A small, well-defined story space is preferable, since toddlers like clear boundaries in their worlds and find it easier to concentrate in smaller spaces. It should be cozy and slightly larger than the seating space needed for the group. Provide designated places for the children and parents to sit. Rug spots (carpet samples) or small flat cushions work well, even in a carpeted room. Arrange these in a semicircular pattern facing the storyteller, thus ensuring that everyone can see and hear and that the storyteller is close enough to keep the toddlers' attention from wandering. See figure 2 for a suggested arrangement of the story space.

Make a ceremony of entering the story space together as a group, giving parents and children a strong signal that the program has started. If you only have one room and parents and children are already waiting in the story space, create an activity to empty the space and to reenter it as a group. Lining up and marching in a circle around the room as you sing a song or chant a nursery rhyme provides a clear message that the program has begun. Allowing parents and children to gather in the story space encourages parents to chat with each other once the program has started, and tod-

Participants sitting in a semicircle during program

FIGURE 2   Suggested Story Space Arrangement

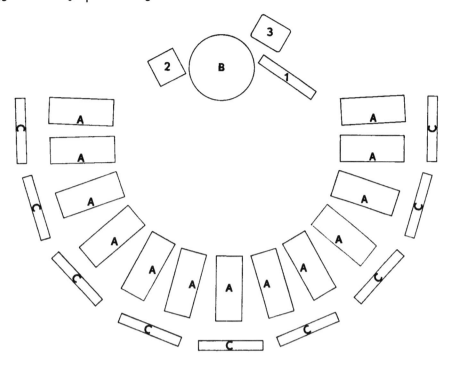

A. Rug spots (carpet samples) are placed in a semicircle close enough to the storyteller so that all parents and children can see and hear. Each parent and child shares one rug spot.

B. The storyteller sits on a low stool or on the floor with the following within an arm's reach: (1) flannelboard on a low easel, (2) a low table or stool for display, and (3) storytime materials (books, puppets, flannelboard figures, handouts, etc.) in the order they will be used and kept out of view behind the flannelboard until needed.

C. Books are displayed around the perimeter of the story space on low shelves, tables, book carts, or the floor. They are to be used in quiet time activities, and they can help define the story space in a larger room.

dlers find it difficult to settle down once they have been running and playing in the area.

Display books around the perimeter of the story space and behind the rug spots where children and parents will be sitting. Leave enough room between the books and the rug spots so that children and parents can get up and down comfortably without knocking them over . . . yet close enough that even shy toddlers can get to them. Books displayed around the space provide a festive environment for the program and make parents aware of other titles appropriate for their toddlers. Exhibit these books on low shelves, tables, or in a semicircle on the floor behind your audience. Displayed books can be used to define the story space in a larger room. At some point in the program children should be encouraged to select a book to examine with their parents, and occasionally restless children will find focus by retrieving a book to hold in their hands while listening to the program.

Format

Toddler storytimes are 20–25 minutes in length and can be presented in six- to eight-week sessions, building one upon another. Libraries commonly offer six sessions a year (two in the fall, two in the winter/spring, and two in the summer), taking short breaks between sessions. Often several toddler programs are presented each week. The preferred group size is ten to fifteen toddlers with accompanying adults in each program. Each storytime is filled with fast-paced action and visual stimuli divided into short (3–5 minute) segments.

It is no surprise that toddlers are more alert and cooperative in the morning than later in the day. Programs offered between 9:00 and 11:00 AM are most successful. Toddlers need naps and do not concentrate well in the afternoon. Early evening programs between 5:00 and 6:30 PM also work well and are popular with working parents. When selecting a day of the week, canvass other agencies and organizations offering activities for this age group to avoid conflicts and to let them know your program exists.

One of the most important considerations is to choose a time when there will be as few distractions as possible. Take the telephone off the hook if it can be heard in the story space. Do not schedule a program on the morning the trash truck picks up outside. Take every precaution to keep from being interrupted.

Be consistent with your program. Start on time. A vicious cycle develops when programs are delayed because people consistently arrive late. This penalizes those who arrived on time, rewards the behavior of latecomers, and encourages everyone to arrive later the next time. After all, "They never start on time." Take your program seriously and start when it is scheduled to begin. If special circumstances exist (bad weather or parking problems), ask the group if they mind waiting a few minutes.

Be firm about your program. If you decide that latecomers will not be admitted to the story space once a program is in progress (and this is *strongly* recommended, if it is possible to enforce), state so from the beginning . . . and

make no exceptions. It is unfair to those who have arrived on time to have their concentration interrupted by latecomers. The program is designed so that the opening routine prepares toddlers to focus their attention and to participate. When someone arrives late, you must start from the beginning to reorient everyone into the routine or deal with a restless child out of sync with the others.

This rule may seem harsh for parents caught on the outside with a disappointed toddler. Latecomers are usually harried and embarrassed. If possible, another staff member should interact with them, explaining the problems caused by entering the story space after the program has begun. Invite parents to wait until the program is over so the child can get a handout and talk with one of the storytime puppets. Offering a puzzle or toy to distract the child and giving the parent assistance selecting books helps time pass more quickly. Most parents are cooperative and understanding once they calm down, but a few are not.

If a parent chooses not to wait until the program ends and leaves the library, mail the handout to the child with a note that they were missed. Mention how much you appreciate their cooperation in keeping the program's high level of quality and how eager you are to see them next time. Enforcing a rule about latecomers is to everyone's benefit. Some people will arrive as much as 15 minutes late for a toddler program scheduled to last 20 minutes! That is unfair to you, to others in the group, and to the tardy child who has missed most of the program. Rarely will a latecomer miss a second program when this rule is enforced.

Program Themes

Planning each program around specific themes makes selection of materials easy and helps toddlers keep their attention focused throughout the storytime. Themes can be specific (Halloween, dogs, or picnics), or they can be more general in nature (spring, family, or weather). Choose them carefully and center them around objects and events familiar to toddlers: family members, daily routines, play activities, animals, holidays, etc. Support the theme with all other program elements: books, fingerplays, flannelboards, activities, songs, and puppets.

Create your own themes, taking a rhyme from one and stories from another and adding a favorite song or activity. Toddler programs work best when you use materials you personally enjoy. Include your favorite stories, flannelboard presentations, activities, and fingerplays. Create a general theme and call it, "My Favorite Things."

Program Handout

Provide a printed handout for parents listing books, fingerplays, and rhymes for each program. Include follow-up ideas, a craft for the parent and child to do together at home, and a mention of other library materials or services that might be of interest to them. The fifty thematic programs found elsewhere in this book were designed to help create program handouts for parents as well as create toddler storytime programs in libraries.

Program handouts have several benefits that outweigh the cost and time needed to produce them.

1. Parents and children are encouraged to talk about the storytime program and to repeat the fingerplays and rhymes at home when they have a printed reminder of them. Including follow-up and craft ideas keeps the library "at their fingertips" for weeks to come.
2. Handouts help parents select appropriate books, making future visits to the library more successful for them even after storytime programs have ended. Parents often use program handouts to look for books or make recommendations to other parents months after they attended their last toddler storytime.
3. Include in the program handout the following: titles of the stories used in the program or other appropriate books with the same theme (including authors' names and call numbers); words and directions for selected fingerplays, rhymes, and songs used in the program; follow-up ideas for parents and children to do at home together; a simple craft idea including instructions; and the title of a parenting resource: book, magazine, video, or audiotape available at the library or a related library service, such as interlibrary loan or other programming.
4. Handouts can be used over and over again, since themes are repeated from one year to the next.

Program Record-Keeping and Materials

Keep a written record of what materials and activities were used in programs and how they were received by your audience. Record the exact order in which stories and activities were shared along with notes about the success (or lack thereof) to make preparation for the program the next time it is offered much easier and more successful.

Gather together all materials to be used in a toddler storytime session so they are on hand when needed. One library uses magazine storage boxes (one box for each theme) and places all books, puppets, handouts, flannelboard figures, and other items needed for that program inside the box. Any notes the storyteller made following the last time the program was done are also included. Thus, storytellers do not have to scramble to find scattered materials, and in the event of emergency, another programmer can step in knowing what was planned for the storytime that day.

—————— Troubleshooting ——————

The most difficult part about working with toddlers can be interacting with their parents. Several common complaints plague most toddler programs, as outlined in the following sections.

Some appear during program registration, and others crop up as programs progress each week. Most problems can be solved easily by talking with the parent. Taking the parent aside, out of earshot of others, helps avoid embarrassment and encourages cooperation. Without laying blame, simply state, "I need your help," and explain the problem. The two of you are partners with a problem to solve together. Speak to parents immediately following the program if the problem surfaced there. Face-to-face contact is best, but make a phone call before the next program if you cannot talk to the parent immediately.

Too Young

The first issue encountered is usually the parent who wants to enroll a child younger than the guidelines of your program, with the familiar refrain, "But *my* child is so mature for her age." When your program is filled to capacity and has a waiting list, it's easier to stick to your guns than when you have space for more children. However, parents can be very persistent. Explaining that the program is designed for children to attend for one year, graduating into a preschool storytime when they turn three, often helps the parent understand. Starting too young means the child will be repeating part of the toddler storytime program. (Actually, the toddler couldn't care less. They like lots of repetition, but precocious parents do not.) As a last resort, invite the parent to visit a storytime with the young toddler to see if the child is really ready to participate.

Twins and Triplets

Another problem that appears at enrollment is that of multiple births. A parent will want to enroll twins or triplets with only one adult accompanying them. Toddler storytimes are designed for one child and one adult to interact together, or as one library puts it, "one lap, one child." The most successful solution for this problem is to ask the parent to recruit another adult (grandparent, neighbor, or friend) to enroll and accompany one of the children or to

enroll in an evening session when the other parent can also attend. The siblings enjoy the extra attention, can actually trade adults during the program, and never have to vie for one parent's attention. A second solution is for one child to be enrolled in toddler storytime and the other in a different activity (preschool, recreation center program, etc.) and then switch places for the next storytime session. We have heard reports where twins attending with one parent has worked out fine, and yet in other situations, it was disastrous.

Siblings

Since toddler storytimes are intended for one child and one adult to attend together, they are not the place for older or younger siblings. Occasional emergencies will necessitate that a sibling accompany storytime participants, but this should not be an ongoing situation. Make certain parents understand this part of the program when they enroll. Common solutions to child care problems include bringing along a friend, neighbor, or relative to watch the sibling in the library while the parent and toddler are in storytime; forming a baby-sitting co-op with neighbors or friends so that one parent and toddler can attend one session, then trade off with the baby-sitting parent and toddler for the next session; and Mom's Day Out programs offered at churches and child care centers (some may even form cooperative programs with the library to provide child care in exchange for an occasional storytime program). Make clear to parents that leaving siblings unattended in the library is *not* a solution.

Talking Parents

The most frequent complaint from toddler programmers (as well as from other children's programs where parents are in attendance) is that of parents talking during programs. For example, two friends who have not seen each other for a while may decide to sit together in storytime and chat throughout the program, especially during the "quiet time" activity intended for parent and child to bond with a book. The easiest way to break it up is to direct the child to share a book: "Michael, give that book to your Mom and show her the cats in it." Following the program, approach both parents and ask for their "help." Acknowledge that they are good friends, but ask that they please not visit during the program. If the problem persists, use your influence with their children as they are entering the story space, guiding them to sit in places that are not close to each other: "Mary, here is a red rug spot for you and Mom to sit on. Look Michael! The green rug spot you like is over there." Sneaky, but it works. Most parents do not mean to be intrusive. They simply do not realize they are causing a distraction, or they do not understand they should be interacting with their children. Be direct.

Child Discipline

Disciplining toddlers is a tricky business, and it is the parent's responsibility. When one child becomes restless or disruptive, continue with the program by staying focused on the other children. This lets the parent of the unhappy child know that you are not going to discipline the child. However, if the parent does not attempt to improve the situation, you should quietly suggest, "Perhaps you could step outside with her for a few moments until she is ready to return."

Children Who Are Not Ready

Toddlers mature at a widely varying rate. Occasionally a child who is chronologically two years old is not yet ready to participate in group activities. Such children can be very disruptive: squirming, squealing, and running around the story space, even attacking others or knocking over program materials. Most parents quickly realize this is a problem and voluntarily withdraw their children from the program. Once in a while you will find a parent who is totally engrossed in storytime activities and seems to be oblivious to the child's behavior. Talk with the parent after the storytime and explain that you have noticed the child doesn't seem to be getting much out of the program. Acknowledge that toddlers' interests often change dramatically within a few weeks or months and suggest that the parent enroll the child in the next session.

Forcing Participation

Toddlers enjoy watching others, and they will participate when they are ready. Some parents become anxious (especially if they are in a group where other children participate while theirs do not), and they push their children to join in activities or contact with a storytime puppet. This is usually met with strong resistance from the toddlers, and it can lead to a screaming showdown. Quietly encourage these parents during the program to "just do the activity yourself, and your children eventually will, too." If it is an ongoing problem, talk with the individual parents after the program, reassuring them that their children are perfectly normal. Watching others is one way toddlers learn about and take stock of unfamiliar situations. Stress again how important it is for the parents to participate, acting as role models for their children.

Measuring Results

Keeping statistical records (enrollment, waiting list numbers, day and time of programs, attendance, etc.) should be done for all library programming. Athough time- and labor-intensive, children's programming is one area for which statistics and population-service information can be collected, protecting the services during cutbacks in a budget crunch. Statistics can show which days or times work best in your community and can indicate where additional programs are required.

Take program surveys periodically. Asking participants what elements of the program they like best (and least) can be very enlightening. Inviting suggestions can lead to additional programs or library services and always strengthens your base of support among patrons.

Surveys and statistical data allow you to evaluate services and programming in terms of community needs and expectations. Surveys can be taken before offering a toddler program to determine the level of interest in the community or at the end of a storytime series to evaluate how the program is meeting your patron's needs. Design questions based on what you want to know. Examples of survey questions are

What day of the week is better for your child and you to come to storytime?

Do you prefer morning programs or early evening programs?
What part of the storytime do you like best?
What part of the storytime does your child like best?

Always leave a space for comments and suggestions.

2
Program Elements

The toddler storytime begins when children enter the library and ends when they leave. In the 45–60 minutes intervening, a series of well-planned elements come together to form an enjoyable program that promotes trust and learning for children, supports and informs parents, and puts another feather in the library's programming cap. Beginning with the simple acts of greeting the child and pinning a name tag on a shirt . . . continuing through opening routines to the actual storytelling program and quiet time activity . . . and ending with closing routines and final good-bye hugs given to a puppet, toddler storytimes can become the favorite children's program offered in your library.

When asking for cooperation or giving instructions in this program, it is important that you speak to the children and not to the adults. Talking to the children directly, making eye contact, and smiling at them as you do lets them know that this is *their* program. It makes them feel special and the center of attention, and toddlers like that. Tell children what you want them to do, and parents will listen and help their children comply. Do not rush them. Toddlers need time to hear and assimilate what you are saying. Repeat your request if necessary. When you begin giving directions to the parents, you are telling the children that they are no longer important, and their behavior will mirror that.

Toddler storytimes must be fast-paced and highly structured to hold the short attention spans and developing listening skills of young tots. Do not expect a lot of response from toddlers at first. The program should flow smoothly from one element into the next without delays. The following program elements have proven effective and combine easily to create a well-balanced toddler storytime.

When interacting with toddlers, physically get down on their level whenever possible. Greet them sitting in a small chair, and conduct the program from a low stool or sitting on the floor. Toddlers can be very shy, and they feel threatened by adults who are standing or walking toward them. It is important for them to see your face so they can begin to know and trust you. Consider the world from their point of view: Everything looks enormous, and most of what they see is taken up with people's bottoms, knees, and feet. They hear disembodied voices coming from above them, and they rarely are eye-to-eye with people who are talking to them. Can you remember the last time you talked with someone much taller than you, how uncomfortable it was, and how hard you found it to concentrate on what they were saying? Stay low. Sit still. Let them come to you.

Don't let toddlers be pushed into situations or participation in activities. They learn much about their worlds by observing, and they need to feel very comfortable before participating. You must be their advocate. Whether the children are receiving name tags, participating in activities, or getting their fingers "tasted" by a puppet, well-meaning parents compare their children with others in the group and will sometimes push toddlers into situations where the children feel uncomfortable. Your awareness of the child's response and a constant reassurance, "It's okay if you don't want to have your finger tasted today," help both parents and children relax and enjoy the experience.

Avoid "yes or no" questions when interacting with toddlers before and during programs. Rather, offer them choices. Don't ask, "Do you want me to pin your name tag on?" which can legitimately be answered, "No!" Instead ask, "Where do you want your name tag pinned?" or offer alternatives, "Shall we pin your name tag on your collar today or on your pocket?"

Name Tags

Ask participants to arrive 10–15 minutes early so they have ample time for children to settle down, get their name tags, and feel comfortable. Everyone in the program should wear a name tag: the storyteller to set an example, the parents to remind them of their participation, and the children to give the storyteller a handle (each child's name) with which to conduct the program. The first close contact between child and storyteller is the name tag encounter.

As parent and child enter the library, ask "Are you here for the toddler storytime?" After they have removed their jackets, invite them to come to you to get their name tags. Ask for the child's name, speaking to the child and looking at the parent only for confirmation or for an answer if the child is shy. Giving children name tags is an excellent way to greet them, and it provides a one-to-one bonding experience for child and storyteller. Be patient. Resist the urge to go to the child who is reluctant or slow. Letting the child come to you reduces stress for the child and promotes trust.

To encourage children to approach you, point to the name tag you are wearing and tell them you have one just like it for them. If some children are still reluctant, involve them in another way by asking them to "help" by coming to get their parents' name tags: "Here is Daddy's name tag. You can give it to him." (This is another good

reason for parents to wear name tags.) Children will approach, take the name tag from you, and give it to their parent. Then the tots watch carefully to see what the parent does with it. Toddlers love to help. Don't rush this process—trust takes time. They will want to assist you each week in handing out parents' name tags.

Attach the name tag to a child's clothing with a small safety pin, or thread the name tag with loops of yarn that slide over the child's head. Resist well-meaning parents when they attempt to take name tags from you directly—it is important for you to interact with the child as much as possible. Once a child is close to you, show the name tag and ask where he or she would like you to pin it. For very shy children, let them watch you pin name tags on others. As a last resort, let the parents pin the name tags, saying how much you will enjoy doing that next time.

Name tags should be colorful and durable, laminated if possible to prevent them from being pulled apart or chewed into pulp. A simple clown name tag made from basic shapes lends itself very well to this program and creates several opportunities during the storytime to draw attention to it. Print the child's name in large letters on *both* sides of the name tag. This way it can be read if it flips over during the program. Parents' name tags do not have to be elaborate: A square or circle is sufficient. Printing the

Toddler giving name tag to parent

child's name in small letters on the back of the parent's name tag helps get the tags paired together again at the end of the program.

—— Before the Program ——

Toddlers need time to "shift gears" before the program begins. They are very sensitive to changes: from being cooped up in a car seat to the freedom of moving on their own, from being bundled in layers of clothing to less restrictive attire, or from outside temperatures to inside ones. After they have received their name tags, encourage them to browse for books or play until it is time for the program to begin. Provide appropriate puzzles or toys with which they can play while they are waiting. Have enough toys or puzzles because toddlers do not readily share. Toddlers expel a lot of restless energy before entering the story space, and parents can use this time to chat with friends and select books, making their active participation in the program easier.

Start the program on time, and enter the story space together as a group. Letting parents and children straggle into the space where your program will be held robs toddlers of the structure

Parent and child at wall-size flannelboard waiting for storytime

they need in storytime. The clearer the boundaries and the stronger the signals, the more secure toddlers feel and the better their cooperation will be. If parents and children must wait in the same space you use for storytime, make it part of your opening routine to call them out of that space, reentering it as a group.

Within the story space you should have arranged seating markers to indicate where you want parents and children to sit. Rug spots (carpet samples) are perfectly sized and economical for this purpose. Children choose where they will sit with their parents.

—— Opening Routine ——

Opening and closing routines are the "security blankets" for toddlers during storytimes. Young children feel comfortable and safe knowing exactly how programs will begin and end. Parents benefit from observing how structure and repetition can be used to calm and focus the attention of toddlers. Opening routines have four basic parts.

1. Come with me! entering the story space and getting settled
2. Look at me! refocusing toddler's attention on you
3. Do with me! a participation activity done with you
4. Watch me do! directing children's attention elsewhere yet still under your control.

This progression moves toddlers from concrete concepts to abstract thinking, step-by-step.

Come with Me!

Use a sound maker (bell, tambourine, favorite song, etc.) to signal that it is time for storytime to begin and that you are ready to enter the story space together. Have the children gather their parents and line up for storytime. Reassure children who are involved in a puzzle or toy that they can return to it after storytime is over. By making children responsible for getting their parents lined up, you continue to reinforce that this is their program. Create a ritual for entering the story space, marching to recorded music, singing a song, or chanting a nursery rhyme together. As children enter the story space, they choose where to sit that day. If you have children who only want to sit on one color of rug spot, make sure there are a couple of rugs in that color to avoid conflicts. Use this opportunity to separate "talkative" parents by encouraging their children to sit on opposite sides of the room.

Look at Me!

As children and their parents are getting settled, there is some confusion and you must redirect their attention back to you to continue the program. Although a sharp, loud sound would accomplish this purpose, it can also excite or frighten young children. The method recommended is to provide stimulation that children can actually feel against their skin as you move among them. The puff of air from a folded fan, the tickle of a feather, or dangling ribbons and placing a pretend "something" in their hands all provide physical sensations that can be delivered in a gentle, nonthreatening manner and from a slight distance. Children's attention will become riveted on you, and their curiosities will be piqued. Continue talking throughout this process, calling each child by name and explaining that this is bringing *listening dust* to make them better listeners.

Do With Me!

Immediately follow the attention-getter with a participation activity that can be done while everyone is seated: a welcoming song with everyone vigorously waving, a fingerplay, or a hand-clapping rhyme. Whatever the activity, it should be the same every week. Keep movements large, and don't go too fast. This keeps toddlers' attention focused on you and releases restless energy. Making eye contact with par-

Toddlers getting listening dust and sharing it

ents lets them know you expect them to do the activity with you. Children will follow their parents' leads. A favorite opening fingerplay is "Open Them! Shut Them!" (see figure 3). The "Hello!" song found in the theme pages for Friends also works well.

FIGURE 3   An Opening Fingerplay

Open Them! Shut Them!

Open them! *(hands held in front, fingers extended)*
Shut them! *(close fingers tightly)*
Give a little clap. *(clap hands)*
Open them! Shut them! *(repeat)*
Put them in your lap. *(lay hands in lap)*
Creep them, creep them *(wiggle fingers slowly up the front of the body)*
Up to your chin. *(stop hands at chin)*
Open your mouth, *(open mouth wide, keeping fingers on chin)*
But don't put them in! *(fling hands outward and upward)*
Open them! Shut them! *(repeat first actions)*
Give a little clap.
Open them! Shut them!
Put them in your lap.

Toddler joining in the opening fingerplay

Keep it simple. One easy flannelboard is a shape puzzle that has seven basic shapes (two circles, a rectangle, a triangle, two stars, and a crescent). When the puzzle pieces are re-arranged, they form a clown that matches children's name tags. Name each piece as it is moved on the flannelboard, and explain how its relationship to other pieces has changed. For example, "I put the triangle above the circle. The rectangle goes between the triangle and the circle." Then direct children's attention to the matching name tags, having children point out one of the shapes to their parents. While they are thus engaged, remove flannelboard pieces and put them away. When their attention returns to you, be ready to begin the first story. (Clown name tags and the shape puzzle patterns can be found in appendix A.)

Watch Me Do!

Follow the participation activity immediately by redirecting their attention to a flannelboard activity. Flannelboards combine tangible elements, which can be moved and touched, with abstract concepts such as counting, colors, and story structure. This process is necessary for children to listen and understand the stories that will follow. This will be the first introduction to the "watch and listen" storytime model for toddlers. It is here they will first practice their listening skills and their abilities to concentrate.

The assembled clown shape puzzle

Story Program: ── Story, Activity, Story ──

The body of each storytime, sandwiched between opening and closing routines, is the story program—the part that changes from week to week. Including two or three short stories that are alternated with activities to get children up and moving, the story program must flow smoothly and quickly to hold toddlers' attention. The following chapter includes fifty thematic story programs that have been assembled, complete with suggested books, songs, and fingerplays, for programmers to use.

Stories can be presented and repeated through a variety of formats: books, fingerplays, flannelboard presentations, creative dramatics, music, puppets, and realia. Alternate stories (any aspect of the program where children are sitting and listening) with activities that allow children to move and release pent-up energy. This story-action-story pattern should continue in quick succession throughout the program. It will allow toddlers to gradually improve their listening skills and lengthen their attention spans without overtaxing their need for physical activity.

Books

The selection of books to use in toddler story-times has gotten easier, and books are more plentiful. There are many fine books for this age group, and the criteria for choosing the best to use in storytimes follows:

1. Illustrations should be simple and clearly defined against the backgrounds, making them easy to see from a distance. Objects and characters with bold outlines are best. If illustrations are questionable for toddlers, adapt the story to another format: fingerplay, flannelboard presentation, creative dramatics, or puppets.
2. Characters should be kept to a minimum; no more than three or four.
3. Stories should be repetitive, either in the actions of the characters or with repeating refrains or dialogue.
4. The story should move quickly from beginning to end in a linear fashion. For longer stories, drop some of the characters to shorten the story for use with the group.
5. The plot (if there is one) should be very simple with no subplots. Books without plots (concept books or those identifying familiar objects or animals) can also be used.

Storyteller holding book in proper position

Repetition is essential for toddlers to help them understand what is happening (comprehension), to recall events and characters (using memory and imagination), to anticipate action in the story (reading readiness), and to hear words used to tell the story (expanding vocabulary). Children greet a familiar story as an old friend and are eager to share it again and again. This means the same story can be used more than once during the program. Varying the format (first as a book, then through a flannelboard presentation or creative dramatics) makes the repetition less tedious for parents and the storyteller. Toddlers enjoy the same story presented in a new package.

Fingerplays

Fingerplays and action rhymes are essential to toddler storytimes. Interspersed between stories, they help channel restless energy, allowing toddlers to concentrate better on the stories that follow. The combination of movement, rhythm and rhyme, and following directions are welcome additions to any storytime.

Standard fingerplays must be adapted for use with toddlers. Their fine-motor skills are not yet developed enough for them to succeed with the small finger movements most fingerplays employ. Recall the last time you saw a toddler struggle to display two fingers when asked his age, and you better understand the problem. Convert favorite fingerplays into large motor activities, with broad movements using arms, legs, and the entire body to replace smaller finger motions. These bigger motions also help toddlers release more restless energy.

Whenever possible, incorporate sign language (American Sign Language or Signed English) into action rhymes. Many signed words are appropriate for use with toddlers, and teaching them a motion to use with a spoken word is more meaningful when the motion has added meaning. They are learning another language.

Toddler in stretching activity

Flannelboard Presentations

Flannelboards come in many sizes, small enough to hold in one hand or large enough to be placed on an easel. They can be purchased commercially or made from cardboard covered with felt or a carpet sample glued to a piece of wood.

Flannelboard figures can be simple shapes or elaborate characters, made from paper, felt, or fabric. Flannelboard stories offer great freedom and variety to a storytime program.

1. Flannelboard stories help hold the attention of toddlers, providing movement and action not only within the action of the story but in the telling of it as well. Toddlers like to watch the storyteller put figures on the flannelboard, move them around, and take them off again. They also like to help with this process.

2. Pictures in books are abstract concepts. Toddlers do not always recognize and respond to a two-dimensional illustration as being representative of a "real" object. Although flannelboard figures look two-dimensional, they can be held and moved, thus forming a bridge for toddlers between the concrete and abstract.

3. Flannelboard figures allow the use of stories that are too long or have illustrations inappropriate for use with toddlers in group situations. When converting a book to a flannelboard format, always display the book so that parents will know they can take that story home to share one-to-one with their children. Illustrations that do not work in group

"Old MacDonald Had a Farm" on carpet-sample flannelboard

situations are usually appropriate for use individually with children.

4. Flannelboards allow the expansion of fingerplays, songs, and rhymes into visual formats, enhancing storytime themes, reinforcing language, and providing additional material for toddler programs.

5. Flannelboard activities allow the use of elements unavailable in appropriate book form. For example, use a flannelboard traffic light during programs about colors and cars.

6. The flannelboard presentation expands a story or rhyme into a different format, giving toddlers the repetition they crave while keeping the material fresh for the storyteller and parents.

Easy flannelboard figures can be made from pictures cut from magazines or discarded books. Gluing pictures to felt or to strips of sandpaper will hold them in place on a flannelboard. The pictures in coloring books are simple enough to make good flannelboard patterns, cutting them out of felt and decorating them with wiggly eyes or trim. Examine some of the excellent books on creating flannelboard figures listed in the professional bibliography, and make some of them part of your children's programming collection.

Store flannelboard figures in large clasp envelopes, and keep them in a file box or file drawer with the contents noted on the outside. Rather than making duplicate figures, note on the outside of the envelope which figures are "borrowed" from another set.

After using felt figures in a storytime program, remove them from the flannelboard and put them out of view of the children. "Out of sight, out of mind" is an excellent adage when working with toddlers.

Creative Dramatics

Creative play comes naturally to toddlers who love to play and pretend, but it needs to be encouraged in their parents. Acting out events in a story or pretending to be one of the characters

Children "watering" seeds during garden program

allows children the opportunity to stretch, get the "wiggles out," and concentrate better when they return to their rug spots. Keep it simple. Encourage parents and children to hop like bunnies, fly like butterflies, or chug around the room as train cars. Creative dramatics can quickly be added to a program if children still seem restless after a planned action rhyme, reinforcing the theme in children's minds.

Creative drama can also be used as an integral part of telling the story. When using *The Carrot Seed* by Ruth Krauss in a garden-theme program, toddlers can actively mimic the action in the story as they hear it, planting the seed, watering it, pulling the weeds, and finally harvesting the giant carrot from the garden. They stay focused on the story and involved in it from beginning to end.

Acting out certain elements of a story carries it beyond the moment of telling. By helping toddlers recall what they have seen and heard, you are leading them through the steps of using their memories, filing and retrieving information, as well as letting them reexamine, practice, and play with the vocabulary they heard. Parents are encouraged to participate in creative play with their children while the storyteller is modeling the process for them.

Music

Toddlers like to listen to music, dance and march to it, and sing. Music can be used upon entering or leaving the story space as children line up and march with their parents. It can accompany storytelling, fingerplays, stretching activities, and creative play.

Music can be made by the storyteller, by the entire group, or by using recorded tapes or compact discs. Include as many different opportunities as possible to share music in your storytime program. Give children the opportunity to play purchased or handmade musical or rhythm instruments.

If you play an instrument, share that talent in at least one storytime program. Children need to be exposed to music in all its varieties and sources. Also include singing a cappella so parents realize that music made without instruments or recording devices has value as well. *Everybody* can sing . . . some of us just don't carry tunes as well as others. Children do not care if you sing on key, and parents will be encouraged by your enthusiasm to sing out loud also, regardless of what they think of their own singing voices.

Action songs with movements and songs with lots of repetition work great with toddlers. Words (instructions) should be sung clearly and slowly. Keep actions simple enough for toddlers to follow along, or demonstrate the actions before introducing the song. Songs with choruses and refrains, such as *Old MacDonald Had a Farm,* are popular and a great deal of fun for everyone.

Realia

Realia are any objects used to enhance or illustrate a program theme. Many objects work well in toddler storytimes: A toy rake and watering can are perfect additions to the gardens program, allowing children to take turns tending a pretend garden. A basket of artificial fruit makes the colors in *Mr. Rabbit's Lovely Present* more real. Toddlers also enjoy musical instruments, holiday items, and costume pieces.

Since toddlers are still in the tactile phase of learning, give them ample opportunities to explore objects by touching and holding them. Keep two considerations in mind when using realia in toddler programs. The first is safety. Choose objects that do not have sharp points or edges, small pieces that can fall off or be removed by tiny prying fingers, or toxic surfaces that might find their way into a small child's mouth. The second consideration is planning enough time in your program for children to touch and handle the objects.

Because they are fascinated by new and unfamiliar objects, toddlers are sometimes reluctant to release them or to move on to the next part of the program. Keep the object in your control. When you let them hold it, ask that it be returned to you. You then pass it to the next child. Young children will relinquish an object to an adult, but they will not always do so to another child. Put the object out of sight before moving on to the next part of the program.

Puppets

Puppets are one of the most popular elements in toddler storytimes for many reasons. Puppets provide a nonthreatening introduction to a new environment, to new routines, and to a new group situation. They allow close, physical contact between the storyteller and the child, which builds trust and friendship. Puppets provide another tactile element to a program that stimulates senses, as each child can touch or be touched by them.

Puppets are usually smaller than toddlers, who are accustomed to being smaller than everyone else. This gives children a feeling of importance, power, and self-confidence. Talking and listening to puppets give children the opportunity to practice their language and listening skills. Because they are so popular, the use of puppets helps children recall the storytime program and its elements better after children get home.

Several different kinds of puppets are used in toddler storytimes: story puppets, storytime mascots, and fingertasters. Story puppets are

Storyteller introducing a sock puppet fingertaster

those used in sharing a story in the program, such as a glove puppet used with *Caps for Sale* by Esphyr Slobodkina or stick puppets used with *Freight Train* by Donald Crews. Storytime mascots are familiar figures present in all storytime programs, and they perform specific duties, such as introducing stories or participating in the opening routine. Fingertasters are sock puppets that "taste" children's fingers, again stimulating another of their senses and bringing them into close contact with the storyteller.

Storytime mascots and fingertasters are not toys. They are powerful programming tools that should be used only by the storyteller. Allowing children to play with them (other than interacting with them while they are controlled by the storyteller) robs the puppets of their effectiveness and confuses children as to the roles the puppets play in the program. If children are interested, make sure there are some washable, kid-sized puppets in with the puzzles and toys that they play with before and after the program.

Giving puppets specific jobs to do during storytime helps define their purpose and personalities.

1. A host puppet says "hello" and "good-bye" or leads participants into the story space and through opening or closing routines.
2. An assistant puppet introduces the storytime theme, brings books for the storyteller to share, gives directions for what comes next, and leads songs, creative play, or fingerplays.
3. A role-model puppet displays either preferred behavior (following directions and using listening skills) or undesirable behavior (putting clothes on wrong or playing unsafely). Children enjoy correcting the puppet's behavior.

Toddler getting her finger "tasted" by a sock puppet

4. A puppet can participate in telling the story, becoming a character in it or narrating it.

The most popular puppets in most children's programs are fingertasters. Made from socks (the pattern is in the Mealtimes program and appendix A), the only necessary features are button eyes . . . and *no teeth!* A fingertaster can be hidden in a pocket or a small box and emerge toward the end of the program to "taste" fingers and say good-bye to children. To say young children *love* getting their fingers "tasted" is an understatement. They become ecstatic! The puppet "licks" or gently "sucks" on children's fingers, then tells them what "flavor" they are that day . . . and it changes every day! For toddlers, the experience of having their fingers "licked" is more appealing because of the vicarious stimulation of their senses of taste. But they don't really care what they taste like. They will come back again and again to have their fingers, elbows, noses, and toes "tasted."

It is very important to have a puppet say good-bye to children as they leave. Toddlers need time to interact with the storyteller and each other. Often children are still processing the storytime program and what they heard and saw. They need time to "shift gears" again, preparing to leave the premises. As they interact with a puppet at the end of the program, parents can gather their belongings or engage in a friendly chat with a neighbor. A puppet can provide a gentle prodding, saying "Good-bye! Good-bye!" when parents are ready to go and children are still reluctant to leave.

Inexpensive puppets can be purchased or easily made from old toys, material scraps, or throwaway items. When purchasing a puppet, look at its face and particularly the eyes. Are they visible? Is the puppet inviting to look at, so that children will be drawn to it? Big puppets are enjoyable for older children, but they may overpower toddlers who prefer smaller characters. Puppets should be sturdily constructed with no small pieces that might become dislodged and be swallowed. They should be made from washable materials (felt cannot be washed). Avoid puppets with teeth, or remove the teeth, as they are threatening to young children.

When making puppets, keep the eyes close to the mouth to make the puppet more vulnerable. Do not add teeth.

Puppets are gentle creatures that often act shier of the children than the children are of the puppets. Puppets should never be used to rough-house, make loud noises, or hit each other. When children strike at a puppet, immediately pull the puppet away saying, "Oh, please do not hit him. He does not like being hit." Then give the puppet back to the child saying, "But he does like to be petted and hugged." Children will respond with appropriate behavior.

Do not let parents force toddlers into contact with the puppet. Move the puppet away from the child if you sense resistance or fear.

Quiet Time

A quiet time may seem out of place in a highly structured program for active toddlers. However, it fits in well as a transition between the last story and the closing routines, and it serves several purposes.

1. Quiet time is an opportunity for parents and children to interact one-to-one, reinforcing what they've been doing throughout the program and encouraging them to re-create it at home. A few moments of sharing language works well, such as reciting nursery rhymes or playing a color-, parts of the body-, or clothing-identification game. Letting children choose a book from those displayed in the story space and share it with the parent guarantees success, since the books on display are all appropriate for the age group.

2. A few quiet moments allow children and parents to process the storytime experience before they face the flurry of activity associated with leaving the library. They

*Parent and child sharing
a book during quiet time*

will retain more of the program and will talk about it more at home when they have this opportunity.

3. Quiet time is a good change-of-pace for toddlers. Storytime was filled with fast-paced, highly structured, and very active elements. This relatively unstructured time lets them begin to return to their own schedules, pacing, and agendas.

4. Quiet time allows the storyteller a few moments to gather program materials together, to ready handouts and giveaway items for distribution, and to prepare for the closing routine.

Be aware that some parents may use this time to chat with each other rather than interact with their children. Give instructions to their children to get the parents involved again: "Bobby, ask Dad to sing the *Twinkle, Twinkle* song with you." Make it clear to parents that quiet time is an integral part of the storytime program, and be firm about it.

This quiet activity will be short, and children will react to it based upon their own levels of maturity. Usually during the first program of the session, you give directions for the quiet activity, and within 30–60 seconds you will notice some children already growing restless from inactivity. It is very rewarding to see these same children's tolerance and willingness to spend quiet time with parents extending every week. By the last program in the session, you may have to interrupt them to close the program. Use the appearance of restless behavior in two or more children as your cue to start the closing routine.

Closing Routine

As with the opening routine, the closing routine should be the same every week. Begin by removing name tags and trading them for program handouts. The fingertasting puppet then appears, tastes fingers, and says good-bye as children leave the story space.

Name Tag Removal

As you notice children getting restless during the quiet time, ask them to have their parents remove both name tags, and have the children bring them to you. Start with the restless children. This is a low-key activity that allows others to finish their quiet time activity and to remove their name tags. Exchange each set of name tags for a program handout.

The only changes to routines in the final program of a session is that the children can take their name tags home with them. Instead of asking for the name tags to be removed, tell children they will be able to wear them home, then distribute the handouts. Be prepared for some children to "insist" that you take the name tags back. Toddlers like their routines to be consistent! If this happens, simply hand the name tags back to the parent when the child is not looking. Tell the children that you will still be at the library when they come to visit, even when there is no storytime. Invite parents and children to attend any future programs being offered for families.

Returning Listening Dust

When all name tags have been returned, refocus attention on you by asking that the children return the listening dust you gave them in the opening routine. Tell them to brush all that dust off their clothes and their hair and to give it back to you. Cup your hands to receive the "dust" from them, and then pour it into the pocket or box (or wherever) in which the fingertasting puppet is hiding.

Fingertaster

Carefully remove the fingertaster from its hiding place and place it on your hand. For the first session, the puppet should be very shy and frightened of the children. Let them coax it out to interact with them. Explain that the fingertaster has no teeth (open its mouth so they can see) but that it loves to lick fingers (demonstrate on yourself). Ask the nearest parent if he or she would like to have a finger tasted. Move the puppet very slowly toward the parent for a "taste." Make the flavor something fun that will cause the parents to laugh and make the children want to participate. Then sit still and ask who wants their fingers tasted. Let children come to you, taking as much time as they

want. Call on those who have not come forward, but if they decline it is okay.

Saying Good-Bye

When all children who want their fingers "tasted" have come forward, tell them it is time to say good-bye for the day. Tell them that the fingertaster would like to give them a hug and say farewell before they leave the story space. This allows parents time to gather belongings together. Singing a good-bye song or chanting a rhyme, have everyone line up at the door and exit the story space together.

This final activity is the least structured part of the program. Some children need more time to talk with the puppet or have their fingers caressed repeatedly. Letting parents and children leave the story space as they are ready is an acceptable alternative, while you remain seated and let the puppet chat with children or say good-bye. If children are reluctant to leave, the puppet gets involved, waving farewell, calling out "Bye Bye!" and "See you next week!" or even directing the child's attention to something outside the story space. The parent will be grateful for your assistance, and you won't have a crying child leaving your building.

———— Follow-Up ————

Check to see if anyone arrived late and might be waiting in the children's area to receive the week's handout. Let tardy children interact with the fingertaster, and show parents the books used in the program and displayed in the story space. This helps them feel that they didn't miss out on everything.

After gathering together and storing all storytime materials, record attendance and absences for your statistics. Make notes in your story file or in this book about which stories and activities worked well (and which didn't). This saves you a lot of time and recrimination when you repeat the program theme.

Match parents' and children's name tags together so they are ready for the next program. If you mail handouts to absent children, do so immediately. Children love to get mail, and parents will soon see the value of having a list of appropriate materials and activities for their children. It also encourages them to come the following week. If postage is a problem, clip the handout to the name tags of the absent children so they can be distributed the next week when name tags are handed out. If children are absent for the final program, mail their name tags and handouts to them with a note that you hope to see them soon in the library.

3
Program Themes

Gathered together in this chapter are fifty thematic programs for toddler storytimes. Each theme includes sixteen titles appropriate for toddlers for use in the storytime program or to be recommended to parents and caregivers. Next are fingerplays/action rhymes, including at least one song. These are followed by suggestions of activities to enrich the theme and a craft for parents and toddlers to pursue together at home. Any of these components can be shared with parents in program handouts for each theme.

To reflect the multicultural world in which we live and work, books, rhymes, and crafts representing different cultural heritages were included for each theme wherever possible. Editions of recommended titles in languages other than English are noted in the bibliography of titles used in the programs, as are differing formats such as pop-up and big-format books. Special consideration was also given to varying abilities within themes, including a sign language word for each theme, books with textures and movable parts for children with visual impairments, and books in which characters with disabilities are prominent.

The titles were selected with the intent of broadening the way themes could be used. For example, in the spring theme you will find titles for a program on spring, on Easter and Passover holidays, and on eggs. This format will give you flexibility and additional ideas to make the storytimes individual and keep them fresh.

Although some titles would be appropriate with several themes, they have been included in only one place. Feel free to trade titles between themes as appropriate. An effort was made to include the work of as many authors as possible, again to broaden choices. The "in print" status was checked on all titles. A few "out of print" titles were knowingly included if they were titles common to most children's collections.

Because the selection of stories and activities is a very personal issue, dictating which materials should be used is a disservice to storytellers and audiences alike. Therefore, in this edition program notes are less structured and include *suggestions* of how certain titles or elements can be used instead of a sequential, step-by-step outline for each program.

Program notes include a sign language word, with directions for introducing it into storytimes, as well as giveaway ideas and instructions for each theme. However, giveaways should be used sparingly so they do not become the primary focus of storytimes for toddlers or parents.

Space has been provided in each theme for you to make your own program notes. Record which stories worked best for you and which did not. Make note of new titles appropriate for use with the theme or of old favorites that were not included in this edition. Jot down the unplanned things that happened during the program that you want to repeat the next time, and write ideas shared with you by others. Feel free to leave out verses of rhymes and songs that do not work in your situation and to create new verses of your own. Add pages and create your own themes, using favorite books and activities or subjects of interest to toddlers in your community. A wealth of information and ideas passes by us every day. When you find something interesting, make a note of it. Who knows where it will lead? That is how the first edition of this book began.

Autumn (Halloween)

Books

Be Brave Baby Rabbit
FRAN MANUSHKIN

Clifford's First Halloween
NORMAN BRIDWELL

*Corduroy's Halloween:
A Lift-the-Flap Book*
B. G. HENNESSY

A Dark, Dark Tale
RUTH BROWN

Georgie (Also in Spanish:
    Jorgito)
ROBERT BRIGHT

Go Away, Big Green Monster
ED EMBERLEY

Humbug Witch
LORNA BALIAN

It's Pumpkin Time!
ZOE HALL

Marmalade's Yellow Leaf
CINDY WHEELER

On Halloween Night
FERIDA WOLFF

One Dark Night
EDNA MITCHELL PRESTON

One Fall Day
MOLLY BANG

Red Leaf, Yellow Leaf
LOIS EHLERT

Where the Wild Things Are
MAURICE SENDAK

Who Goes Out on Halloween?
SUE ALEXANDER

Word Bird's Halloween Words
JANE BELK MONCURE

Rhythms, Rhymes, and Fingerplays

Autumn Leaves

Leaves are falling from the trees *(flutter fingers down)*
Yellow, brown, and red.
Falling, falling from above.
One landed on my head! *(hands on head)*

Jack-O'-Lantern   (tune: "I'm a Little Teapot")

I'm a jack-o'-lantern, *(arms form large circle)*
Big and fat.
I have two eyes, a nose, and a hat. *(point to eyes
    and nose, put hands on head)*
Children come at Halloween *(make beckoning motion)*
From miles and miles.
Put in a candle and *(mimic the action)*
Watch me smile. *(fingers to corners of mouth, smile big)*

Two Little Ghosts

A very old witch was stirring a pot, *(make stirring motion)*
Ooo-oooo! Ooo-oooo!
Two little ghosts said, "What has she got?" *(shrug shoulders)*
Tippytoe, tippytoe, tippytoe . . . *("walk" fingers up arm
    or tiptoe in circle)*
Boo! *(clap hands sharply)*

Parents' Follow-Up Ideas

Take an autumn walk and talk about the changes in the seasons.
Collect leaves that have fallen from trees and sort them by size or
color. Help your child notice changes in temperature that require different clothing or changes in play habits.

Together visit a pumpkin patch or a supermarket to choose a pumpkin, the traditional autumn vegetable. Even if you do not want a traditional jack-o'-lantern, cut a design in the pumpkin and introduce your
child to a vegetable lantern. Your toddler can help scoop out the seeds
and push the cut-out pieces out of the pumpkin shell. Put a votive candle inside and light it. Then turn out the lights to enjoy your pumpkin
lantern. Do not leave children alone with a burning candle.

Keep a "dress-up box" filled with old clothes, hats, scarves, shoes,
and handbags for children to use while pretending.

Paper bag costumes are fun and economical. Two books to help
you with ideas and construction of them are Goldie T. Chernoff, *Easy
Costumes You Don't Have to Sew,* and Nancy Renfro, *Bags Are Big! A
Paper Bag Craft Book.*

Craft

Wild Thing Sack Puppet

You will need: small paper sack (lunch sized or smaller)

glue

scraps of material, paper, yarn, felt

crayons or magic markers

pipe cleaners, trim, buttons

Using the bottom flap of the paper bag as the face of your puppet, draw or glue on it features that appear on the upper half of the face: eyes, brows, nose, cheeks, and mustache. Under the flap of the bag, draw the mouth so that it is visible only when the flap is raised. Add tongue, lips, and chin. Use teeth sparingly.

Decorate the rest of the bag with your scraps and odds and ends, using glue. Let the glue dry thoroughly.

To operate, place the sack over your hand and move the flap (mouth) up and down as the puppet "talks."

Program Notes

Sign Language

HALLOWEEN   Cover your face with both hands and slowly move your hands apart as though taking off a mask.

Note: Do *not* use this program as the first one in a series. Toddlers need time to develop trust for the storyteller and others in the group before asking them to participate where others are wearing costumes.

The week prior to presenting this program, invite children to attend in costume. If the storyteller is in a costume, do not wear a mask or full stage makeup. Spend time having each child stand and admire costumes, including children who are not in costume ("Jerry is dressed as a happy boy"). Some children may be shy of others in unusual clothes. The storytime puppet wearing a costume (no mask) will reassure them. Have children remove all masks or cumbersome costume pieces before beginning the opening routine.

When using the rhyme "Two Little Ghosts," start by saying "Boo!" together to avoid startling anyone. Next practice the sequence, "Tippytoe, tippytoe, tippytoe . . . Boo!" a couple of times so they will know when the Boo! shows up in the rhyme.

Make a flannelboard jack-o'-lantern for the "Jack-O'-Lantern" rhyme, using familiar shapes: a large orange circle, a green rectangle (hat), three yellow triangles (eyes and nose), and a large crescent (mouth). Let the children help put the face on the jack-o'-lantern.

Give away "ghosts" can be made by covering lollipops with facial tissues and securing them with tape.

Fingertaster "tastes" autumn foods, such as apples, corn, pumpkin pie, nuts, etc.

Children exit the story space in a Halloween parade or as fluttering autumn leaves.

—————————————————————————— Notes ——————————————————————————

Babies

Books

Baby and I Can Play Together
KAREN HENDRICKSON

Baby in a Buggy
MONICA WELLINGTON

A Baby Just Like Me
SUSAN WINTER

Don't Wake the Baby
WENDY CHEYETTE LEWISON

Geraldine's Baby Brother
HOLLY KELLER

Good Night, Baby
CHERYL WILLIS HUDSON

I Am Adopted
SUSAN LAPSLEY

I Heard Said the Bird
POLLY BERENDS

The New Baby (Also in
   Spanish: *El Nuevo Bibi*)
MERCER MAYER

Peter's Chair (Also in Spanish:
   La Silla de Pedro)
EZRA JACK KEATS

Rock-a-Bye Babies
ANNA ROSS

Sweet Baby Coming
ELOISE GREENFIELD

We Have a Baby
CATHRYN FALWELL

What Does Baby See?
DENISE LEWIS PATRICK

Where's My Baby?
H. A. REY

Where's the Baby?
PAT HUTCHINS

Rhythms, Rhymes, and Fingerplays

The Baby

Shhh! *(finger to lips)*
Baby is sleeping *(hands to cheek, palms together)*
Don't wake her up! *(waggle finger and shake head)*
Shhh! Baby is sleeping *(repeat motions each time)*
Don't wake her up!
Shhh! Baby is sleeping
Don't wake her up!
We don't want to make Baby cry. *(crying motion:
   fists to cheeks, rotating back and forth)*

Walk on tippy toes *(touch fingers lightly to knees)*
Don't make a sound. *(finger to lips)*
   [repeat both lines twice more]
We don't want to make Baby cry. *(crying motion:
   fists to cheeks, rotating back and forth)*

The baby's AWAKE! *(eyes wide open, make "surprise"*
motion with hand near shoulders, palms out)
She's crying, boo-hoo *(fists to cheeks, rotate back*
and forth) [repeat both lines twice]
Baby, sweet baby, don't cry! *(gently pat cheeks*
and shake head)

We'll tickle the baby *(wiggle fingers under chin)*
Under her chin . . . [repeat both lines twice]
Baby, sweet baby, don't cry! *(make "crying" motion)*

Baby's stopped crying! *(stop "crying" motion)*
She's starting to smile *(make BIG smile)*
[repeat both lines twice]
I LOVE my baby. *(make hugging motion)*
Bye, bye! *(wave)*

Hush Little Baby   (song)

Hush, little baby! Don't say a word.
Mama's gonna catch you a mocking bird.
And if that mocking bird won't sing,
Mama's gonna buy you a kite and string.
And if that kite and string won't fly,
Mama's gonna bake you an apple pie.
And if that apple pie is sour,
Mama's gonna grow you a yellow flower.
And if that yellow flower has bugs,
Mama's gonna give you kisses and hugs.
Hush, little baby! Hush.

Parents' Follow-Up Ideas

Tell your toddlers stories of when they were little babies and how they
changed as they grew. Use photographs or videos but also tell stories
without pictures. Talk about how excited you were when they came into
your family, how you needed to do almost everything for them, and how
happy you were with each of their "firsts" (coo, smile, word, and step).
Snuggle your toddlers close as you talk about how they are changing.
Emphasize that you love them the same through all stages of their lives.

Toddlers should have soft toys to cuddle and play with regardless
of their gender. They are never too young to learn to show tender, loving care for toys, pets, or other children.

Animal babies are called by many different names. Expand your
toddler's vocabulary by sharing these names in a game. Use a picture
book or coloring book for animal pictures and say, "Here's a dog!
Baby dogs are called puppies. What are they called? Puppies!"

cat—kitten	bird—chick	cow—calf
horse—colt	duck—duckling	bear/lion—cub
goat—kid	sheep—lamb	rabbit—bunny

Craft

Bubble Cup

You will need: small plastic/paper cup (5 oz. size)

old washcloth or piece of terry cloth

rubber band

plastic straw

hole punch

liquid soap

spray bottle with water in it

Punch a hole in the side of the cup one inch from the top. The straw should fit snugly in this hole. From the washcloth cut a circle larger than the mouth of the cup and secure it over the top of the cup with the rubber band. Spray water on the cloth to moisten it and smear a little liquid soap over it with your finger.

Have your child blow into the straw and bubbles will erupt from the top! Since there is only air inside the cup, the child will not get soap or water in the mouth if he or she sucks on the straw instead of blowing. If the bubbles stop, check to see if the straw is bent, cutting off the air supply. Also, check the cloth to determine if more water or soap is needed.

Cups can be labeled with the child's name and decorated with markers, fabric scraps, or pictures. The cloth can be removed and washed or replaced as needed.

Program Notes

Sign Language

> BABY   Form a cradle with your arms, as if holding a baby, and gently swing arms side to side.

Introduce the theme with a storytime puppet or doll dressed as a baby. Let each child who responds with a baby-type behavior (cooing, fussing, no talking) hug the puppet or rock a doll in a shoe box cradle. As this is happening, talk about what "big boys" and "big girls" the toddlers are and how different they are from babies who can do very little for themselves.

Peter's Chair is a good story for a flannelboard.

Giveaways are big boy/big girl medallions made from posterboard circles glued to ribbon loops.

Fingertaster "tastes" soft foods, such as mashed bananas, oatmeal, mashed potatoes, etc.

Children exit the story space taking their "babies" for a walk.

─────────────── Notes ───────────────

Bath Time

Books

Babar's Bath Book
LAURENT DE BRUNHOFF

Bathtime
MAUREEN ROFFEY

Clifford's Bathtime
NORMAN BRIDWELL

Dirty Larry
BOBBIE HAMSA

Ernie's Bath Book
MICHAEL SMOLLIN

Harry the Dirty Dog (Also
   in Spanish: *Harry,
   el Perrito Sucio*)
GENE ZION

I Am Water
JEAN MARZOLLO

Max's Bath (Board book)
ROSEMARY WELLS

Messy Baby
JAN ORMEROD

Nice and Clean
ANNE AND HARLOW ROCKWELL

No More Water in the Tub!
TEDD ARNOLD

Paddington Takes a Bath
MICHAEL BOND

*Rub-A-Dub-Dub: What's
in the Tub?*
MARY BLOCKSMA

Sam's Bath
BARBRO LINDGREN

Spot Goes Splash!
ERIC HILL

Taking a Bath
MARCIA LEONARD

Rhythms, Rhymes, and Fingerplays

Rub-A-Dub-Dub

Rub-a-dub-dub, one child in the tub.
   (rub knuckles lightly up and down on the chest)
Tell me what you see.
One foot with toes, *(point to parts of the body)*
A hand, a nose,
As clean as they can be. *(rub hands together)*

Rub-a-dub-dub, one child in the tub.
Tell me what you see.
Two ears, a cheek, *(point)*
So clean they squeak, *(rub cheeks gently)*
A chin, a tummy, a knee. *(point)*

Rub-a-dub-dub, one child in the tub.
Tell me what you see.
Legs and arms, *(extend legs and arms)*
So clean and warm, *(wiggle arms)*
Do they have a hug for me? *(cross arms
      over chest, giving "self" a hug)*

Washing   (tune: "Mulberry Bush")

This is the way we wash our face *(hands make
    washing motion over face)*
Wash our face, wash our face.
This is the way we wash our face,
Early in the morning.

[Verse 2]
   . . . brush our teeth *(brushing motion)*
   . . . after we eat breakfast.

[Verse 3]
   . . . wash our hands *(hands make washing motion)*
   . . . after we've been playing.

[Verse 4]
   . . . take a bath *(rub knuckles on chest)*
   . . . before we say "Goodnight."

Float My Boat   (tune: "Row, Row, Row Your Boat")

Float, float, float my boat,
In a soapy tub.
Together we are getting clean,
Rub-a-dub-a-dub.

Parents' Follow-Up Ideas

Take your children to a drive-through car wash to experience how
cars "take baths." Talk about the process before you go and take time
to watch other cars go in dirty and come out clean. Once inside, some
children may be frightened, so be prepared to offer reassurance and
talk about what is happening. You may find yourself washing the car
often once they decide it is safe and fun.

Put red, stick-on dots on hot water handles to help your children
stay safe. Red means "hot" and "hands off," and only grownups
should touch red-dotted handles. Put dots on water faucets in bathrooms, the kitchen, and the laundry room. Also use them on stoves,
crock pots or other heated appliances, and other "hands off" areas.

To keep bath time fun, throw some Ping Pong balls with faces on
them into the bath water. Add a few drops of food coloring to change
the color or float a couple of ice cubes in a warm bath. [*Note:* Some
toddlers develop urinary or vaginal infections from commercial bubble bath preparations. Save them for when they are older.]

A simple hand-washing routine in which your children help gather
items, prepare themselves, and put items away will give them pride in
their abilities and lessen struggles over getting cleaned up:

1. child gathers needed items (soap, towel, nail brush, chair, or low stool)
2. rolls up sleeves and steps up to sink on a chair or low stool
3. fills sink half way with warm water (adult turns on the hot water)
4. wets hands and rubs soap on them, returning the soap to the soap dish
5. lathers hands well and gets the soap between fingers and on the backs of hands (If necessary, use a nail brush on nails and on tough spots.)
6. rinses hands well in basin, and drains sink
7. dries hands, front and back, working one finger at a time
8. climbs down from stool
9. puts away towel, soap, stool, brush, etc.

Craft

Clean Clara (Clem), a Bath Mitt

You will need: 2 washcloths or an old hand towel

scissors and pins

needle and thread

yarn

small buttons

Photocopy or trace the mitt shape on page 34 to use as a pattern. With washcloths together, pin the pattern to the middle with the bottom edge (the opening) lined up along the edges of the washcloths so you don't have to hem them. Cut through both washcloths, and sew them together along the sides and top of the mitt. Turn it inside out. Sew several pieces of yarn to the top for hair and buttons on the front for eyes.

When your child is taking a bath, show how Clara (Clem) can help her or him get clean. Put the mitt puppet on your child's hand and lather it with soap. Be sure the eyes are on the back of your child's hand so they do not scratch when washing. Your toddler can use Clara (Clem) to wash his or her face, legs, and arms, and you can wash the child's back. Clara (Clem) can also wash toys, friends, etc. For a no-sew version, use a ready-made mitten for a "one-armed" Clara (Clem).

Program Notes

Sign Language

BATH   Rub your closed hands up and down lightly on your chest as though washing the chest during a bath.

Have several towels, washcloths, a plastic tub, and a plastic pitcher on hand. Between stories, talk with the storytime puppet about how eating, playing, and other things can make us dirty or sticky. With a plastic wash tub, give the storytime puppet or some of the library toys a "pretend" bath. Let the children help wash, rinse, and dry them. As children are busy, talk about other things that get "baths," such as cars, animals in the zoo, and pets, and mention that some people take showers instead of sit-down baths. Use words and phrases like "slippery," "still soapy," and "rinsing." Explain that baths do more than make you clean; they help you get warm in the winter and cool off in the summer.

Giveaways can be little soaps solicited from a motel chain and decorated with a colorful sticker.

Fingertaster "tastes" foods that must be washed, such as carrots, cherries, apples, etc.

Children exit the story space singing the first verse to "Washing."

——————————————— Notes ———————————————

Bears

Books

Are You There, Bear?
RON MARIS

Baby Bear
PATRICK YEE

Bears, Bears, and More Bears
JACKIE MORRIS

Bears, Bears, Everywhere
    (Also in Spanish: *Osos,*
    Osos, Aqui y Alli)
RITA MILIOS

Bears in Pairs
NIKI YEKTAI

Blueberries for Sal
ROBERT MCCLOSKEY

Goldilocks and the Three Bears
JANE DYER

He Bear, She Bear
STAN AND JAN BERENSTAIN

Moon Bear
FRANK ASCH

My Brown Bear Barney
DOROTHY BUTLER

Numbears: A Counting Book
KATHLEEN HAGUE

Sleepy Bear
LYDIA DABCOVICH

Ten Bears in My Bed:
A Goodnight Countdown
STANLEY MACK

This Is the Bear
SARAH HAYES

We're Going on a Bear Hunt
MICHAEL ROSEN

Where's the Bear?
CHARLOTTE POMERANTZ

Rhythms, Rhymes, and Fingerplays

Five Bears in Bed   (tune: "Ten in a Bed")

There were five bears in her bed, *(hold up five fingers)*
And the little one said,
"Roll over! Roll over!" *(roll hands over each other)*
So they all rolled over,
And one fell out. *(one hand rolls to one side)*

[Repeat with four, three, two, and one]

There were no bears in her bed, *(hold up fist)*
And the little one said,
"Good night!" *(lay head on hands and close eyes)*

Bears Everywhere

Bears, bears, bears everywhere! *(point in different*
    directions)
Bears climbing stairs. *(make climbing motion)*
Bears sitting on chairs. *(sitting motion)*
Bears collecting fares. *(reach out, as if taking money)*

Bears giving stares. *(eyes wide open, look around)*
Bears washing hairs. *(hair-washing motion)*
Bears, bears, bears everywhere! *(point)*

Going on a Bear Hunt

We are going hunting for a bear. *(shade eyes with hand and peer around)*
We will walk down the sidewalk; *(pat hands on knees for walking)*
Push our way through tall grass; *(alternately push hands away from body side to side)*
Swim a river; *(make swimming motions)*
And climb a tall tree. *("climb" as if pulling self up a rope, hands alternating)*

Keep looking!! *(shade eyes and peer all around)*
What do you see?? A bear???? *(act surprised)*
We have to get out of here! *(repeat above motions faster)*

Climb down that tree, and run!
Swim that river, and run!
Push through that grass, and run!
Now run up the sidewalk . . . and in the door . . .
And shut the door tight! *(clap hands loudly)*
Whew . . . I'm glad we are home safe!! *(wipe forehead with fingers and sigh)*

Parents' Follow-Up Ideas

A guess-what-I-am game uses the sounds and motions of different animals. Toddlers like to guess and act out the different animals with you. Start with a picture book about animals found on farms, in zoos, or at home. Initially choose animals that are familiar to your child. The book will give you ideas, and you can talk with your toddler about the animal's appearance, where it lives, and how it is different from others.

Watch for bears when shopping or traveling. This activity is fun because bears are plentiful. You will find them on clothing, linens, toys, and most products. Help your child become more observant by being on the look-out for bears. Name the different kinds of bears as your toddler finds them: polar bears, pandas, brown bears, etc. Examine displays of teddy bears in toy stores together. Can your child find the largest one? The smallest?

Cut pictures of bears out of magazines, catalogs, brochures, advertising flyers, and cereal boxes. Let your child sort them by size or color and then count them. Make a bear book, a bear mobile, or bear magnets for the refrigerator.

Craft

Kitchen Clay

You will need: 2 cups baking soda

1 cup cornstarch

1⅓ cups water

pinch of salt

sauce pan

waxed paper

towel

plastic bag

This recipe feels almost like *real* clay. Put all the ingredients in a saucepan and mix well. Stir over medium heat until the mixture bubbles and thickens. Turn out onto a board or waxed paper and let cool. Knead until smooth. Wrap in a damp towel and place in the refrigerator for 10–15 minutes.

Help your child learn how to squeeze, roll, pat, and make balls from clay and to put them together to make many different objects.

Store the clay in a tightly closed plastic bag in the refrigerator, and add a few drops of water to the bag to keep it from hardening.

To preserve a special creation, let the object harden in the air for a day or two. Paint with tempera or acrylic paints and cover with shellac. The result: a work of art!

Program Notes

Sign Language

BEAR Cross your arms over your chest with hands on shoulders and scratch twice.

Introduce the theme using a picture of a bear or a teddy bear toy.

Use flannelboard bears for the song, "Five Bears in Bed." Place the bears in a row on the flannelboard, then remove them one at a time as you chant or sing the song. In more mature groups, children can help remove bears during the song.

A bear puppet or teddy bear can give "bear hugs" to children, and children pass the hugs along to their adults.

Giveaways are bear straw caddies, a bear picture with holes punched in the top and bottom and threaded on a straw.

Fingertaster "tastes" honey-related flavors: bread and honey, honey cake, honey pancakes, etc.

Children exit the story space as lumbering bears.

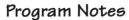
Notes

Bedtime

Books

Bedtime
JOHN RICHARDSON

Bedtime for Bear
SANDOL STODDARD

Clifford's Bedtime
NORMAN BRIDWELL

Going to Bed
SANDRA BOYNTON

Goodnight Moon (Also in
   Spanish: *Buenas Noches,
   Luna*)
MARGARET WISE BROWN

Joshua's Night Whispers
ANGELA JOHNSON

Just a Nap
MERCER MAYER

*K Is for Kiss Goodnight:
A Bedtime Alphabet*
JILL SARDEGNA

The Napping House
   (Also in Spanish:
   La Casa Adormecida)
AUDREY WOOD

Pajamas
LIVINGSTON AND MAGGIE TAYLOR

*Sheep, Sheep, Help Me
Fall Asleep*
ARLENE ALDA

Sweet Dreams, Spot!
ERIC HILL

Ten, Nine, Eight
MOLLY BANG

Twinkle, Twinkle Little Star
IZA TRAPANI

When It's Time for Bed
NICK BUTTERWORTH

*Where Does the Brown
Bear Go?*
NICKI WEISS

Rhythms, Rhymes, and Fingerplays

Going to Bed

This little child is going to bed *(point to self)*
Down on the pillow he lays his head. *(rest head
   on hands)*
He wraps himself in covers tight, *(wrap arms
   across body)*
And this is the way he sleeps all night.
   (close eyes, rest head on hands)
Morning comes, he opens his eyes. *(raise head,
   eyes wide open)*
Off with a toss the covers fly. *(fling arms wide)*
Soon he is up and dressed and away, *(jump up)*
Ready for fun and play all day. *(clap hands,
   turn in circle)*

Japanese Lullaby

	[translation]
(chant softly while parents rock their children on laps; use soothing sounds)	
Nen-ne-n ko-ro-ri-yo [Nehn-neh-nnn koh-roh-ree-yoh]	*Please go to sleep, la-la-la*
O-ko-ro-ri-yo [Oh-koh-roh-ree-yoh]	*La-la-la*
Bo-ya-wa yo-i-ko-da [Boh-yah-wah yoh-ee-koh-dah]	*Baby is a good baby*
Ne-n-ne-shi-na [Neh-nnn-neh-shee-nah]	*Please go to sleep.*
Bo-ya-no O-mo-ri-wa [Boh-yah-noh Oh-moh-ree-wah]	*Baby's nursemaid*
Do-ko-e-i-ta [Doh-koh-eh-ee-tah]	*Where did she go?*
An-o Ya-ma Ko-e-te [Ahn-oh Yah-mah Koh-ee-teh]	*Over that mountain*
Sa-to Ko-e-te [Sah-toh Koh-eh-teh]	*Over to a village*
Sa-to-no Mi-ya-ge Ni [Sah-toh-noh Mee-yah-geh Nee]	*What present will she bring?*
Na-ni Mo-ro-ta [Nah-nee Moh-roh-tah]	*What will you get from her?*
Den-den Da-i-ko-ni [Dehn-dehn Dah-ee-koh-nee]	*A toy drum*
Sho-u No-fu-e [Shoh-oo Noh-foo-eh]	*And a toy flute*

Rock-a-Bye-Baby   (song)

Rock-a-bye baby on a tree top. *(sway side to side, arms folded in a "cradle," as though holding a baby)*
When the wind blows, the cradle will rock. *(extend hands above head and keep swaying)*
When the bough breaks, *(clap hands on "breaks")* the cradle will fall. *(hands, palm upward, move apart)*
And down will come cradle, baby, and all. *(slowly lower hands, returning arms to "cradle" motion)*

Parents' Follow-Up Ideas

Take a walk outside with your toddler near sunset. Talk about the sun moving lower in the sky and changes in the light: sky colors, amount of light, silhouettes, and stars appearing. Notice objects you can see clearly earlier but not later. Help your child recognize the various stages of dimming light and realize that the object is still there although you can no longer see it.

If you can see the horizon, encourage your child to watch the sun's final moments of descent. What are other changes as day becomes night? Talk about lights appearing in houses and buildings and on streets. Are there changes in the wind, sounds, or smells? What other changes show your neighborhood is preparing for night and for bedtime?

Examine the night sky with your child. Talk about the things you see there: the moon, stars, meteor showers, or aircraft lights. What shape is the moon? Can you see only a few stars or many? Are there other lights? Are they moving, blinking, or standing still? Let your toddler point to a bright star and make a wish upon it together. "Star light! Star bright! First star I see tonight. I wish I may, I wish I might, Have the wish I wish tonight." All wishes are better when sealed with a kiss.

Bedtime is easier with a set routine. As in the story *Goodnight Moon*, toddlers need time to shift gears and settle down. A familiar routine, followed the same each night, will help your child feel more secure and relaxed, whether he or she is at home in bed or in a motel room. Baths; brushing teeth; putting on sleeping clothes; saying goodnight to family, pets, and toys; and sharing a book or two are all components of a good bedtime routine.

Craft

Bedtime Mobile

You will need: branch with several smaller twigs

            string (several pieces 12″ long)

            scissors

            index cards

            glue

            pictures from magazines, photos, tinfoil shapes, small toys, or items from nature

Cut out pictures, photos, or shapes and glue to both sides of an index card. Trim around the edges, and punch a small hole in the top of the card. Push one end of a piece of string through the hole and tie

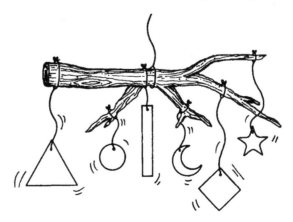

it in a knot. Tie the other end of the string to the branch and keep adding pictures, varying the length of the string and placement on the twigs. Hold the branch up often to see how it balances when hanging.

Find the center of the branch and tie a string there. Attach the mobile to the ceiling over your toddler's bed with a nail or plant hanger. It will move in the air currents, helping little ones fall asleep as they watch it. Change the items on the mobile or make a new one as seasons change or holidays approach. Use small objects (toys, pine cones, leaves, and so on) light enough to balance each other. Let your child help you accumulate the items to be added to a new mobile and decide where they will be placed.

Program Notes

Sign Language

SLEEP   With palms together, place your hands next to your cheek and lean your head against them as if on a pillow.

Introduce the theme with a sleepy storytime puppet. Provide a bed for the puppet (a pillow, box, or small blanket). The book *The Napping House* makes a good flannelboard or flip-chart story for toddlers. Between stories, the puppet can ask children to participate in its bedtime routine: changing clothes, brushing teeth, saying goodnight, etc. Share *Goodnight Moon*, and the puppet can give all children goodnight hugs, then they tuck it in bed. Place the "Asleep" doorknob hanger on the puppet's bed.

Giveaways are awake/asleep doorknob hangers made with index cards and yarn.

Fingertaster "tastes" bedtime snacks, such as milk, cookies, hot chocolate, etc.

Children exit the story space on tiptoe to keep from waking the puppet.

———————— **Notes** ————————

Birds

Books

Black Crow, Black Crow
GINGER FOGLESONG GUY

The Chick and the Duckling
MIRRA GINSBURG

The Chicken Book
GARTH WILLIAMS

Fluffy Little Duckling
TONY HUTCHINGS

Good-Night, Owl!
PAT HUTCHINS

Here a Chick, There a Chick
BRUCE MCMILLAN

*Little Robin Redbreast:
A Mother Goose Rhyme*

Look Out Bird!
MARILYN JANOVITZ

Mama Bird, Baby Bird
ANGELA JOHNSON

Our Yard Is Full of Birds
ANNE F. ROCKWELL

Pop-Up Little Duck
PEGGY TAGEL

Rosie's Walk
PAT HUTCHINS

Round Robin
JACK KENT

Season of Swans
MONICA WELLINGTON

*What Does the Rooster Say,
Yoshio?*
EDITH BATTLES

Where's That Duck? (Also
in Spanish: *Dónde Está
el Pato?*)
MARY BLOCKSMA

Rhythms, Rhymes, and Fingerplays

Five Little Red Birds

Five little red birds, *(hold up five fingers)*
Pecking at my door. *(mimic actions)*
One flew away, and
Then there were four. *(hold up four fingers)*

[Repeat with]
    Four . . . sitting in a tree. One pounced on
        a worm . . . three.
    Three . . . calling "Coo-coo-coo." One flew
        to a nest . . . two.
    Two . . . sleeping in the sun. One woke and
        hopped away . . . one.
    One . . . as lonely as could be. When it flew
        away, all that's left was me!

I'm a Little Chick

I'm a little chick who goes "Bawk, bawk, bawk!"
   (hands in armpits, flap arms like wings)
I dip my head when I walk, walk, walk.
   (lean front and back)
I scratch for a worm going "Bawk, bawk, bawk!"
   (one hand forms claw, make scratching motions)
Then I fly on home from my walk, walk, walk.
   (make flying motion)

I'm a little baby bird who goes "Peep, peep, peep!"
   (open and close fingers like a mouth)
I close my eyes when I sleep, sleep, sleep.
   (close eyes and rest head on hands)
I sing for my mommy going "Peep, peep, peep!"
   (open and close fingers like a mouth)
Then I ruffle my feathers and sleep, sleep, sleep.
   (close eyes and rest head on hands)

I'm a little duck who goes "Quack, quack, quack!"
   (open and close fingers like a mouth)
I waddle when I walk in the back, back, back.
   (put backs of hands on hips and wiggle side to side)
I swim in the water going "Quack, quack, quack!"
   (open and close fingers like a mouth)
Then I shake off my tail in the back, back, back.
   (wiggle rear)

Six Little Ducks   (traditional folk song)

Six little ducks that I once knew,
Fat ones, skinny ones, they were, too.

[Chorus]
   But one little duck with a feather in his back
   Led all the others with a quack, quack, quack.
   Quack, quack, quack! Quack, quack, quack!
   He led all the others with a quack, quack, quack!

Down to the water they did go,
Wibble, wobble, wibble, wobble to and fro.

[Chorus]

Home from the water they did come,
Wibble, wobble, wibble, wobble ho-hum-hum.

[Chorus]

Parents' Follow-Up Ideas

Tossing or dropping bean bags into a container (laundry basket, large pan, waste basket, or shoe box) is a good coordination exercise. Bean bags can be dropped from above by standing directly over containers, or they can be tossed from a short distance. To make bean bags, put a small amount of rice or beans in a plastic bag (newspaper bags work well) and tie the top closed. Slip the plastic bag inside a sock or mitten and sew the opening. Store bean bags inside a coffee can or shoe box.

Use cans with plastic lids (coffee, potato chip, or tennis ball containers) to make a bank for your child. Decorate the can with paint, photos, fabric, or contact paper, and cut a slot in the plastic lid. Show your toddler how to drop coins into the bank to "bank" any spare change. Keep the bank out of your child's reach, and supervise your toddler closely to prevent him or her from swallowing coins.

Compare real objects and animals with toys and pictures in books or magazines. Encourage your child to talk about the differences he or she sees in them. If you live in a city, visit a petting zoo to see real ducks and chickens and other farm animals.

Craft

Bean Bag Chickens

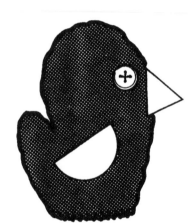

You will need: old mittens or hot mitts

buttons

fabric scraps or felt

glue

needle and thread

dried beans or rice

Hold the mitten up in front of you; the thumb will become the tail of the chicken and the opposite side is the chicken's head. Sew a button on each side for eyes and glue on a fabric triangle for a beak. Cut two semicircles of material for wings and glue them to each side of the body.

Fill a plastic bag loosely with dried beans or rice and close it securely. Slide the plastic bag in the mitten and sew the opening so that the beans will not fall out if handled roughly. Use scraps or yarn to create other animals or people out of other mitts.

Program Notes

Sign Language

BIRD Pinch your index finger and thumb together and place them in front of your mouth, opening and closing them like a beak.

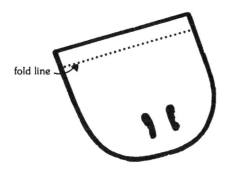
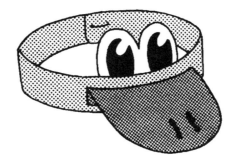
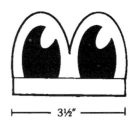

fold line

3½"

Storytime puppet introduces the theme wearing a duck headband and making quacking noises.

When using *Rosie's Walk,* make clucking noises throughout the book as Rosie walks. Good stories for flannelboards are *Goodnight Owl!* and *The Chicken Book.*

Giveaways are duck headbands made with a strip of construction paper that has eyes and a beak glued to it. Distribute the duck headbands and then sing the "Six Little Ducks" song.

Fingertaster "tastes" things birds like to eat, such as corn, sunflower seeds, nuts, etc.

Children leave the story space flapping their "wings" like baby birds.

——————————————— **Notes** ———————————————

Birthdays

Books

Birthday Monsters
SANDRA BOYNTON

Birthday Party
HELEN OXENBURY

Corduroy's Party
LYDIA FREEMAN

Dandelion
DON FREEMAN

Handtalk Birthday
REMY CHARLIP

Happy Birthday, Little Bear
HARRIET ZIEFERT

Happy Birthday, Sam
PAT HUTCHINS

Happy Birthday to Me
ANNE AND HARLOW ROCKWELL

Happy Birthday, Word Bird
JANE BELK MONCURE

Hello, Amigos!
TRICIA BROWN

I Can Do It by Myself
LESSIE JONES LITTLE AND
ELOISE GREENFIELD

*Mary Wore Her Red Dress and
Henry Wore His Green Sneakers*
MERLE PEEK

Max's Birthday
ROSEMARY WELLS

The Secret Birthday Message
ERIC CARLE

Spot Goes to a Party (Also
in Spanish: *Spot Va a
una Fiesta*)
ERIC HILL

Will It Ever Be My Birthday?
DOROTHY COREY

Rhythms, Rhymes, and Fingerplays

A Birthday

Today is *(insert child's name)* birthday
Let's make a birthday cake *(form circle with fingers)*
Mix and stir *(make stirring motions)*
Stir and mix,
Then into the oven to bake. *(palm up, make
    sliding motion)*

Peeking through the window *(shade eyes with hands)*
I like to see it bake.
Sniff, sniff, sniff. It smells so good! *(sniff)*
Hurry, hurry, cake! *(clap hands sharply)*

Here's our cake so nice and round *(form circle
    with fingers)*
We'll frost it pink and white. *(make frosting motions)*
We'll put two candles on it *(hold up two fingers)*
To make a birthday light.
And then, blow them out!! 1, 2. *(blow on fingers)*

It's Your Birthday   (tune "Skip to My Lou")

It's your birthday, *(point to a child)*
What'll I do? *(point to self)*
It's your birthday, what'll I do? *(repeat actions)*
It's your birthday, what'll I do? *(repeat actions)*
What'll I do for you, dear? *(point to self and then to child)*

[Verse 2]

  . . . Share my cookie, *(both hands together, fingers
    curled and touching)*
Break it in two. *(make breaking motion)*
That's what I'll do for you, dear.

[Verse 3]

  . . . Wrap your present in ribbons blue. *(one hand
    circles around the other, as though wrapping
    ribbon around a present)*
That's what I'll do for you, dear.

[Verse 4]

  . . . Give you a big hug and kisses, too. *(arms
    reach across body as though hugging someone,
    and blow a kiss)*
That's what I'll do for you, dear.

Balloon

This is the way we blow our balloon *(hold hands,
  palms together, in front of mouth)*
Blow!! Blow!! Blow!! *(blow into hands, pulling them
  apart slowly)*
This is the way we break our balloon *(hands wide apart)*
Oh!! Oh!! Oh!! *(clap hands 3 times)*

Parents' Follow-Up Ideas

Have a pretend birthday party (great for bad weather days). Invite pets, toys, or TV characters. Let your child help you put up decorations and set a "party" table. Wrap one of your child's old toys in Sunday comic pages or a decorated grocery sack. Devise a pretend birthday cake (sandwich, muffin, or cookie) and sing "Happy Birthday" to the lucky person or toy. Everybody helps blow out the pretend candles, and your child can open the gift.

Toddlers like to pretend. Sometimes this pretense helps them prepare for new situations, like taking a trip, Sunday School, parties, doctor visits, etc. When confronted with a new situation, try acting it out at home ahead of time to help your child feel more comfortable and know what is expected.

If your child has a birthday close to a major holiday like Christmas or Hanukkah, you can quietly celebrate on the actual date, then have an "unbirthday" party a few months later when the social calendar isn't as full.

One of the *best* presents you can give a toddler is a subscription to a magazine. Magazines are relatively inexpensive and arrive "new" every month, keeping reading material at hand and providing pictures to use in crafts. Besides, children love to get mail! There are many great magazines created especially for young children, such as *Your Big Back Yard* (nature topics) and *Sesame Street* (which comes with a separate parents' issue each month). Most libraries have *Magazines for Children*, a book that lists magazines and subscription information, grouping them by subject and age levels. Ask your librarian for help choosing the best magazines for your children.

Craft

Birthday Clown

You will need: scissors

colored paper

3 rubber bands (cut in half to make 6 pieces)

tape

glue

2 paste-on stars (for eyes)

From the colored paper, cut these shapes:

1 large heart (body)

2 small hearts (hands)

1 large circle (head)

3 small circles (pompoms)

1 small crescent (mouth)

2 small rectangles (shoes)

Using these shapes, assemble the head, hat, body, and pompoms to match the figure as shown. Glue a piece of rubber band to each shoe and hand, and then glue the other end to the back of the body as shown. Attach another rubber band to the top of the hat.

When you dangle the clown, it will dance for you! To make the clown more durable, reinforce each shape with light cardboard (3″×5″ card) before assembling.

Program Notes

Sign Language

BIRTHDAY With your right hand open on your chest, move your right hand out and down to lay, palm up, in open left hand.

Introduce the theme by singing "Happy Birthday" to the storytime puppet who is wearing a party hat. The puppet invites the children to join in its birthday celebration.

Use a flannelboard birthday cake with felt candles that can be added later. Let children take turns putting candles on the cake flannelboard, "blowing them out," and taking them down.

Although this theme lends itself to snacks, like cookies or cupcakes, some children have food allergies (to milk, flour, sugar, or peanuts). Check with parents the week before to see if you can offer a treat. If there is a child who cannot have the snack you've planned, cancel the snack or ask the parent for a suitable alternative for that child.

Giveaways are balloons, inflated and tied with ribbon or string. Put one balloon in a touch box (see appendix A), and invite children to reach inside to guess what is there.

Fingertaster "tastes" birthday party foods, such as cake, ice cream, raisins, etc.

Children exit the story space singing "Happy Birthday" to the puppet.

—————————— Notes ——————————

Boats

Books

Big City Port
BETSY MAESTRO

Boats
BYRON BARTON

Boats
ANNE ROCKWELL

Boats, Boats, Boats
JOANNA RUANE

Ferryboat
BETSY AND GIULIO MAESTRO

Four Brave Sailors
MIRRA GINSBURG

Harbor
DONALD CREWS

I Love Boats
FLORA MCDONNELL

Little Boat
SIAN TUCKER

Moon Bear's Canoe
FRANK ASCH

Mr. Gumpy's Outing
JOHN BURNINGHAM

My Blue Boat
CHRIS L. DEMAREST

Noah's Ark
LUCY COUSINS

Sail Away
DONALD CREWS

Ship
CHRIS L. DEMAREST

Who Sank the Boat?
PAMELA ALLEN

Rhythms, Rhymes, and Fingerplays

Boats! Boats!

[Chorus]
　　Boats! Boats! Lots of boats! *(clap hands in rhythm)*
　　Watch them go! Watch them float!

Row! Row! *(rowing motion, both arms extended,*
　　pull hands to chest together)
To and fro,
I am a ROW boat.

Toot! Toot! *(pretend to blow diesel horn)*
Chug-chug-chug, *(arms push and pull in piston motion)*
I am a TUG boat.

Come on wind *(blow air, hands form peak over head)*
Blow a gale!
I am a SAIL boat.

Going fast! *(hands alternately shoot across body)*
Whee! Whee!
I am a SPEED boat.

Back and forth, *("boat" sign; hands go right then left)*
People I carry
I am a FERRY boat.

Under water, *(make diving motion, palms together)*
Blub, blub, blub
I am a SUB-marine boat.

Row, Row, Row Your Boat   (song)

Row, row, row your boat,
Gently down the stream.
Merrily, merrily, merrily, merrily,
Life is but a dream.

Parents' Follow-Up Ideas

Sit on the floor with your legs open and with your toddler sitting in-side your legs facing you and holding your hands. Rock backward, gently pulling your child toward you. Then lean forward, having him or her rock backward. Sing "Row, Row, Row Your Boat" as you rock back and forth in a rowing motion. Do not rock so far backward that you pull your child's bottom off the floor. If necessary, move the child closer to you.

In the sink, bathtub, or wading pool, try floating different objects with your child to see which make good boats. Give your child lots of objects (plastic cup, jar lid, cork, and a rock). Experiment to see what floats and what doesn't. Styrofoam meat trays float well and can carry nonfloating cargo. After a rain storm or washing the car, float boats made of paper or leaves on water streams and puddles. *Safety tip:* Never leave children alone with even a few inches of water nearby.

Go on pretend boat rides with your toddler. Help your child use blocks, boxes, or pillows to make a boat shape or designate a bed or the couch as today's boat. Decide where you will journey to-gether and talk about the objects, animals, or people you "see" there. Take along a snack for a boat picnic, and re-member to "swim" anytime either of you leaves the boat.

Craft

Bathtub Boats

You will need: bottle cap or jar lid, bar of floating soap, cork, or empty walnut shell

toothpicks

dab of clay or clay dough

scissors

crayons

paper

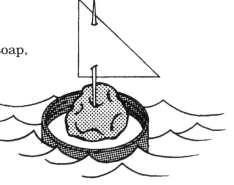

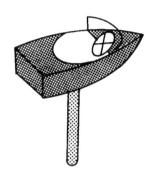

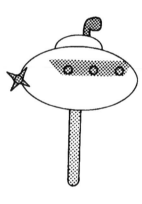

Cut a sail from the paper (triangle shape) and decorate it. Put your child's name on it. Poke a toothpick through the sail, through one side and out. Leave one end of the toothpick sticking down below the sail to anchor it to the boat. Stick a dab of clay inside the jar lid or shell, and press the toothpick into it. Your boat is now ready to sail.

If using cork or soap, the clay is not needed. Press the toothpick mast into the boat and set sail. If using a cork, cut a slit in one side and push a penny into it for balance.

Program Notes

Sign Language

BOAT   Cup your hands at waist level. Raise and lower your hands slightly as you move them away from your body (like a boat on the waves).

Introduce the theme using a toy boat or pictures of boats. Or create stick puppets of different boats and giving one to each child, let them float around the room before coming back to "port" and parking their boats in the "marina."

The "Boats, Boats" rhyme and *Mr. Gumpy's Outing* work best as flannelboards.

Giveaways can be boat stick puppets made with craft sticks and pictures cut from magazines or photocopied and colored. Folded paper boats also make good giveaways.

Fingertaster "tastes" watery flavors: sea water, bath water, fish, boiled potatoes, etc.

Invite children to carefully leave the story space in their favorite pretend boat. Remind them that even speedboats must go slower when other boats are around!

——————————— **Notes** ———————————

Bugs and Caterpillars

Books

Butterfly Kiss
MARCIAL BOO

Buzz! Buzz! Buzz!
BYRON BARTON

Inch by Inch
LEO LIONNI

The Itsy-Bitsy Spider
IZA TRAPANI

Ladybug, Ladybug
RUTH BROWN

Lift a Rock: Find a Bug
CHRIS SANTORO

Oh My, a Fly!
JAN PIENKOWSKI

Peek-a-Bug

Pooh and Some Bees
A. A. MILNE

Spider Magic
RUTH YOUNG AND MITCHELL ROSE

Spider on the Floor
RAFFI

Ten Flashing Fireflies
PHILEMON STURGES

Ugly Bug
DONALD CHARLES

The Very Hungry Caterpillar
    (Also in French: *La Chenille
    Affamee*, Spanish: *La Orga
    Muy Hambrienta*, and
    Vietnamese: *Chú Sâu Rọm
    Quá Đôi*)
ERIC CARLE

The Very Quiet Cricket
ERIC CARLE

*What's That Sound,
Woolly Bear?*
PHILEMON STURGES

Rhythms, Rhymes, and Fingerplays

Eency Weency Spider

Eency weency spider went up the water spout,
    (wiggle fingers upward in front of body)
Down came the rain and washed the spider out.
    (sweep arms down and to one side)
Out came the sun and dried up all the rain,
    (arms form circle over head)
And the eency weency spider went up the spout again.
    (wiggle fingers upward again)

Baby Bumble Bee   (traditional song)

I'm bringing home a baby bumble bee.
    (hold hand in front with fingers closed)
Won't my mommy be very proud of me?
I'm bringing home a baby bumble bee.
Buzzzz, buzzzzzz, buzzzzzzzzz . . .
Ouch! It stung me. *(open hand quickly and shake it)*

Caterpillar

This is the egg, found not far away.
>   *(point with index finger to center of other palm)*
This is the caterpillar, who one sunny day,
>   hatched from the egg, found not far away.
>   *(wiggle index finger like caterpillar)*

This is the cocoon all snuggled away,
>   that covered the caterpillar, who one sunny day,
>   hatched from the egg, found not far away.
>   *(form fist, cup other hand over it, peek inside)*

This is the butterfly, who did sashay
>   out of the cocoon all snuggled away,
>   that covered the caterpillar, who one sunny day,
>   hatched from the egg, found not far away.
>   *(palms toward you, hook thumbs together*
>   *and wiggle fingers)*

These are the wings, on bright display
>   worn by the butterfly, who did sashay
>   out of the cocoon all snuggled away,
>   that covered the caterpillar, who one sunny day,
>   hatched from the egg, found not far away.
>   *(raise and lower arms at sides like butterfly wings)*

Beautiful butterfly . . . Can I watch you play?
>   *("fly" your butterfly up, down, and around)*

Parents' Follow-Up Ideas

Make a butterfly sandwich for lunch. Cut one slice of bread diagonally, and lay the halves on a plate with the crust tips facing each other, forming wings. Spread jelly, cream cheese, or peanut butter on the bread and arrange cheese slices, carrot rounds, banana circles, or raisins to make the design on the wings. For the butterfly's antennae, cut celery or green pepper strips. Encourage your child to help think of other ways to decorate butterfly sandwiches or to make other "butterfly" lunches. How about a small pizza cut into quarters and re-arranged on a plate with a carrot as the butterfly's body?

Create a nesting game using different sizes of cans from mushrooms, soups, vegetables, etc. Cleanly cut open one end of cans so there are no sharp edges. Remove the contents and the labels; wash the cans thoroughly and dry them. Cover the cut edges with adhesive or cloth tape to protect small fingers from accidental cuts. Cans may be stacked upside down on top of each other to build things or nested inside each other for storage. For more-colorful cans, cover them with bright contact paper.

To make a quick finger puppet, cut a finger from an old glove. Decorate it with markers, fabric, or yarn scraps to make ears, mouths, hair, etc. To make eyes, sew on buttons or glue on small wiggle-eyes. Make a caterpillar finger puppet, then add some wings to turn it into a butterfly.

Craft

Colorful Butterfly

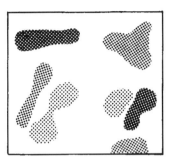

You will need: paper towels

newspapers

food coloring or tempera paint

sponge or small paintbrush

pipe cleaners

small containers (baby food jars, margarine containers, muffin pan)

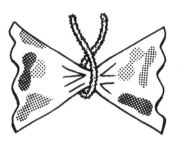

Cover the table with newspapers, several layers thick. Lay a paper towel flat on the newspapers. Pour food colors into separate containers for each color. With the sponge or paintbrush, help your child dab or drop each color on the paper towel. Help your child notice how the colors spread through the towel. Where they mingle, new colors are created. Clear water can be sprinkled on the towel to lighten or spread the colors more. Hang the towel and let it dry thoroughly.

When dry, fold the towel lengthwise in accordion pleats. Pinch the pleats together at the center and twist a pipe cleaner around to hold them. Curve the ends of the pipe cleaner to look like antennae, and fluff out the paper towel on both sides of the pipe cleaner to form wings. Decorate your windows or room with beautiful butterflies.

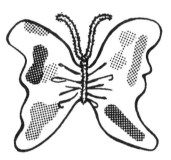

Program Notes

Sign Language

BUTTERFLY Cross your hands at the wrists, palms facing chest. Link your thumbs and wiggle your fingers like butterfly wings.

Storytime puppet introduces the theme with butterfly stickers or one of the storytime books about insects.

Use a finger puppet with *Inch by Inch,* having it measure the birds in the book. Following a stretching activity, the inchworm can measure children's arms, hands, etc.

Use stick puppets or a flannelboard of "Eency Weency Spider" and let children help the spider climb the spout.

After sharing *The Very Hungry Caterpillar,* introduce a sock puppet caterpillar that turns into a butterfly (instructions are in appendix A).

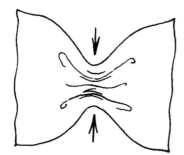

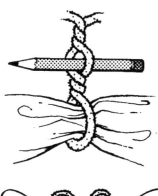

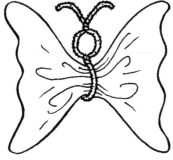

Shorten the number of insects in *The Very Quiet Cricket*. Giveaways are pipe-cleaner and facial tissue butterflies. Fingertaster "tastes" foods from *The Very Hungry Caterpillar*. Children exit the story space as butterflies.

——————————— **Notes** ———————————

Cats

Books

Calico Cat's Year (Also in
  Spanish: *El Año del
  Gato Galano*)
DONALD CHARLES

Do You Like Cats?
JOANNE OPPENHEIM

Find the Kitten
STEPHEN CARTWRIGHT AND
CLAUDIA ZEFF

Have You Seen My Cat?
ERIC CARLE

The Kitten Book
JAN PFLOOG

Kitten for a Day
EZRA JACK KEATS

Kittens Love
LISA MCCUE

Little Kitten
JUDY DUNN

My Cats, Nick & Nora
ISABELLE HARPER

One Little Kitten
TANA HOBAN

Pat the Cat
EDITH KUNHARDT

Soft as a Kitten
AUDEAN JOHNSON

The Three Little Kittens
PAUL GALDONE

What's Maggie Up To?
DURGA BERNHARD

*When One Cat Woke Up:
A Cat Counting Book*
JUDY ASTLEY

*Where's My Fuzzy Blanket?
A Lift-and-Touch Book*
NOELLE CARTER

Rhythms, Rhymes, and Fingerplays

I Have a Cat

I have a cat *(one hand strokes the other)*
My cat is fat! *(arms form large circle)*
I have a cat. *(stroking motion)*
It wears a hat. *(hands on head)*
I have a cat. *(stroking motion)*
It caught a bat. *(make grabbing motion)*
I have a cat. *(stroking)*
Purrrrrrrrrrrr,
Meeeooowww!

Pretty Kitty   (tune: "Frere Jacques")

Pretty kitty. Pretty kitty.
Where are you? Where are you?
With your fur so silky,
And your tickly whiskers.
Meow, me—ow. Meow, me—ow.

Five Little Kittens

One, two, three, four, five *(count fingers on one hand)*
Five little kittens standing in a row. *(stand up straight)*
They nod their heads to the children, so. *(nod head)*
They run to the left, *(run in place, turning left)*
They run to the right, *(run in place, turning right)*
They stand and stretch in the bright sunlight.
   (stretch arms over head)
Along comes a dog, looking for some fun.
   (hunch shoulders)
Meowwww! Meowwww! *(fingers cupped, reach out
   quickly in scratching motion)*
See that doggie run! *(clap hands quickly)*

Parents' Follow-Up Ideas

Trace your children's hands and feet on a paper sack. Cut out the tracings and hang them where they can be admired. Indicate which cupboards or drawers your children are allowed to get into by taping one of their handprints to the outside. This works well for clothes and toy storage areas also. Trace hands from other members of the family and compare them. How are they alike and different? Write on handprints short notes dictated by your toddler or let your toddler decorate them and mail them to friends and relatives as impromptu greeting cards.

Our familiar house cats are part of a much larger family that includes lions, tigers, pumas, and panthers. Introduce your children to a neighbor's cat (if you do not have one at home), helping them learn how to treat animals smaller than they are. As a field trip, visit a pet store or humane shelter to observe cats. Watch how they move and what they do. Let your child mimic cats and talk about their behavior: cleaning, moving tails, stretching, jumping, etc. Visit the big cat exhibit at a local zoo or watch a nature program on television together and see if your child notices some of the same behaviors in the much larger cat cousins.

When your toddlers are in stubborn moods, chanting will help distract them and get them to cooperate. Start with a nursery rhyme, such as "Jack and Jill," "Humpty Dumpty," or "Little Boy Blue," and gradually change the words to what you want them to do: "Little Boy Blue, we're putting on your shoe; your shoe, shoe, shoe. There's two, two, two, shoes, shoes, shoes." Play with the words and the rhythms, keeping your voice lighthearted. Chanting often helps uncooperative and restless children refocus their attentions.

Craft

Yummy Gelly Animals

You will need: 2 envelopes of unflavored gelatin

2 small boxes of flavored gelatin (with or without sugar)

$1\frac{1}{2}$ cups cold water

$1\frac{1}{2}$ cups hot water

flat cake pan or cookie sheet with sides

cookie cutters

covered container for storage

Dissolve the unflavored gelatin in the cold water. Add the hot water to the flavored gelatin and stir until dissolved. Add flavored gelatin mixture to cold water mixture and stir until thoroughly mixed.

Pour gelatin into a flat cake pan or cookie sheets with rims. Chill in the refrigerator until firm, then cut with cookie cutters to make animals and shapes (or cut gelatin into blocks with a knife). Save all the scraps to nibble on later.

Store shapes in a covered container in the refrigerator. Although the mixture is as wiggly as traditional Jello, it is easier to handle with fingers and fun to eat. Use some caution when your child is eating gelly animals; the coloring may stain some fabrics.

Program Notes

Sign Language

CAT   Pinch your thumbs and index fingers together parallel to the edges of your mouth and move your hands outward, as though stroking a cat's whiskers.

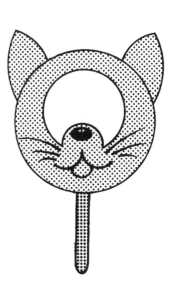

Storytime puppet introduces the theme making purring and meowing noises and asking the children to guess what the animal is.

Three Little Kittens makes a good flannelboard story. *Pat the Cat* and *Soft as a Kitten* are good for children with visual difficulties since they can feel the kitten's fur. The rhyme "Five Little Kittens" can become a full action rhyme, as children act it out.

Giveaways are kitten masks made from paper plates and wooden sticks, making the ears out of the center of the plate that was cut away.

Fingertaster "tastes" foods cats enjoy, such as milk, tuna fish, melted ice cream, catnip, or catsup (ketchup).

Children exit the story space purring like cats.

 Notes

Circus

Books

Animals, Animals in the Circus

At the Carnival
KIRSTEN HALL

Bearymore
DON FREEMAN

Carousel
DONALD CREWS

Circus Baby
MAUD AND MISKA PETERSHAM

Clifford at the Circus
NORMAN BRIDWELL

Clown Caboose
JOANNE BARKAN

Come to the Circus

Do You See What I See?
MATHEW PRICE

Harry Goes to Fun Land
HARRIET ZIEFERT

Little Chicken Chicken
DAVID MARTIN

Paddington at the Circus
MICHAEL BOND

Peter Spier's Circus
PETER SPIER

Spot Goes to the Circus (Also in Spanish: *Spot Va al Circo*)
ERIC HILL

Up & Down on the Merry-Go-Round
BILL MARTIN

Word Bird's Circus Surprise
JANE BELK MONCURE

Rhythms, Rhymes, and Fingerplays

Five Circus Elephants

Five circus elephants waiting near the door.
   (hold up five fingers)
One jumps through a hoop, *(jump in place)*
And now there are four. *(hold up four fingers)*

Four circus elephants looking up to see.
   (four fingers)
One walks around the ring, *(walk in place)*
And now there are three. *(three fingers)*

Three circus elephants waiting for their cue.
   (three fingers)
One dances to a song, *(dance in place)*
And now there are two. *(two fingers)*

Two circus elephants looking for some fun.
   (two fingers)
One bounced a yellow ball, *(bouncing motion)*
And now there is one. *(one finger)*

One circus elephant standing all alone.
   (one finger)
He waved his trunk to say goodbye,
   (wave arm side to side in front of body)
And slowly walked on home. *(walk in circle)*

Circus (tune: "Sailing, Sailing")

Circus, circus,
Under the tent so high,
Prancing ponies and dancing dogs
Merrily go by.

Lions roaring,
Ladies flying high!
Elephants and silly clowns
All at the circus. Oh, my!

Five Little Clowns

Five little clowns all in a row, *(hold up five fingers)*
Wearing funny hats *(pat head)*
And polka-dotted bows. *(hands make motion
   like fixing a bow tie)*
One little clown hopped away, *(hop in place)*
Back to the circus to laugh and play.
   (wave "good-bye")

[Repeat with]
   Four . . . danced away *(dancing motion)*
   Three . . . somersaulted *(turn around)*
   Two . . . zoomed *(shoot hand quickly in
      front of body)*
   One . . . tiptoed *(tiptoe in place)*

Parents' Follow-Up Ideas

Draw three large circles on a sidewalk or driveway with chalk or
arrange a hose in looping circles in the grass. Number each circle (or
label them with colors, alphabet letters, shapes, etc.). Let your toddler become the performer as you play the part of the ring master describing the action. "In ring number one are prancing horses. See
them march around the ring . . . and jump high . . . and turn 'round
and 'round. Listen to them neigh!" This is a fun activity for play
groups. For a change of pace, let a child be the ring master and you
become one of the performers.
   Draw a simple picture of a chubby clown or copy one from a coloring book. Give your child a page of colored dot stickers and let her
decorate the clown's costume. When the costume is finished, count

the number of dots of each color. As an alternative, make several clowns, one with red dots, one with blue, etc.

Tie a short piece of clothesline between the backs of two chairs, pulling the chairs apart until the line is taut. Using clip clothespins, show your child how to hang things on the line, to display artwork, favorite animal pictures, or pretend to hang some clothes out to "dry." *Safety tip:* Push the chairs up against a wall so no one will walk between them and get caught in the line.

Craft

Clown Poncho

You will need: a rectangular piece of fabric, an old
                    pillowcase cut up two sides, or a bath towel

scissors

needle and thread or fabric glue

fabric circles in bright colors

pompoms

ribbon (optional)

Fold the fabric in half, lengthwise. Fold it again, keeping the folded edges together, as shown. Cut a semicircle at the center fold and open the cloth. Cut a 2″ slit from the circle at the front of the poncho. (If circle is too small to go over child's head, fold the cloth again and cut a larger semicircle or make the slit longer.) Sew or glue pompoms down the front of the poncho and attach colored fabric circles randomly to the front and back. Do not use felt for circles if the poncho will be washed.

Optional: To make ties for the sides of the poncho, cut ribbon into four pieces. Sew two to the front sides and two to the back sides. Make other circus ponchos for lion tamers, circus master, acrobats, members of the circus band, etc.

Program Notes

Sign Language

CIRCUS   Your left hand forms a curved "c" shape, palm down. Your right hand, fingertips together, touches the back of the left hand, then it moves out and around to create a circle, like a circus ring.

Mention the clown/circus connection during the opening routine as you assemble the clown shape puzzle described in the opening routine. Storytime puppet can help introduce the theme wearing a clown hat or red nose. If there is a clown troupe in your town, invite a clown to come *at the end* of your program to make balloon animals

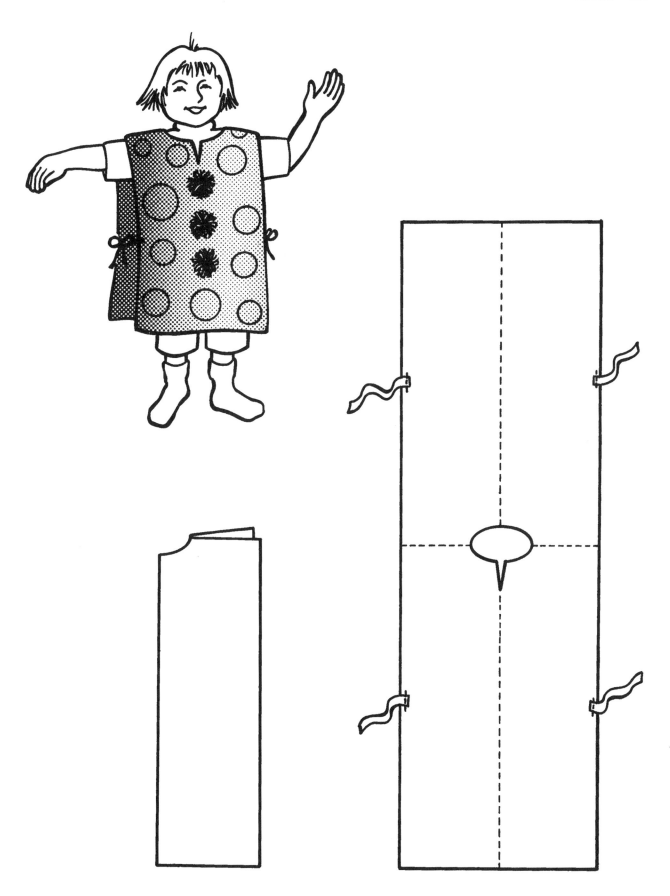

for children. Remember, most toddlers are afraid of clowns, so interview your clown visitor before to be certain the person has experience with this age and is sensitive to their needs. Before a clown visits, talk about clowns as people who like to dress up in silly clothes and put on makeup to make children laugh. Have the storytime puppet lead the contact with the clown, shyly approaching the clown, examining the makeup and costume, and finally taking a balloon or giving a hug. *Note:* No child should be forced to participate. Let the puppet be the intermediary for those who do not want to get near the clown.

The "Five Circus Elephants" and "Five Little Clowns" rhymes work well as flannelboard presentations.

Giveaways are clown stickers (or balloon figures if there is a clown visitor).

Fingertaster "tastes" foods from circuses or fairs, such as corn on the cob, cotton candy, corn dogs, popcorn, etc.

Children exit the story space prancing like circus ponies.

———————————— **Notes** ————————————

Colors

Books

Baby's Colors
NAOMI MCMILLAN

Big Bird's Color Game

*Brown Bear, Brown Bear,
What Do You See?*
BILL MARTIN

*Brown Cow, Green Grass,
Yellow Mellow Sun*
ELLEN JACKSON

Colors
HEIDI GOENNEL

Fuzzy Yellow Duckling
MATTHEW VANFLEET

In the House
ANGIE SAGE

Mouse Paint
ELLEN WALSH

My Very First Book of Colors
ERIC CARLE

Paddington's Colors
MICHAEL BOND

Pink, Red, Blue, What are You?
LAURA MCGEE KVASNOSKY

Purple Is a Part of a Rainbow
    (Also in Spanish: *El Morado
    es Parte del Arco Iris*)
CAROLYN KOWALCZYK

Spot Looks at Colors (Also in
    Spanish: *Spot Mira los
    Colores*)
ERIC HILL

What Color? ¿Qué Color?
ALAN BENJAMIN

White Rabbit's Color Book
ALAN BAKER

Who Said Red?
MARY SERFOZO

Rhythms, Rhymes, and Fingerplays

What Are You Wearing?
(tune: "Mary Had a Little Lamb")

Martin* has a red shirt on,
Red shirt on, red shirt on.
Martin has a red shirt on.
I see him here today.

[*Use the names of your children
and the colors of their clothes.]

Green Says Go

Green says, "Go!" *(march in place quickly)*
Go! Go! Go!
Yellow says, "Slow!" *(march slowly)*
Slow . . . slow . . . slow.
And red says, "Stop!" *(stop suddenly)*
Go, go, go! *(move fast)*

Slow . . . slow . . . slow. *(move slowly)*
And STOP! *(stop)*

[Repeat go, slow, stop instructions several times,
giving children the opportunity to pretend they
are cars driving down the street.]

Purple Song   (tune: "Twinkle, Twinkle Little Star")

Purple, purple
I see you.
Purple is a grape,
And a flower, too.
Part of the rainbow,
Up in the sky.
Purple's a color
On a butterfly.
Purple, purple,
I see you.
Purple is a grape
and a flower, too.

Parents' Follow-Up Ideas

It is a fact of life that crayons break, and the smaller pieces get scattered or worse (crushed under foot). Recycle broken crayons into multicolored "cookies" that are easy for small hands to hold and fun to use. Cut broken pieces into ¼″ lengths and place three or four pieces in each section of a muffin pan. Bake at 250° for 5 minutes or until the pieces just start to melt together. Turn off the oven and let the muffin pan cool inside. Remove it when it is completely cooled and store the crayon cookies in a covered container.

Fingerpainting can be messy, so wear an old shirt for a smock and put newspaper under the surface where you'll be working.

To make fingerpaint combine:

liquid laundry starch or paste mixed with an equal amount
   of liquid dishwashing detergent

food coloring

Add the food coloring to the starch. dampen a piece of paper (shelf or butcher paper works best) and drop several teaspoons of fingerpaint on it. Use one or more colors. With fingers, hands, and wrists, encourage toddlers to swirl the paint around and around, making and changing the designs. Lay it on newspapers to dry.

For toddlers who don't like getting their hands messy, put the paint inside a zipping plastic bag and close it. Another idea is to let your toddler paint on a cookie sheet with a plastic spoon or paintbrush. The results are the same as above but without the mess.

Craft

Traffic Light

You will need: black construction paper or felt

green, yellow, and red construction paper or felt

scissors

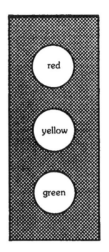

Cut a 4″×9″ rectangle from the black paper or felt. Using a can or glass as a pattern, draw circles on the green, yellow, and red construction paper or felt and cut them out.

Take turns with your toddler putting the colored circles onto the traffic light. As you do, talk about each color and what it means for safety.

Program Notes

Sign Language

STOP   Bring the edge of the right hand down sharply in the palm of the left hand.

Introduce the theme by naming the colors of the shape puzzle pieces in the opening routine. Point out matching colors in the room or children's clothing.

Storytime puppet can lead the "What Are You Wearing?" song as everyone stands and claps.

With the traffic light on the flannelboard, share the rhyme "Green Says Go," then have children be cars as you call out the colors (with hints like "Go! Go! Go!"). Repeat several times before "slowing" them down for the quiet activity.

Giveaways are colorful stickers or gummed stars.

Fingertaster "tastes" colorful foods, such as red apples, yellow bananas, purple grapes, etc.

Children exit the story space with the traffic light showing yellow so they are going slowly.

––––––––––––––––––––––––– Notes –––––––––––––––––––––––––

—————— Counting ——————

Books

AfroBets 1 2 3
CHERYL WILLIS HUDSON

Corduroy's Day
LYDIA FREEMAN

Count on Calico Cat (Also in
    Spanish: *Cuenta con
    Gato Galano*)
DONALD CHARLES

*Fish Eyes: A Book
You Can Count On*
LOIS EHLERT

Max's Toys: A Counting Book
ROSEMARY WELLS

One Crow
JIM AYLESWORTH

*One Good Horse: A
Cowpuncher's Counting Book*
ANN HERBERT SCOTT

One Wet Jacket
NANCY TAFURI

*One White Sail: A
Caribbean Counting Book*
S. T. GARNE

*One Yellow Lion: Fold-Out
Fun with Numbers*
MATTHEW VANFLEET

Over in the Meadow
JOHN LANGSTAFF

Paddington's 1 2 3
MICHAEL BOND

Splash!
ANN JONAS

Spot Counts 1 to 10
ERIC HILL

Who's Afraid?
CARLA DIJS

Willie Can Count
ANNE F. ROCKWELL

Rhythms, Rhymes, and Fingerplays

Inside the Space Shuttle

Inside the space shuttle *(crouch down low)*
Just enough room. *(pull hands close to body)*
Here comes the countdown,
1, 2, 3, 4, 5—
ZOOOOOOMMM! *(Jump up, throwing hands
    above head)*

A-Counting We Will Go   (tune: "A-Hunting We Will Go")

A-counting we will go. *(clap in rhythm)*
A-counting we will go.
1-2-3
4 and 5
A-counting we will go.

We're going to count our fingers. *(wiggle fingers)*
We're going to count our fingers.
1-2-3 *(count on fingers)*

4 and 5
A-counting we will go.

We're counting as we jump.
(bounce up and down)
We're counting as we jump,
1-2-3 *(count as you bounce)*
4 and 5,
A-counting we will go.

Count With Me

Count with me in Spanish.
Count with me and see.
Counting in Spanish
Is as easy as can be!
One is uno [oo-no]
Two is dos [dose]
Three is tres [trace]
Four is quatro [kwa-tro]
Five is cinco [seen-ko]
Count with me in Spanish:
Uno, dos, tres, quatro, cinco.
It's as easy as can be!

[Verse 2]

   . . . Swahili.
   One is moja [mo-jah]
   Two is mbili [im-bee-lee]
   Three is tatu [tah-too]
   Four is nne [nah-nay]
   Five is tano [tah-no]

[Verse 3]

   . . . Japanese.
   One is ichi [ee-chee]
   Two is ni [nee]
   Three is san [sahn]
   Four is shi [shee]
   Five is go [goh]

Parents' Follow-Up Ideas

Counting in rhymes and listening to numbers and their sequence is vitally important for young children. Count everything! Don't expect or push your children to count with you. It is the sound of the number words and the sequence in which they are spoken that is important and entertaining for toddlers.

   The strong rhythms in poetry and nursery rhymes help your children develop a sense of rhythm, which will make it easier for them to learn to count and to read later on. Recite favorite nursery rhymes, sing songs, and chant (even nonsense sounds) often to your child.

Identify the numbers 1–9 by name wherever you see them: in stores, on billboards or street signs, on price tags, etc. Don't push your children to understand the *math* that makes 2 into 3. Help them learn the word *two* means the numeral 2 and both of them represent two objects on the table.

Craft

Counting Balls

You will need: construction paper or colorful magazine pages

scissors

tape

string (optional)

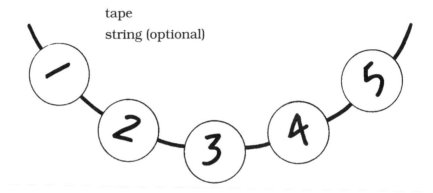

Trace around a glass or bowl to make five circles on different colors of paper. Cut out the circles and number them 1 to 5. Tape them to a door, refrigerator, or wall low enough that your child can touch them or make a mini-clothesline with a piece of string tied between two objects on which the circles are hung.

Each time you pass them, count the circles. Don't draw too much attention to yourself; just nonchalantly count, "1, 2, 3, 4, 5" and touch each circle as you pass by. Soon your child will be copying this activity and counting, too. Use these circles to talk about colors and line relationships (front, middle, and back).

Program Notes

Sign Language

ONE   Your index finger is extended (the palm faces forward on all numbers).

TWO   Your index and middle fingers are extended.

THREE Your thumb, index finger, and middle finger are extended.

FOUR   Fingers extended, thumb folded across palm.

FIVE   Your thumb and all fingers are extended.

Introduce the theme by counting the pieces of the shape puzzle in the opening routine before rearranging them into the clown. Point out the "two" stars and have the children find them on their name tags and count them. Encourage parents to count with you as you share today's books.

Put five objects on the flannelboard and use them as you recite "Count with Me." Count things in twos with children and adults standing. Count: eyes, ears, feet, knees, hands, etc. Then do actions and count them: 2 hops, 2 claps, 2 big steps, 2 little steps.

Giveaways are bee bookmarks made by copying the pattern on this page.

Fingertaster "tastes" small foods and includes numbers, such as three raisins, two grapes, one cookie, etc.

Children exit the story space counting in cadence: 1, 2; 1, 2 . . .

—————————— Notes ——————————

———————— Dancing ————————

Books

Barnyard Dance
SANDRA BOYNTON

Bertie and the Bear
PAMELA ALLEN

Best Dressed Bear (Also in
    Spanish: *El Oso Más Elegante*)
MARY BLOCKSMA

Boom-De-Boom
ELAINE EDELMAN

Color Dance
ANN JONAS

Come Dance with Me
CAROL NICKLAUS

Dance Away
GEORGE SHANNON

Dancing Class
HELEN OXENBURY

Dancing Daisy
KAY GALLWEY

Hop Jump
ELLEN WALSH

Jiggle, Wiggle, Prance
SALLY NOLL

Red Dancing Shoes
DENISE LEWIS PATRICK

Moondance
FRANK ASCH

Stamp Your Feet
SARAH HAYES

Word Bird's Rainy-Day Dance
JANE BELK MONCURE

Wibbly Pig Can Dance!
MICK INKPEN

Rhythms, Rhymes, and Fingerplays

Me and My Shadow   (tune: "Me and My Shadow")

Me and my shadow, *(sway side to side)*
Dancing down the avenue.
I raise my arms up, *(raise arms)*
And my shadow does it, too. *(raise arms, again)*

I kick my legs out, *(kick legs)*
Then I bend down very low. *(bend down)*
My shadow's with me, *(sway)*
Dancing fast—*(sway fast)*
Or . . . dancing . . . slow. *(sway slow)*

My dancing partner *(sway)*
Is with me when the sun does shine. *(arms
    form circle over head)*
My shadow's dancing, *(sway)*
With me, and it's mine, all mine! *(hands on chest,
    sway side to side)*

Clap Your Hands

Clap, clap, clap your hands, *(clap hands*
in rhythm with words)
Clap your hands with me.
Clap them fast! *(clap quickly)*
Clap—them—slow. *(clap slowly)*
Clap your hands with me. *(return to*
original rhythm)

[continue with]

Stomp, stomp your feet
Pat your knees
La-la, sing a song

Dancing Animals   (tune: "Mulberry Bush")

This is the way the horses prance,
("trot" in place, knees high)
The horses prance, the horses prance.
This is way the horses prance,
Dancing in the morning.

[continue with]

ducks waddle
bunnies hop
worms wiggle
cats stretch

Parents' Follow-Up Ideas

Dancing is a celebration of motion. Help your children discover the rhythms of the world around them by pointing out rhythm, movements, and cadences in familiar things. Imitate the movement of flags or a wind-tossed tree, the actions of machines (large and small), or dancers on television. Capture the rhythms of poetry and music using your feet, hands, arms, head, or whole body.

There are many opportunities to dance:

- Mirror dances: Dance and sing together in front of a full-length mirror. Toddlers love watching themselves and others as mirror images. Once your children have the hang of it, dance facing them, becoming their "mirror" and copying the things they do. Trade places, and let them "mirror" you.
- Shadow dances: In a place with a strong light source behind your children so that their shadows will be prominent, encourage them to dance, hop, jump, skip, etc., and watch their shadows do it, too. Give them ribbon streamers, hoops, or a cape to make the shadow more intriguing. This is a good outside activity when the sunshine is bright and shadows can be seen on the ground or on a wall.

- Animal dances: Imitate the movement of animals, especially those that move fast or slow or have quick, jerky movements.

Save musical crib toys for dancing. Let children hold the toys and make the music as they move. If the toy is the type with a cord to make it play, let your toddler start it and both of you dance when the music plays. If the music slows down before stopping, encourage toddlers to slow their movements to match. When the music stops, stop dancing.

Crafts

Hand Streamers and Ankle Bells

You will need: 2 drapery rings (or other small circles like canning or shower curtain rings)

strips of colorful cloth, ribbons, or crepe paper streamers

yarn

2 pipe cleaners

small jingle bells

Hand Streamers (make 2): Tie a bell to the metal eye of the drapery ring, forming the bottom of the hand streamer. Gather several strips of cloth together and tie them to one side of the drapery ring so the tails of the strips hang freely. Repeat on other side, leaving room at the top of the ring for the child's hand. Using materials of different weights (nylon, cottons, blends, tulle) or combining materials (cloth, plastic, paper) will make the streamers float and reflect light in different ways. Holding one ring in each hand, children can twirl and run with the streamers floating behind them.

Ankle Bells (make 2): Thread several small bells on a pipe cleaner, and attach it around your child's ankle so it jingles with every step. Use these dancing props with some of the follow-up suggestions.

Program Notes

Sign Language

DANCE   Place your left hand, palm upward, with fingers toward right (becomes the dance floor); your right hand, with the index and middle fingers extended downward over your left palm, swings side to side (as though dancing)

This is an excellent time to include music in your program. If you do not play an instrument, bring a tape recorder or portable CD player and play favorite children's songs between stories. Sing and chant together as everyone dances. Between stories introduce shadow dancing with a bright desk light or film projector aimed at a wall or if you have a full-length mirror, encourage children and adults to mirror-dance.

Giveaways are small bells threaded on pipe cleaners.

Fingertaster "tastes" beverages, such as orange juice, Kool Aid, lemonade, etc.

Children exit the story space dancing.

— Notes —

——————— December ———————

Books

Christmas Cookies
WENDY CHEYETTE LEWISON

Claude, the Dog
DICK GACKENBACH

Clifford's First Christmas
NORMAN BRIDWELL

*Corduroy's Christmas:
A Lift-the-Flap Book*
B. G. HENNESSY

Dear Santa
ALAN BENJAMIN

Hanukkah
ALAN BENJAMIN

Happy Christmas, Gemma
SARAH HAYES

Kente Colors
DEBBIE CHOCOLATE

Let's Trim the Tree
BERNICE CHARDIET

Max's Christmas (Also in
    Spanish: *La Navidad de Max*)
ROSEMARY WELLS

My First Kwanzaa Book
DEBORAH M. CHOCOLATE

Sammy Spider's First Hanukkah
SYLVIA A. ROUSS

Spot's First Christmas (Also in
    Spanish: *La Primera Navidad
    de Spot*)
ERIC HILL

*What Is Hanukkah?
A Lift-the-Flap Book*
HARRIET ZIEFERT

*Where's My Christmas Stocking?
A Lift-and-Touch Book*
NOELLE CARTER

Word Bird's Christmas Words
JANE BELK MONCURE

Rhythms, Rhymes, and Fingerplays

Hanukkah Candles   (tune: "Ten Little Indians")

One little, two little, three little candles,
Four little, five little, six little candles,
Seven little, eight little Hanukkah candles,
Shining on my menorah.
Eight little, seven little, six little candles,
Five little, four little, three little candles,
Two little, one little Hanukkah candle,
Shining on my menorah.

[*Note:* This rhyme can also be used for Divali, the Indian
Festival of Lights, which is also celebrated in December.
Change "Hanukkah candles" to "candles for Divali," and
the last line to "A festival of lights."]

Looking for Santa

We are looking for Santa *(arms form circle in front
   of belly and laugh "Ho-Ho-Ho!")*
Is the North Pole that way? Or that way? *(point in
   several directions)*
We will walk down the sidewalk, *(pat hands on knees)*
Don't fall on the ice! *(hands slide off knees left and right)*
We will swim across the ocean, *(make swimming motions)*
Climb up a snow bank, *(make climbing motions)*
And slide down the other side. *(hands slide from the
   knees down and away from the body)*

I see a little house. *(hand shades eyes)*
Knock on the door. Knock, knock, knock. *(make
   knocking motion)*
And there's Santa Claus! *(arms circle big belly and
   laugh "Ho, Ho, Ho!")*
Say, "Hi, Santa!" *(wave and call out greeting)*
Wait! He says we should hurry home to bed so he
   can come visit us.
Say, "Bye, Santa!" *(wave and say good bye)*

We'd better run! *(pat knees quickly)*
Climb up that snow bank *(fast climbing motion)* and run!
Slide down the other side *(fast sliding motion)* and run!
Swim across the ocean *(fast swimming motion)* and run!
Careful not to fall on the ice. *(fast slipping motion)*

Run in the house and shut the door *(clap hands sharply)*
Jump in bed and go to sleep. *(lay cheek on hands)*
Merry Christmas, Santa, and good night. *(close eyes
   and snore)*

Merry Christmas   (tune: "We Wish
   You a Merry Christmas")

We wish you a merry Christmas,
We wish you a merry Christmas,
We wish you a merry Christmas,
It's that time of year.

We'll decorate our Christmas tree,
We'll decorate our Christmas tree,
We'll decorate our Christmas tree,
With ornaments dear.

We'll bake up some Christmas cookies,
We'll bake up some Christmas cookies,
We'll bake up some Christmas cookies,
To bring you good cheer.

We'll sing songs with fa-la-la's,
We'll sing songs with fa-la-la's,
We'll sing songs with fa-la-la's,
Christmas is near.

Parents' Follow-Up Ideas

Involve your toddlers in holiday preparations, such as shopping for foods and gifts and putting up decorations. Talk about the coming celebrations and take time to play-act happenings for family or community ceremonies. Encourage them to be a part of appropriate activities but be aware that young children may become overwhelmed with the sights, sounds, and large crowds involved with holiday festivities. Help them focus on smaller components of the celebration. They will absorb and understand much of the broader traditions, but not in the same way as older children and adults do. That will come later.

Many cultures celebrate holidays in December. Use this opportunity and festive atmosphere to learn more about other people in your community and the holidays they celebrate.

Craft

Hanukkah Dreidel

You will need: cardboard egg carton

orange stick or pencil

small square of poster board

glue

poster paints

washable markers

beans, pennies, raisins, or counting pieces

> Note: It is important to use *cardboard* egg cartons for this craft because they have four-sided dividers (pyramids) that separate the rows of egg cups.

Cut one of the divider pyramids from the egg carton and trim the edges so that the sides are the same length. Poke a hole through the narrow end of the pyramid and insert an orange stick or small sharpened pencil through the hole with the pointed end on the outside. Cut a square of poster board the same size as the open end of the pyramid. Punch a hole in the middle of the poster board for the blunt end of the stick to fit through snugly. Glue the poster board to the open end of the pyramid. Make certain the pointed end of the stick extends beyond the tip of the pyramid and the other end of the stick extends beyond the poster board far enough to make the dreidel twirl. Paint the dreidel. When it is dry, draw or paste one of the Hebrew symbols on each side. The four symbols represent the first letters in the phrase "A great miracle happened there," recognizing the event celebrated during Hanukkah.

Children play the dreidel game using beans, pennies, raisins, or any "counting" pieces. Children sit in a circle. Each child places one piece in the center. Children take turns spinning the top and following the directions that each symbol indicates:

Nun = do nothing; miss a turn

Gimel = take all the pieces

Hay = take half the pieces

Shin = put in two pieces

When all pieces are gone, each child places one piece in the center again. The game is over when one child has all the pieces (or in a timed version, the winner is the one with the most pieces after a set amount of time). Toddlers may not have the patience to play the game to the end, but they like to participate.

Program Notes

Sign Language

CANDLE   Place the tip of the right index finger at the lips (as though blowing out a candle). Move it to the base of your outstretched left hand with palm facing out and fingers wiggling (like flickering candle flames).

Note: Be very relaxed at this time of year. Children are excited and can find it difficult to concentrate.

Flannelboard activities include the "Hanukkah Candles" song, adding candles as you sing; a plain pine tree, letting each child add a Christmas ornament; and round circles (enough so each child can participate) that become candle holders as each child adds a flannelboard candle.

Invite children to participate in "Looking for Santa." Introduce each action before beginning the activity. This is a perfect activity to lead into a surprise visit by a Santa impersonator. If you invite a Santa to your toddler program, plan for it to happen at the end of your program. Enlist another staff member to meet the Santa and to bring him into the story room just as the "Looking for Santa" activity is finished. Keep in mind that some toddlers are afraid of costumed characters. Let the storytime puppet act as a buffer between Santa and those children.

Giveaways are holiday stickers.

Fingertaster "tastes" holiday foods, such as candy canes, Christmas cookies, potato latkes, etc.

Children exit the story space singing a simple holiday song, like "We Wish You a Merry Christmas."

NUN

GIMEL

HAY

SHIN

——————————— Notes ———————————

Dogs

Books

Doggies
SANDRA BOYNTON

Good Dog, Carl
ALEXANDRA DAY

My Dog Rosie
ISABELLE HARPER

My New Boy
JOAN PHILLIPS

The New Puppy
LAURENCE ANHOLT

Our Dog
HELEN OXENBURY

Pat the Puppy
EDITH KUNHARDT

Puppies Love
LISA MCCUE

The Puppy Book
JAN PFLOOG

Roly Poly Puppies
ELAINE MOORE

Sam's Wagon
BARBRO LINDGREN

What a Hungry Puppy!
GAIL HERMAN

Where's Al?
BYRON BARTON

Where's Spot? (Also in
    Spanish: *Dónde esta
    á Spot?*)
ERIC HILL

Who Said Meow?
MARIA POLUSHKIN

Who's Counting?
NANCY TAFURI

Rhythms, Rhymes, and Fingerplays

My Little Dog   (tune: "Where Has My Little Dog Gone?")

Oh, where? Oh, where has my little dog gone?
   (look all around)
Oh, where? Oh, where can he be? *(keep looking)*
With his ears cut short *(hands on ears)*
And his tail cut long. *(wave hand behind like a tail)*
Oh, where? Oh, where can he be? *(look all around)*

Here! Oh, here is my little lost dog! *(clap hands)*
He's right here behind me! *(point over shoulder)*
With his ears cut short *(hands on ears)*
And his tail cut long. *(wave hand behind like a tail)*
He's right here behind me! *(point over shoulder)*

Puppy's Doghouse

This is puppy's doghouse. *(hands form peak over head)*
This is puppy's bed. *(hands out in front, palms up)*
This is puppy's pan of milk, *(cup hands together
    like a bowl)*
Where he can be fed. *(make licking motion)*
This is puppy's collar *(encircle neck with fingers)*
His name is on it, too. *(nod)*
Take a stick and throw it! *(throwing motion)*
He'll bring it back to you. *(rapidly pat leg with hand)*

I See a Doggie   (tune: "How Much Is That Doggie in the Window?")

I see a doggie out the window, *(hands frame face
    as though peering out a window)*
In a box at the lady's yard sale. *(arms form large
    circle in front of body)*
I see a doggie out the window, *(hands frame face)*
And he has a waggily tail. *(arm sways side to side
    like a wagging tail)*

I wave to the doggie out the window, *(wave excitedly)*
And he wags his wiggily tail. *(arm sways side to side)*
I wave to the doggie out the window, *(wave)*
And he licks some milk from a pail. *(make
    licking motion)*

Mom hands me the doggie through the window,
    (arms outstretch as though receiving something)
She bought him at the lady's yard sale. *(arms
    folded across the chest)*
Together we are looking out the window, *(hands
    frame face)*
Just me and my dog and his tail. *(arm sways
    side to side)*

Parents' Follow-Up Ideas

Talk about animal safety to help your child understand caution when meeting unknown animals for the first time. Talk about the difference between wild animals and pets. Practice how the child will be "introduced" to someone's pet by pretending before this happens. *Note:* Animals are unpredictable; never leave children alone with unknown animals. Check with the local animal shelter for guidelines for children (and adults) to avoid being bitten or frightened by dogs.

Toddlers tend to generalize animals. If your children are familiar with dogs, they may call all four-footed animals "dogs." Take every opportunity to help your toddlers learn there are many different kinds of animals. Some are called dogs even though they look very different from each other, and even more are not dogs (cats, cows, horses, etc.).

Gather pictures of dogs from advertising, magazines, and photographs. Make a dog book, letting your child sort the pictures by color, by height (dogs with long legs or short legs), long hair or short hair, pointy ears or droopy ears, long tails or short tails, etc. Practice dog noises: barking, whimpering, panting, growling. Examine your family dog, a neighbor's dog, or dogs in pet shops or humane shelters to see how they move, sound, smell, etc.

Craft

Dog Finger Puppets

You will need: paper

scissors

washable markers or crayons

tape

Trace these patterns, cut them out of paper, and color them. Wrap the tabs around your child's first and second fingers and tape the ends together. By moving these fingers, the puppies can walk, jump, run, and so on. With a small box you can make a doghouse in which your "pets" can live.

Make additional finger puppets by cutting pictures from magazines or greeting cards, leaving tabs on them to wrap around fingers.

Program Notes

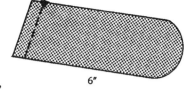

Sign Language

DOG   Pat your leg with your hand, as if calling a dog to you.

Storytime puppet introduces the theme with dog noises (barks, whimpers, panting) and asks children to guess what animal the stories are about that day.

Following the "My Little Dog" rhyme, "discover" a dog puppet or stuffed dog who likes to be petted, to lick fingers and noses, and to be hugged gently. The puppet teaches everybody how to swim doing the dog paddle (palms down, hands paddle in front of chest), and then it retires for a puppy nap.

Giveaways are puppy ears made by gluing construction paper ears to a headband that is tied on the child with string.

Fingertaster "tastes" things dogs would enjoy eating, such as hamburgers, hot dogs, dog biscuits, etc.

Children exit the story space by dog paddling.

─────────────── Notes ───────────────

Family

Books

Abby
JEANNETTE CAINES

Abuela's Weave (Also in
    Spanish: *El Tapiz de
    Abuela*)
OMAR CASTAÑEDA

Brothers and Sisters
DEBBY SLIER

Clifford's Family (Also in
    Spanish: *La Familia
    de Clifford*)
NORMAN BRIDWELL

Daddies
DIAN CURTIS REGAN

Grandma & Grandpa
HELEN OXENBURY

I Love My Mommy Because . . .
LAUREL PORTER-GAYLORD

Jafta's Father
HUGH LEWIN

Jonathan and His Mommy
IRENE SMALLS

Just Like Daddy
FRANK ASCH

Mama Zooms
JANE COWEN-FLETCHER

My Family
JANE CONTEH-MORGAN

One of Three
ANGELA JOHNSON

Spot Visits His Grandparents
ERIC HILL

Twins: Two by Two
CATHERINE AND LAURENCE ANHOLT

Whose Mommy Is This?
CHARLES REASONER

Rhythms, Rhymes, and Fingerplays

This Little Family

This little mommy is working. *(wiggle thumb)*
This little daddy's at the store. *(wiggle index finger)*
This little brother rides his bike. *(wiggle middle finger)*
This little sister's at the door. *(wiggle ring finger)*
And this little child is me! *(wiggle little finger)*
Me, me, me, me, me, me, me! *(wiggle little finger)*
My family loves me *(close hand)*
And I love them! *(open fingers wide)*
Who could ask for anything more? *(tickle the palm
    with fingers of other hand)*

Am I Your Little One?

[rhyme to use with animal pictures]
Am I your little one? *(point to self)*
Look at you. *(point to animal picture)*
You have *horns,*
Do I have them, too?

You say *"Moo"* and it's *grass* you eat.
You're not my mommy,
You have cow's feet.

[Verse 2]
    . . . feathers . . . say "Quack"
       . . . bugs you eat . . . have duck feet.

[Verse 3]
    . . . whiskers . . . say "Meow"
       . . . mice you eat . . . have cat feet.

[Verse 4]
    . . . ten fingers . . . say "I love you"
       . . . pizza you eat.
You ARE my mommy! You can't be beat.

My Baby Bopping   (tune: "Bye Baby Bunting")

My Baby Bopping.
Daddy's gone a-shopping,
To buy a little blanket warm
To wrap up Baby Bopping.

Parents' Follow-Up Ideas

Family and friends are very important to your toddlers as their awareness of the world gradually spreads outward from the immediate family. Knowing who their families are makes children feel more secure in the world. Helping them see relationships from different points of view is a good way to broaden their awareness.

Who's who in your family? Help your children learn how people in their families are related to your toddlers. Use photographs of family members. Before showing your children photos of adults-as-children, help them understand the time lapse by looking at their baby pictures, talking about how they used to look, and how much they have grown and changed. When talking about relatives, use family nicknames, such as "Nana," "Grammy," or "Da," but also explain kin names, like grandfather, cousin, or aunt. Help your children see that the same person can belong to several groups in the generations of a family.

Some of the most important stories your children will ever hear are stories of things that happened to you as a child. Everyone has stories to share, and the most interesting stories for your children are about the "little things" in life. Talk often about your memories from your childhood: pets, your room, favorite foods or toys, chores, friends, toys, holidays, getting into trouble, visiting relatives, or taking vacations. Share songs and rhymes you remember. Children are fascinated that adults were once children, too, and they gain a sense of security by knowing that you have been through similar trials and tribulations. Don't be surprised when they ask for a favorite story again and again.

Craft

Ping-Pong Family

You will need: 6–12 Ping-Pong balls

empty egg carton (cardboard preferred)

permanent markers

poster paints (optional)

Draw faces on the Ping-Pong balls to represent various family members (including pets). After letting the markers dry thoroughly, the Ping-Pong family is ready to move into their egg carton house, where they can be stored or transported. The "house" can be decorated inside and out with poster paints. Encourage your child to play with the Ping-Pong family and make up stories about them. The permanent markers allow the "family" in bathtubs and wading pools. New family or friends can be easily added.

Program Notes

Sign Language

FAMILY   Lightly pinch together your thumb and index finger on both hands and bring them together in front of your chest, palms facing and fingers up (looks like eyeglasses). Rotate your wrists outward until little fingers touch, forming a small circle.

Note: Be sensitive that families come in many different sizes and configurations.

This is a good program to include guests, such as grandparents, siblings, cousins, etc. Children who do not bring guests can bring a photograph of a family member.

Storytime puppet introduces another puppet or a stuffed animal as a sister, cousin, father, mother, etc.

Use flannelboard pictures of animals with the rhyme "Am I Your Little One?" Nesting dolls also fit well with this theme.

Giveaways are construction paper bracelets for child and adult made from strips of construction paper decorated with matching stickers. One sticker should be kept aside to hold the bracelet ends together around the wrist.

Fingertaster "tastes" different kinds of soups, such as chicken noodle, tomato, potato, etc.

Children exit the story space holding hands with the adults who brought them.

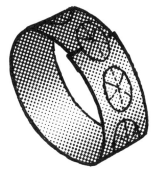

————————— Notes —————————

Farms

Books

Big Red Barn (Also in Spanish: *El Gran Granero Rojo*)
MARGARET WISE BROWN

Clifford's Animal Sounds
NORMAN BRIDWELL

Farm Morning
DAVID MCPHAIL

Going to Sleep on the Farm
WENDY CHEYETTE LEWISON

Mary Had a Little Lamb
SARA HALE

My Farm
JANE CONTEH-MORGAN

Old MacDonald Had a Farm
HOLLY BERRY

On My Horse
ELOISE GREENFIELD

Open the Barn Door
CHRISTOPHER SANTORO

Pop-Up Farm Animals
ROD CAMPBELL

Spot Goes to the Farm (Also in Spanish: *Spot Va a la Granja*)
ERIC HILL

This Is the Farmer
NANCY TAFURI

What Do Lambs Say?
DOROTHY ROSE

Who Owns the Cow?
ANDREW CLEMENTS

Who Sees You? On the Farm
CARLA DIJS

Wonderful Feast
ESPHYR SLOBODKINA

Rhythms, Rhymes, and Fingerplays

Here Is a Farmer

Here is a farmer,
What does he do?
He feeds the cows
And milks them, too.

Chickens and pigs,
Horses and sheep,
He puts in the barn
To eat and sleep.

He drives the tractor,
Fields to sow.
Plants the seeds
So they will grow.

Here is the farmer,
At work or play.
He keeps busy
All through the day.

The Scarecrow

The old scarecrow is a funny
old man.
He flaps in the wind as hard as
he can.
He flaps to the right, *(lean right)*
He flaps to the left, *(lean left)*
He flaps back and forth *(lean
forward and back)*
'Til he's 'most out of breath.
His arms swing out; *(swing arms)*
His legs swing, too. *(swing legs)*
He nods his head *(nod head)*
"How do you do?"
See him flippity flop *(swing arms
and legs)*
When the wind blows hard,
That old scarecrow
In our backyard.

Old MacDonald   (traditional song)

Old MacDonald had a farm, E-I-E-I-O!
And on that farm he had a cow, E-I-E-I-O!
With a moo-moo here, and a moo-moo there.
Here a moo! There a moo! Everywhere a moo-moo.
Old MacDonald had a farm, E-I-E-I-O!

[Repeat using other farm animals and the sounds
they make]

Parents' Follow-Up Ideas

Make animal sounds with your toddler or sing "Old MacDonald Had
a Farm." Some fun sounds are

chicken *(cluck)*	bird *(chirp)*	goose *(honk)*	cat *(meow)*
lamb *(baa)*	snake *(hiss)*	pig *(oink)*	donkey *(hee-haw)*
crow *(caw)*	duck *(quack)*	lion *(roar)*	
dog *(rruf)*	horse *(neigh)*	rooster *(cock-a-doodle-do)*	

Singing should be a part of your daily routine. Sing together to TV,
the radio, or music from your stereo. Sing without accompanying music. Singing makes time go by faster: dressing, bathing, waiting in line,
and riding in the car. You don't have to "carry a tune" to sing. No matter how good (or bad) you think your voice sounds, your voice is beautiful to your child. Ask your librarian to help you find books with
children's songs in them or make up your own words to familiar tunes.
Who cares if they don't rhyme or make sense. Your child will love it!

Create a farm animal sound game using a paper plate, clip clothespins, and pictures of farm animals. Cut pictures from magazines,
brochures, advertising, etc. Find two pictures of each animal. Glue
one picture of each animal around the rim of a paper plate. Glue the
other picture to a clip clothespin. Help your child match the pictures
and talk about the sounds the animals make, the foods they eat,
where they live, etc. If you cannot find two animal pictures, color the
clothespins with markers, and let your child match the color to the
corresponding color behind the animal.

Craft

Old Scarecrow Flannelboard

You will need: felt pieces

scissors

markers

Cut the following pieces from different colors of felt:

        1 stick, the length of the scarecrow

        1 pair pants

        1 shirt

        2 hands

        1 hat

        1 circle, for head

Draw a face on the circle and make patches, buttons, and pockets on the shirt and pants. Assemble the pieces, beginning with the stick and ending with the hat, using a flannelboard or a cushion from the sofa. Recite "The Scarecrow" rhyme with your child and act out the motions.

Program Notes

Sign Language

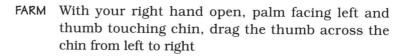

FARM With your right hand open, palm facing left and thumb touching chin, drag the thumb across the chin from left to right

Storytime puppet or the storyteller introduces the theme wearing a straw hat.

The "Old MacDonald" song works well as a flannelboard story or with stick puppet animals, which children can then return to the "barn" when finished.

Assemble the scarecrow on the flannelboard, beginning with the stick, and talk about how scarecrows flap their arms and legs to keep birds away from the farmer's seeds. After reciting "The Scarecrow" rhyme, repeat it for the children to act out.

Giveaways are farm animal finger puppets made by photocopying and enlarging this page and cutting them out, then taping the flaps in a circle.

Fingertaster "tastes" foods that farm animals eat, such as carrots, corn, oats, milk, hay, chicken feed, etc.

Children exit the story space making farm animal sounds.

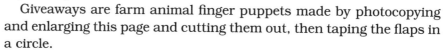

——————————————————— Notes ———————————————————

Feelings

Books

A Is for Angry: An Animal and Adjective Alphabet
SANDRA BOYNTON

If You're Happy and You Know It
JO LODGE

I'm Green and I'm Grumpy!
ALISON LESTER

Jafta
HUGH LEWIN

Making Faces
NICK BUTTERWORTH

Monster Faces
TOM BRANNON

No! No! No!
ANNE F. ROCKWELL

On Monday When It Rained
CHERRYL KACHENMEISTER

Paddington's Things I Feel
MICHAEL BOND

Shake My Sillies Out
RAFFI

Shy Charles
ROSEMARY WELLS

So Happy, So Sad
JULIE PASCHKIS

This Is Betsy
GUNILLA WOLDE

This Is the Bear and the Scary Night
SARAH HAYES

This Is the Way We Make a Face
JO LODGE

What Sadie Sang
EVE RICE

Rhythms, Rhymes, and Fingerplays

If You're Happy   (traditional song)

If you're happy and you know it, clap your hands.
(clap hands twice)
If you're happy and you know it, clap your hands.
(clap hands)
If you're happy and you know it,
Your face will surely show it. *(point to face)*
If you're happy and you know it, clap your hands.
(clap hands)

[Repeat with]
 . . . jump up high
 . . . shout YA-HOO
 . . . blow a kiss, etc.

[Once children are familiar with this song, change the emotions and add appropriate actions: sad = say "Boo-hoo"; silly = shake your head; grumpy = stamp your feet; scared = hide your eyes, etc.]

Old MacDonald Felt So Glad
   (tune: "Old MacDonald Had a Farm")

Old MacDonald felt so glad, HA-HA-HA-HA-HA
And when he's glad, he sounds like this:
   HA-HA-HA-HA-HA.
With a HA-HA here,
And a HO-HO there,
And a HEE-HEE-HEE-HEE everywhere,
Old MacDonald felt so glad, HA-HA-HA-HA-HA.

[Repeat with]
   . . . grumpy, NO! NO! NO! NO! NO!
   . . . sad, BOO-HOO-HOO-HOO-HOO.
   . . . silly, NAH-NAH-NAH-NAH-NAH.
   . . . shy, whisper, whisper-whisper-low.

Parents' Follow-Up Ideas

Everyone has emotions, and they are not "good" or "bad," they are simply *feelings*. Feeling angry is perfectly normal, but throwing a temper tantrum is not the desirable way to express that anger. Helping your child identify and express emotions will make life easier for the entire family.

Talk naturally about your feelings so your children will learn emotions are something everyone experiences. Play with feelings using nursery rhymes: "Say 'Humpty Dumpty' with me and let's pretend like we are very sad . . . now happy . . . now grumpy." A brief burst of activity may help toddlers express strong emotions and change their moods: a twenty-second "angry dance" will let off steam and most likely become a "laughing dance."

Cut pictures from magazines, catalogs, newspapers, and advertising of faces (and bodies) showing emotions. Glue them on index cards and play a matching game with your toddler: "There is a picture of someone who is sad. Can you find another sad face?" Imitate the facial expressions in front of a mirror with your child or make a feelings book with the pictures. Glue happy-face pictures to one page and grumpy faces on another, etc.

Craft

Finger Circle Puppets

You will need: poster board

pill bottle (circle pattern)

scissors

washable markers

masking tape

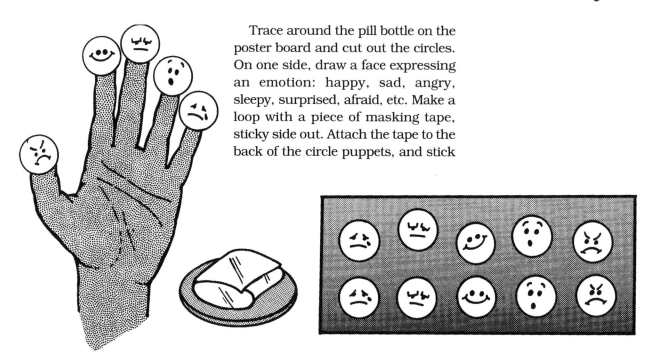

Trace around the pill bottle on the poster board and cut out the circles. On one side, draw a face expressing an emotion: happy, sad, angry, sleepy, surprised, afraid, etc. Make a loop with a piece of masking tape, sticky side out. Attach the tape to the back of the circle puppets, and stick them to your child's fingers. The tape can be easily replaced when it loses its tackiness. Circle puppets can be taped to the ends of straws or sticks if your child does not like having things stuck to fingers.

Other options: Glue pictures to circles instead of drawing faces on them. Make two sets of the circle puppets and play a matching game with them. Or use one puppet to help look for faces with the same expressions in magazines or books.

Program Notes

Sign Language

HAPPY   Bring the flat palm of the right hand, fingers pointing left, upward and outward on the chest.

Bring a mirror to the story space. When assembling the clown shape puzzle, show the children how the crescent smile can become a frown when turned upside down to introduce the theme for the day. Then let them practice making happy faces and sad (pouting) faces in the mirror.

The storytime puppet visits and leads children in the song "Old MacDonald Felt So Glad."

Giveaways are happy-face stickers.

Fingertaster "tastes" flavors that are pleasers, such as bubble gum, peanut butter, cookies, chocolate milk, etc.

Children exit the story space walking as "happy" as they can.

─────────────── Notes ───────────────

Firefighters

Books

All Aboard Fire Trucks
TEDDY SLATER

Big Red Fire Engine (Also in
    Spanish: *Un Carro de
    Bomberos Grande y Rojo*)
ROSE GREYDANUS

*Busy Bears' at the
Fire Station*
JULIA KILLINGBACK

Clifford the Firehouse Dog
NORMAN BRIDWELL

Emergency

Fast Rolling Fire Trucks

Fire Engine
NORMAN GORBATY

Fire Engine Book
JESSE YOUNGER

Fire Engines
ANNE F. ROCKWELL

Fire Fighters
NORMA SIMON

Firehouse
PETER SPIER

I'm a Firefighter
MARY PACKARD

Little Fireman
MARGARET WISE BROWN

Ten Men on a Ladder
CRAIG MACAULEY

*A Visit to the Sesame Street
    Firehouse* (Also in Spanish:
    *Una Visita a la Estación de
    Bomberos de Sesame Street*)
DAN ELLIOTT

*When There Is a Fire, Go
    Outside!* (Also in Spanish:
    *Cuando Hay un Incendio
    Sal Para Fuera*)
DOROTHY CHLAD

Rhythms, Rhymes, and Fingerplays

Sirens

Fire engine, fire engine rolling down the street.
    (hands roll over one another)
With the siren blaring at everyone you meet.
Whoo-ooo! Coming through! *(hands frame
    mouth like megaphone)*
Whoo-ooo! Move aside!
Whoo-ooo, whoo-ooo!
On our way to save the day.
Whoo-ooo, whoo-ooo.

[Repeat with]
    . . . police car
    . . . ambulance

Down at the Station   (tune: "Down by the Station")

Down at the station
Firefighters waiting
Ready to come running
If there is a fire.

The alarm bell starts ringing,
Ding-ding, ding-ding, dinging.
Putting on their boots and hats,
They hurry out the door.

They jump upon the fire truck
Hear the siren wailing,
"Whoo-ooo-ooo-ooo-ooo,
Get out of our way!"

With ladders and hoses,
They put the fire out.
For firefighters it is
Just another day.

The Firefighter

A firefighter's hat keeps head and neck safe.
   (hands on head)
A firefighter's coat helps keep the flames away.
   (hands on opposite arms)
A firefighter's ladder lets her reach windows high.
   (hands reach high)
A firefighter's boots keep his feet warm and dry.
   (hands on feet)
A fire engine carries them quickly to the fire.
   (hands pretend to steer)
A cherry picker's basket will reach above the wire.
   (one arm reaches high)
A firefighter's mask lets her see where smoke is thick.
   (hands frame face)
An ambulance is there in case someone's hurt or sick.
   (one hand twists overhead)
A firefighter's hose, with water from its spout,
   (hands pretend to point hose)
Sprays the fire, sprays the fire,
Until all the flames are out.
Inside the boots and hats, *(touch feet and head)*
Inside the coats and masks, *(touch arms and face)*
Brave men and women are *(hands open, palms up)*
Our friends, the firefighters! *(clap hands)*

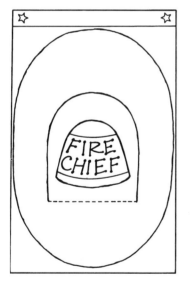

Parents' Follow-Up Ideas

Put a *Tot Finder* sign on your child's window to guide firefighters in case of a fire in your home. They are available at most fire stations, and it is a fun trip with your toddler to see the fire trucks and meet firefighters while picking up the sign.

Every family should have a fire plan. To make certain all smoke detectors are working, test them once a month. Help your toddlers press the button so they will hear the alarm and know what it means. Keep fire extinguishers where they can be easily reached by adults, and check them regularly. Have a fire drill each season, complete with sounding the smoke detector alarm. Acting out emergency situations helps all family members understand what they should do and helps even the smallest child participate.

Keep matches and flammables (like candles and oil lamps) well out of reach of children. They are curious and fascinated by the flames they see when these items are used by adults. Their natural urge to explore for themselves can turn tragic when fire is involved. Put red-dot stickers on anything that could cause a burn, including stoves and irons, and teach your child that red-dot means "Hands off!" or "Will hurt!"

Craft

Firefighter's Hat

You will need: 11″×14″ poster board or heavy construction paper (yellow, red, or black)

pencil

scissors and stapler

washable markers

Cut a 1″ strip from the narrow side of the poster board, draw stars at each end, and set it aside. Draw an oval shape on the remaining paper and a semicircle toward the front of it (see the pattern). Cut out the oval, creating the hat brim, and cut along the semicircle making the top of the hat. Fold along the end of the semicircle so the top stands up. With markers, draw a badge and decorate it on the top of the hat. Staple one end of the 1″ strip to the top of the hat and the other end to the inside brim to stabilize the hat.

Program Notes

Sign Language

FIREFIGHTER With your thumb and index finger curved into a *C* shape, put the thumb on the center of the forehead, fingers pointing upward. Keeping your thumb in place, rotate the hand to the left twice, as though the fingers were encircling the badge on a firefighter's hat.

Note: Invite a firefighter to arrive in the middle of your program. Let adults know in advance that there will be a guest because this program often runs long. Children want lots of time to touch and examine firefighting paraphernalia. Firefighters are happy to have the opportunity to talk with young children, acquainting them with the equipment used to fight fires and talking briefly to parents about fire safety. They will often bring pamphlets, stickers, or coloring pages to hand out.

The storytime puppet introduces the theme wearing a firefighter's hat or carrying a fire engine.

Toddlers love to make a siren sound, so give them the opportunity as you share stories or rhymes. If a firefighter is coming, use only one story and then get the children up to act out one of the rhymes.

Giveaways are stickers or coloring pages (get them from your fire department if no visitor is coming).

Fingertaster "tastes" foods commonly eaten by firefighters (cooked in quantity), such as chili, spaghetti, pizza, beef stew, etc.

Children exit the story space driving fire engines with sirens sounding.

 Notes

Friends

Books

Big Friend, Little Friend
ELOISE GREENFIELD

Do You Want to Be My Friend?
ERIC CARLE

The Doorbell Rang (Also in
    Spanish: *Llaman a la Puerta*)
PAT HUTCHINS

Friends
HELEN OXENBURY

Goodbye Hello (Also in
    Spanish: *Adiós! Hola!*)
BARBARA SHOOK HAZEN

Hi, Word Bird
JANE BELK MONCURE

I Can Share
BONNIE WORTH

If You Give a Mouse a Cookie
    (Also in Spanish: *Si le Das
    Una Galletita a un Ratón*)
LAURA NUMEROFF

Jambo Means Hello
MURIEL FEELINGS

Just Like Me (Also in
    Spanish: *Igual Que Yo*)
BARBARA J. NEASI

My Friends
NANCY TAFURI

Sam's Car
BARBRO LINDGREN

Sitting in My Box
DEE LILLEGARD

Spot's Friends
ERIC HILL

Titch & Daisy
PAT HUTCHINS

*Tom & Pippo Make
a Friend*
HELEN OXENBURY

Rhythms, Rhymes, and Fingerplays

Hello!

Hello, hello, hello! *(wave hand enthusiastically)*
I see you. *(point to children)*
Hello, hello, hello! *(big wave)*
Do you see me, too? *(point to self)*
Hello! I see Danny* here. *(wave to each child,
    making eye contact and letting them wave back)*
Hello! I see Maria* here.
Hello! I see Keisha* here.
Hello, hello, hello! *(wave to everyone)*

[*Repeat until all children have been named. If it
comes out uneven, say "Hello!" to the adults as a
group, to a puppet, or to "my friends." Encourage
parents and children to wave back to you and to each
other as they are named.]

To Have a Friend   (tune: "Pop Goes the Weasel")

To have a friend, we share our toys *(skip around)*
And happily we play.
It's your turn. And now it's mine. *(gesture to child,
    then to self)*
Friends all the day. *(jump)*

[Repeat with other things to share]
    . . . sandbox
    . . . puzzles
    . . . cookies

Goodbye   (tune: "Goodnight Ladies")

Goodbye José. *(wave goodbye to each child)*
Goodbye April.
Goodbye Meiko.
We'll see you all next week. *(wave to everyone)*

[Repeat until all children have been named. See
note with "Hello."]

Parents' Follow-Up Ideas

Use the magic of counting to reinforce sharing in everyday activities.
When serving food at the table, help your children see how the meal
is being "shared": "One for mommy. One for daddy. One for Susie."
Let them help hand out the portions and pass plates or bowls around
the table, taking care to help with hot or heavy plates. When playing
together, take advantage of any opportunity to point out: "Your turn.
My turn." or "You first . . . now me . . . now Max. . . ." Sharing does
not come naturally to young children.

Toddlers are very interested in other children of all ages, but they
may be very shy around them. Help your children get to know other
children by taking them places where there are children about the
same age: library programs, play groups, religious groups, mom's day
out, and family gatherings. Talk about things your toddlers can do
with other children, and talk about ways they can be a good friend to
others. The old adage, "To have a friend, be a friend," is very true.

Reinforce sharing between children, even when it is accidental.
When toddlers play together, provide toys that *share* well: balls,
boats, blocks, a two-child rocking toy, etc. If possible, make sure
there is more than one of a popular toy. Children will often share with
mom when they won't share with others. Use these experiences to
teach the value and fun of sharing with friends.

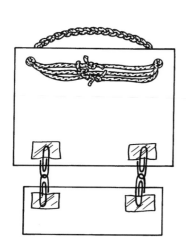

Craft

Welcome Sign with Special Greetings

You will need: 2 pieces of colorful poster board cut into rectangles 8″×12″ and 4″×10″

2 pieces of heavier cardboard cut the same as poster board

glue, pencil, and scissors or craft knife

cloth tape

3 24″ lengths of ribbons or yarn or 2″ strips of cloth

2 clip clothespins

4 large paper clips

washable markers or paints or contact paper

Reinforce the poster boards by gluing them to cardboard and letting them dry thoroughly under a board or books to keep them flat. Decorate the welcome and special greeting signs with paints, markers, or contact paper. Cover the edges of both signs with cloth tape to keep the edges from separating. On the welcome sign, mark two nickel-sized holes on the upper side. Carefully cut out the holes with a craft knife and spread a thin coat of white glue on the inside edges of the holes to reinforce them. While the glue is drying, put the craft knife safely away.

On the back of the welcome sign, glue two paper clips to the lower edge, with the double-loop end of the clip extending beyond the edge. Reinforce the glued clips with cloth tape to help hold them in place. Repeat this process on the back of the upper edge of the special greeting sign, making sure the clips match the distance between those on the welcome sign and being careful not to cover the *open* prong that allows the signs to be connected and changed.

Lay the ribbons evenly together, and clip them together about 4″ from one end with a clothespin. Braid the ribbons, leaving about 4″ at the opposite end unbraided. Thread the ribbon braid through the sign holes (ends in back) and secure them with a clothespin. Tie each of the ribbons together to form a continuous loop at the back of the sign. It is now ready to hang on the front door or in a special place inside the home.

Make other special greetings to use throughout the year: at holidays (Merry Christmas, Happy Hanukkah), welcoming special people (friends, relative, babysitter, Daddy when he's been out of town), or people making expected deliveries (Mail Lady or Pizza Guy). Keep extra greetings in a shoebox, and label the back of them with a drawing, magazine picture, or photograph to help your child identify them. Let your child locate the appropriate greeting and help attach it to the welcome sign.

Program Notes

Sign Language

FRIEND   Hook your right index finger (palm down) over your
curved left index finger (palm down); repeat the action in reverse with your left finger on top. This indicates a close relationship.

Display the welcome sign on flannelboard. The storyteller or story-
time puppet introduces the theme by greeting children with the
"Hello!" rhyme (which can also be part of an opening routine).
Substitute other languages: Spanish = "Hola" (Oh-la); Japanese =
"Oyhyo" (Oh-hah-yo); or sign language = " Hi" (a salute with the right
hand, palm facing out) and sing it again throughout the program.

Giveaways are friendship bracelets made from loops of braided
yarn. (These usually can be bought in bulk quantities at a carnival
supply house.)

Fingertaster "tastes" foods that are easily shared, such as pizza,
orange slices, Popsicles, raisins, etc.

Sing the "Good-bye" song, and encourage children to exit the story
space waving good-bye. (The "Good-bye" song can also become part of
a closing routine.)

─────────────── Notes ───────────────

Frogs and Turtles

Books

April Showers
GEORGE SHANNON

Binyah, Binyah Hide & Seek
JOANNE BARKAN

Caterpillar & the Polliwog
JACK KENT

Frog in the Middle
SUSANNA GRETZ

Frogs Jump
RON MARIS

Jump, Frog, Jump (Also in
    Spanish: *Salta, Ranita, Salta*)
ROBERT KALAN

*One Gaping Wide-Mouthed
Hopping Frog*
LESLIE TRYON

Peeping and Sleeping
FRAN MANUSHKIN

Peter's Song
CAROL P. SAUL

To the Tub
PEGGY PERRY ANDERSON

Tortoise Solves a Problem
AVNER KATZ

Turtle Count
NORMAN GORBATY

Turtle Day
DOUGLAS FLORIAN

Turtle Magic
RUTH YOUNG AND
MITCHELL ROSE

Wake Up, Frog!
ANNIE OWEN

The Wide-Mouthed Frog
REX SCHNEIDER

Rhythms, Rhymes, and Fingerplays

The Little Frog

I am a little frog *(sit with legs crossed)*
Hopping on a log. *(bounce up and down)*
Listen to my song. *("ribbit, ribbit")*
I sleep all winter long. *(lay head against hands)*
Wake up and peek out *(peek between fingers)*
Up I jump, all about. *(bounce up and down)*
I catch flies *(grabbing motion)*
I wink my eyes *(blink)*
I hop and hop *(bounce up and down)*
And then I stop. *(sit down on floor)*

Little Turtle

There was a little turtle *(make fist, cover with other hand)*
Who lived in a box. *(form circle, fingers touching)*
He swam in the water, *(thumbs together, flutter fingers)*
And climbed on the rocks. *("walk" one hand over the other)*
He snapped at a mosquito, *(grabbing motion, up high)*

He snapped at a flea, *(grabbing motion, in front)*
He snapped at a minnow, *(grabbing motion, down low)*
And he snapped at me! *(grabbing motion, under chin)*
He caught the mosquito, *(clap hands up high)*
He caught the flea, *(clap hands in front)*
He caught the minnow, *(clap hands down low)*
But he didn't catch me! *(point to self, shake head)*

Five Little Froggies   (tune: "Ten Little Indians")

One little, two little, three little froggies.
   (count on fingers throughout song)
Four little, five little, green little froggies.
Splashing and croaking and hopping
   are the froggies,
Living in my pond.

Five little, four little, three little froggies.
Two little, one little, green little froggies.
Hopping and croaking and splashing
   are the froggies,
Living in my pond.

Parents' Follow-Up Ideas

Teach your child the game of leap frog using a favorite stuffed animal or a friend. Show your toddler how to crouch low on the floor and jump the stuffed animal over your child. Put the toy on the floor in front of your child and help him or her hop over it. Play in a carpeted area where falls are softened. Leap in a circle or from one point to another (sofa to doorway). Once your children understand the concept of taking turns, they are ready to play this game with friends and with you.

Make a "turtle salad" for lunch using a peach half for the shell, a nut or grape for the head, and carrot sticks for legs and a tail. Serve your turtle on a lettuce-leaf lily pad.

Have fun with a frog friends counting game. Make five "frogs" using pieces of celery or green pepper. A bowl of slightly salted water becomes a pond. Have your toddler hop the first frog up to the bowl and into it. Let him or her play with the frog in the water, swimming round and round, jumping in and out, swimming fast and slow, above and below water, etc. Talk about what the frog is doing. When the frog gets lonely, introduce a second one: "Now there are two." Don't rush this. Let your child explore how two frogs play together (leap frog, taking turns in and out of the water). As you talk, use number words (1, 2, 3, more, less, some, all). When all the frogs have been introduced, let your child become a hungry bird and gobble the frogs down one at a time. *Hint:* When toddlers are faced with many items, they find it hard to concentrate. Keep extra frogs out of sight until it is time to use them.

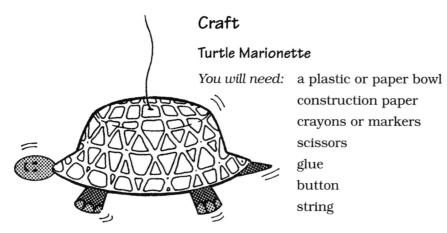

Craft

Turtle Marionette

You will need: a plastic or paper bowl

construction paper

crayons or markers

scissors

glue

button

string

Let your child decorate the bowl, which will become the turtle's shell. Cut from construction paper: 1 circle (head), 4 small rectangles (legs), and 1 triangle (tail). Draw a face on the circle and glue the paper shapes to the edge of the bowl.

Poke a hole in the center of the bowl and thread the string through it. Thread the button onto the string and tie it securely. This helps to keep the string from pulling out of the bowl.

Hold the string, and the turtle will dangle above the floor. It can be made to walk slowly, hop, dance, or even fly.

Program Notes

Sign Language

TURTLE   Cup the left hand over your right fist, extend the right thumb, and wiggle it like a turtle peeking from under its shell.

Note: Avoid using live turtles in your program due to the risks of their carrying salmonella.

Introduce the theme with a frog or turtle puppet or stuffed animal, talking about how they move and turtle's shell or frog's sound.

The "Five Little Froggies" rhyme and the story *Jump, Frog, Jump* make good flannelboard presentations. "The Little Frog" rhyme can be either a lap-sitting or jump-around-the-room activity. Children enjoy hopping and croaking like frogs, as well as crawling slowly and ducking their heads like turtles. The storytime puppet can lead the way.

Giveaways are frog puppets made by sealing an envelope and folding it lengthwise, then cutting a slit in the front of it and gluing on the eyes and body copied from the next page.

Fingertaster "tastes" things frogs and turtles might eat, such as mosquitoes, flies, leaves, little fish, etc.

Children exit the story space hopping like frogs.

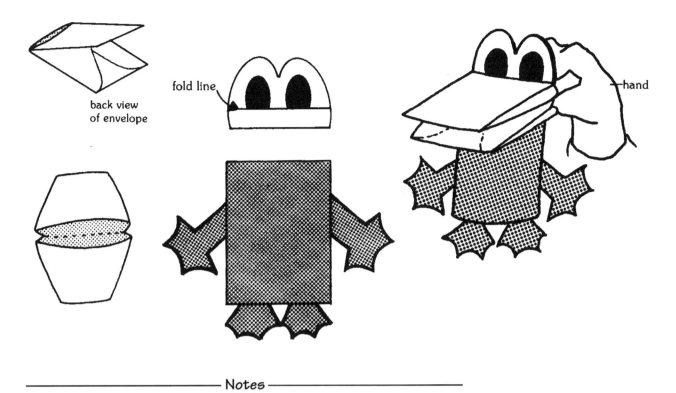

back view
of envelope

fold line

hand

_____ Notes _____

Gardens

Books

Apple Tree
LYNLEY DODD

Apples and Pumpkins
ANNE ROCKWELL

The Carrot Seed
RUTH KRAUSS

Flower Garden
EVE BUNTING

Flower in the Garden
LUCY COUSINS

The Great Big Enormous Turnip
ALEKSEI TOLSTOI

Growing Colors
BRUCE MCMILLAN

Growing Vegetable Soup (Also
   in Spanish: *A Sembrar Sopa
   de Vegetales*)
LOIS EHLERT

How My Garden Grew
ANNE AND HARLOW ROCKWELL

My Father's Hands
JOANNE RYDER

My Garden
JANE CONTEH-MORGAN

Paddington's Garden
MICHAEL BOND

Pop-Up Garden Friends
ROD CAMPBELL

Spot in the Garden
ERIC HILL

Sunflower
MIELA FORD

Tom & Pippo in the Garden
HELEN OXENBURY

Rhythms, Rhymes, and Fingerplays

My Garden

This is my garden *(hands in front, palms up)*
I'll rake it with care *(rake fingers of one hand
   over other palm)*
And then some flower seeds *(twist index finger
   of one hand into center of palm)*
I will plant there. *(pat palm with other fingers)*

The sun will shine *(make circle with arms
   over head)*
And the rain will fall, *(wiggle fingers down
   in front of body)*
And my garden will blossom *(make fists, open
   fingers slowly)*
Growing straight and tall. *(reach hands high
   above head)*

Grow, Grow, Grow (tune: "Row, Row, Row Your Boat")

Grow, grow, growing tall. *(hands raise slowly)*
Flowers growing tall. *(raise hands over head)*
I water my garden *(mimic actions)*
And pull the weeds
And flowers grow from little seeds.
   (cupped hands unfold like blossoms)

Grow, grow, growing wide. *(hands spread outward)*
Pumpkins growing wide. *(arms outstretched at sides)*
I water my garden *(mimic actions)*
And pull the weeds
And pumpkins grow from little seeds. *(cupped hands
   move outward like a pumpkin growing)*

Grow, grow, growing deep. *(hands lower slowly)*
Carrots growing deep. *(hands on the floor)*
I water my garden *(mimic actions)*
And pull the weeds
And carrots grow from little seeds. *(cupped hands
   move away vertically, like elongating carrot)*

I Dig, Dig, Dig

I dig, dig, dig *(digging motion)*
And I plant some seeds. *(planting motion)*
I rake, rake, rake *(raking motion)*
And I pull some weeds. *(pulling motion)*
I wait and watch *(hands on hips)*
And soon I know, *(point to self)*
My garden sprouts *(hands low, palms down)*
And starts to grow. *(raise hands toward ceiling)*

Parents' Follow-Up Ideas

Plant seeds from the fruits you eat (oranges, grapefruits, tangerines, and others). Rinse the seeds and blot them dry with a paper towel. Plant them in a container (flower pot or paper cup) filled with potting soil, labeling each pot with the name of the plant or a picture cut from a magazine. Put the pots in a warm place and keep the soil moist. Let your child feel the differences in the soil before and after you water it. When shoots begin to appear, move the pot to a sunny window and continue to water it regularly. Talk with your child about how seeds grow and how they need light and water to survive. If one wilts slightly, let your child give it water and notice the change when the plant revives later.

Talk about things that grow in gardens when doing grocery shopping. The produce department is the ideal place to start with fresh vegetables and fruits, but also point out similar canned foods or those that begin as seeds. See if you can find foods that grow above and below ground. Name each item as you pass by. If you are unsure, ask the produce manager, showing your toddler that you are learning something new together. Identify items as part of a larger group (fruits, vegetables, above- or below-ground growers, colors, and shapes) and compare the items with others, helping your child be observant and creative in how she or he sees things. "A carrot is a vegetable and an orange is a fruit, but they are the same color. What color is that? Can you find something else that color?"

Make a sponge planter with a piece of sponge. Soak the sponge in water, and sprinkle bird seed or grass seed on it. Put it in a container that holds water, and set it—or hang it with string—in a sunny window. Soak the sponge every day, and soon it will be filled with lovely green plants.

Craft

Funny Potato Face

You will need: 1 large raw potato

cotton balls

grass seed or bird seed

a knife and a tablespoon

7–8 whole cloves

a small dish of water

Scoop some of the pulp out of the top of the potato. Moisten the cotton balls with water and place them in the hollow of the potato. Slice off the bottom of the potato so it will stand by itself; place it in the dish of water. Let your child sprinkle the seed over the cotton. Stick the cloves in the side of the potato to make eyes, nose, and mouth. Keep the cotton moist, and in a few days the potato will sprout a wonderful head of green hair!

Program Notes

Sign Language

GROW   The left hand forms a cup, palm facing you. With tips of fingers together, your right hand comes up through the cupped left hand, with the fingers slowly opening as if a flower were emerging and opening its petals.

Introduce the theme with a plastic watering can and toy garden tools, giving children the opportunity to touch them as you talk about the theme.

When using the story *The Carrot Seed*, bring out a garden box (a large box with a stuffed carrot hidden inside) early in the program. Let children help "rake" or "water" your garden at various stages throughout the program. After sharing the story, insert a green feather duster in the top of the hidden carrot. The feathers become the carrot's leaves. Encourage the children to help you pull the carrot out. Keep your hands *firmly* on the carrot and its "leaves" until time for it to POP out and allow lots of time for them to look and touch the carrot after it has been "harvested." *The Great Big Enormous Turnip* makes a good flannelboard or glove puppet story.

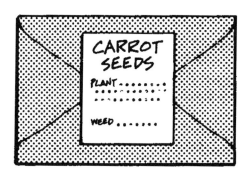

Giveaways are seeds (carrot or other) divided into small envelopes with instructions for planting glued to them. (Radish seeds grow quicker than carrots and are almost foolproof to grow.) Keep a few seeds in a plastic bag so children can see what they look like and how small they are.

Fingertaster "tastes" things grown in gardens, such as carrots, celery, watermelon, corn, tomatoes, etc.

Children exit the story space singing the "Grow, Grow, Grow" song.

—————————— **Notes** ——————————

Getting Dressed

Books

Clothes
SARA LYNN

Dressing
HELEN OXENBURY

How Do I Put It On?
SHIGEO WATANABE

I Can Dress Myself
BONNIE WORTH

Jamaica and Brianna
JUANITA HAVILL

Let's Get Dressed!
HARRIET ZIEFERT

Max's Dragon Shirt
ROSEMARY WELLS

Pocket for Corduroy (Also in
    Spanish: *Un Bolsillo para
    Corduroy*)
DON FREEMAN

Purple Sock, Pink Sock
JONATHAN ALLEN

Red, Blue, Yellow Shoe
TANA HOBAN

Shoes, Shoes, Shoes
ANN MORRIS

Things to Wear
DEBBIE MACKINNON

*Thumpity Thump Gets
Dressed*
CYNDY SZEKERES

Two Shoes, New Shoes
SHIRLEY HUGHES

Whose Shoe?
MARGARET MILLER

*You'll Soon Grow into
Them, Titch*
PAT HUTCHINS

Rhythms, Rhymes, and Fingerplays

Early in the Morning   (tune: "Mulberry Bush")

This is the way we put on our pants,
    (mimic actions)
Put on our pants, put on our pants.
This is the way we put on our pants,
Early in the morning.

[Repeat with]

> put on our shirts
> put on our shoes
> put on our hats

Dressed to Play   (tune: "Three Blind Mice")

Hat, gloves, coat.
Hat, gloves, coat.
Warm socks and boots.
Warm socks and boots.
I'm staying warm while
    I'm out to play

On this cold and snowy day.
I'll have fun as long as I stay.
Hat, gloves, coat.

[Verse 2]

Shorts and sandals. Sunscreen, too.
. . . staying cool . . . bright and sunny day.

[Verse 3]

Boots and umbrella. Raincoats and hat.
. . . staying dry . . . wet and rainy day.

[Verse 4]

Sweater and jacket. Zipped up tight.
. . . staying warm . . . cold and windy day.

Look at Me!

Look at me! *(point to self)*
Upon my head
I wear a hat of brightest red.
  (hands on head)
Look at me! *(point to self)*
Don't I look neat
With shiny shoes upon my feet?
  (point to feet)
Look at me! (point to self)
Hip hip hooray! *(clap hands)*
With shirt and pants *(point to clothing)*
I'm dressed to play. *(jump up and down)*

Parents' Follow-Up Ideas

Set aside definite places in the home for your children's clothes. Put hooks or hangers low enough for your children to hang up their own clothes. Store folded clothes in drawers where they can be easily reached. Your children can help put laundry away and make their own selections when getting dressed.

On laundry day ask your children to remember which of their dirty clothes need washing. Give hints ("What do you wear on your legs?"), and help them give names to specific items of clothing ("Those are called leggings."). Talk about the sequence of laundry actions (gathering, sorting, washing, drying, folding, and putting away). Let your toddlers help sort the laundry by type: underwear, towels, shirts, etc. Help them measure the soap or fabric softener into the washing machine or tear off a softener sheet to put in the dryer. Let them feel a wet sock and a dry one, and talk about the differences in weight, texture, or temperature.

Your children can match socks from the dryer and separate large and small underpants. Use laundry words *(folding, smoothing)*, and talk about colors, shapes (rectangle pillowcases), and parts of clothing (corners, sleeves, collars, buttons). *Safety tip:* Never leave children unattended in a laundry room where they might climb into appliances or "sample" cleaning products.

A good way to avoid right and left shoe mix-ups is to use a waterproof marker or laundry pen. Draw a dot inside each shoe along the inner edges. When shoes are sitting next to each other correctly, the dots are lined up side-by-side.

Craft

Paper Bag Costume

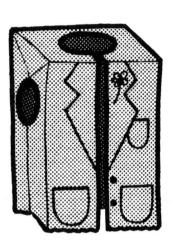

You will need: paper grocery sack

crayons or washable markers

paper or cloth scraps

glue

scissors

With the sack upside down, cut three holes in it: one on the bottom for the head and one on each side for the arms. Cut in a line from the neck hole down the front of the sack to make it easier to get on and off.

Decorate the sack with crayons, markers, or scraps. Add buttons, pockets, collar, belt, sash, or fringe. The costume can look like everyday clothes or be exotic: superheroes, wild creatures, and so on. Hang these costumes from hangers in an area where your child has access to them for fun and pretend play. Don't be surprised if older brothers or sisters want to be part of this, too.

Program Notes

Sign Language

SHIRT   Pinch clothing at the shoulders and pull gently.

Introduce the theme by remarking on the different kinds of clothing worn by adults and children, using clothing words (dress, jumper, overalls, blouse) as well as descriptors (warm, cool, long sleeves, ruffles, etc.).

A simple stretching activity between stories is to pretend to get dressed together to go out to play. The story *How Do I Put It On?* is excellent as a flannelboard presentation, and the clothing can be adapted to cooler weather by making the sleeves and pant legs longer and turning the shoes into boots.

The storytime puppet arrives carrying clothing easy to put on it (hat, collar, scarf) and asks for help getting dressed. Children can help, with the puppet directing them to put the clothing in the wrong places. The storyteller encourages children to help the puppet get dressed correctly.

Giveaways are paper doll bears and clothes, copied from this page.

Fingertaster "tastes" foods appropriate to the season, such as hot soups or frozen yogurt and watermelon.

Children exit the story space marching. Focus their attention on their shoes.

———————————————— Notes ————————————————

Growing Up Safe

Books

Big Like Me
ANNA GROSSNICKLE HINES

The Checkup
HELEN OXENBURY

Corduroy Goes to the Doctor
LISA MCCUE

Eat Up, Gemma
SARAH HAYES

Little Mo
MARTIN WADDELL

Molly
RUTH RADLAUER

My Dentist
HARLOW ROCKWELL

No Diapers for Baby
DENISE LEWIS PATRICK

Pig, Pig Grows Up
DAVID MCPHAIL

Sam's Potty
BARBRO LINDGREN

Say the Magic Word, Please
ANNA ROSS

Sebastian's Trumpet
MIKO IMAI

Step by Step
BRUCE MCMILLAN

The Very Little Girl
PHYLLIS KRASILOVSKY

What's Claude Doing?
DICK GACKENBACH

You Go Away
DOROTHY COREY

Rhythms, Rhymes, and Fingerplays

I Can!

I can! I can! I can! *(clap hands)*
Roll a ball. *(make rolling motion)*
I can! I can! I can! *(clap hands)*
Roll a ball. *(make rolling motion)*
I can! I can! I can! *(clap hands)*
Roll a ball. *(make rolling motion)*
Come roll a ball with me.

[Repeat with]
   throw a ball
   bounce a ball
   jump up high
   turn around
   run so fast
   tippy toe

Stop, Look, and Listen!

Stop! *(hands in front, palms out)*
Look! *(hands shade eyes)*
And listen! *(hands cup ears)*
Before you cross the street,
    (look both ways)
Use your eyes, *(point to eyes)*
Use your ears, *(point to ears)*
And then use your feet. *(point to
    feet and nod head)*

Growing Up Healthy   (tune: "Paw-Paw Patch")

We eat good food,
We're growing up healthy.
We eat good food,
We're growing up healthy.
We eat good food,
We're growing up healthy.
Growing up big and strong.

[Repeat with]

> We help Mommy
> We play outside
> We look both ways
> We get lots of sleep

Parents' Follow-Up Ideas

Children are always in a hurry to "grow up," to be big enough to do things older children do. Help your toddlers realize how much they have already grown. Look at baby pictures together and talk about when they could not eat, crawl, walk, or talk. If there is something they want to do but their skills are not yet good enough, help find things they can do now that will lead into that activity. For example, if they want to ride a two-wheel bike, they need to learn to pedal, and steer, and balance. Those are skills they can perfect now.

Introduce your children to a ruler or cloth measuring tape and show them how to "measure" two objects to see which is larger. Point out the numbers on the ruler to reinforce the concept of counting. Using pictures from magazines, make a chart of the biggest and smallest objects you measure. Remember that sizes in photographs can be confusing; the picture of a refrigerator may look smaller than one of a toy. Make a growth chart for your children and mark their growth progress on it. Use it to compare their height (growth) with others, including smaller pets, toys, and younger children as well as larger examples of different sizes.

Talk about how all living things grow and change. Young children are beginning to notice similarities between themselves and the rest of the world. Notice how flowers bud and then blossom. Visit the petting zoo often to see the progress young animals make over time. Talk about changes in abilities of babies in your home or neighborhood.

Craft

Growth Chart

You will need: a strip of paper, 4–6' long by 6" wide

ruler

permanent marker

glue

photo of child at birth or as young infant

clear contact paper

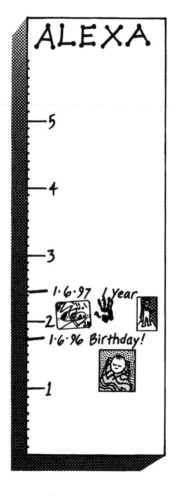

Along the left side of the paper strip, and starting at the bottom, mark inches and feet the length of the paper. Make a large mark at your child's birth length and write the date. Next to it, glue a photo of your child as an infant. Using a baby book or doctor's records, mark growth at various ages and attach a picture of your child taken at that age.

Laminate the growth chart or cover it with clear contact paper on both sides. Mount it on a wall in your child's room where she or he can see it to study the growth rate. Mounting it across from a full-length mirror allows your child to check progress and allows you to introduce the seemingly magical concept of perspective: stand close to the mirror and look taller than the growth chart. Continue to mark growth at milestones, documenting with dates, ages, and photos. Cover additions with clear tape to preserve them and to create a keepsake.

Program Notes

Sign Language

> TALL   The left hand is open, palm forward, fingers upward. Lay the right hand index finger horizontally across the left palm and slide it upward.

The storytime puppet introduces the theme by telling children some of the things it wants to do when it "grows up." The storyteller points out to the puppet some of the things it can do now that it could not do before, such as talking, picking up things, dancing, walking, etc. Make a growth chart for the puppet, marking estimated heights for different "ages" and making it large enough to measure the children against. Mount the growth chart on a nearby wall and invite children to be measured in comparison to the puppet. Focus attention on how much taller each of them is compared with the puppet. Avoid comparing them with each other.

Use flannelboard figures of babies, toddlers, and older children to help toddlers better understand the changes in their growing bodies. Make flannelboard figures from pictures in magazines to illustrate the rhyme "I Can" or the song "Growing Up Healthy."

Giveaways are toothbrushes that you can get free from a local dentist.

Fingertaster "tastes" fruits, such as oranges, bananas, apples, peaches, strawberries, etc.

Children exit the story space walking "tall."

Notes

Hats

Books

Barney's Hats
MARY ANN DUDKO AND
MARGIE LARSEN

Blue Hat, Green Hat
SANDRA BOYNTON

Caps for Sale (Also in Spanish:
    *Se Venden Gorras: La Historia
    de un Vendedor Ambulante,
    Unos Monos y Sus Travesuras*)
ESPHYR SLOBODKINA

Catch That Hat!
EMMA CHICHESTER CLARK

Hats, Hats, Hats
ANN MORRIS

Jennie's Hat
EZRA JACK KEATS

Look, There's My Hat!
MAUREEN ROFFEY

Martin's Hats
JOAN W. BLOS

Mister Momboo's Hat
RALPH LEEMIS

Old Hat, New Hat
STAN AND JAN BERENSTAIN

*Ten Cats Have Hats:
A Counting Book*
JEAN MARZOLLO

This Is the Hat
NANCY VAN LAAN

*Who Took the
Farmer's Hat?*
JOAN L. NODSET

Whose Hat?
MARGARET MILLER

Whose Hat Is That?
RONALD ROY

Word Bird's Hats
JANE BELK MONCURE

Rhythms, Rhymes, and Fingerplays

Hats

A cowboy wears a cowboy hat *(hands
    encircle head)*
As he gallops on his horse. *(galloping
    motion)*
A firefighter's hat keeps her safe *(hands
    encircle head)*
As fires run their course. *(spraying motion
    as with hose)*
A clown wears a pointy hat *(hands form
    point on head)*
And a smile upon his face. *(smile broadly)*
And astronauts wear helmets, *(encircle
    face with hands)*
When blasting into space. *(palms together,
    shoot hands up to sky)*

Paper Hat

Fold the paper just in half *(make folding motion)*
Turn corners down. *(folding motion with right,*
    then left hand)
Now, don't you laugh! *(shake finger)*
Turn up the edges, this way and that.
    (make turning motions)
Now put it on.
It's a paper hat! *(hands form point above head)*

Mary Has a Blue Hat
   ### (tune: "Mary Had a Little Lamb")

Mary has a blue hat on,
Blue hat on, blue hat on.
Mary has a blue hat on
Her head throughout the day.

[Repeat with other names and colors.]

Parents' Follow-Up Ideas

Make a simple strip-hat using a 2"-wide strip of paper, measuring the length around your child's head and securing the ends with tape. Decorate the front with crayons or markers or add a picture of a hat cut from magazines, advertising, or catalogs. Encourage your child to wear the cowboy (police, sports, or Easter) hat when pretending. To better preserve the hat, untape it and cover it with clear contact paper before reassembling it. Store strip-hats on stuffed animals or untaped and lying flat in a box.

Create a hat game using pictures of all kinds of hats cut from magazines, advertising, or catalogs and mounted on index cards. Your child can play a matching game, sort the hat collection by colors or sizes, and put hats on people (or animals) in other books or magazines. Talk about the different kinds of hats (sizes, colors, shapes) and who wears them for work or play. Encourage your toddler to be silly sometimes: "This boy doesn't wear his hat on his head; he wears it on his foot!" Keep the hat collection in a "hat box" made from a plastic container with a lid or a shoe box.

Tired of looking for missing hats and mittens at home? Attach a strip of Velcro (the scratchy, hooked side) along the wall behind the door. When children come home, they'll enjoy pressing their knitted mittens or hats to the strip to hold them in place. Mount the Velcro strip away from high traffic areas since it also sticks to sweaters, scarves, and other fabrics as they pass by.

Craft

Helmets

You will need: plastic milk gallon jug, washed thoroughly

scissors and packing knife

adhesive or cloth tape

glue

permanent markers

cloth and paper scraps

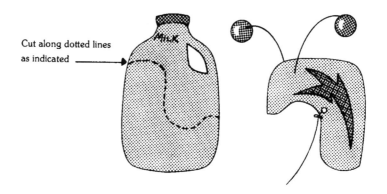

Cut along dotted lines
as indicated

Cut the milk jug in one continuous movement, removing the spout and lid, handle, and top of jug. What is left is a piece of bowl-shaped plastic that will form the body of the helmet. Place it over your child's head and mark where it should be cut away so it does not rub against shoulders, ears, or neck. You may have to stuff a small towel inside it to make it sit right on your child's head. Cover the edges with tape to avoid scratches.

When the helmet fits comfortably, decorate it with markers or scraps to create a motorcycle, football, or astronaut helmet.

Program Notes

Sign Language

HAT   Pat the top of your head with the right hand.

Note: At the end of the previous week, invite children to wear hats to the next program. Have paper hats available for children who come without them, letting them decide whether or not they want to participate.

Reinforce the theme when assembling the clown shape puzzle: the triangle is the clown's hat.

The story *Caps for Sale* can be used several ways: with the book, as a flannelboard story, and as a play with the children being the monkeys and using baseball caps, paper, or pretend hats. The rhyme "Mary Has a Blue Hat" makes a good flannelboard presentation using different-colored hats and a smiling felt face.

Giveaways are paper hats folded from newspaper or wrapping paper with children's names printed on them. Be sure to tape the corners so they don't come unfolded, and if it is windy, remind children to "hold on to your hats" as they leave.

Since some bakers wear chefs' hats, fingertaster "tastes" things made in bakeries, such as bread, muffins, cake, cookies, etc.

Children exit the story space wearing their hats.

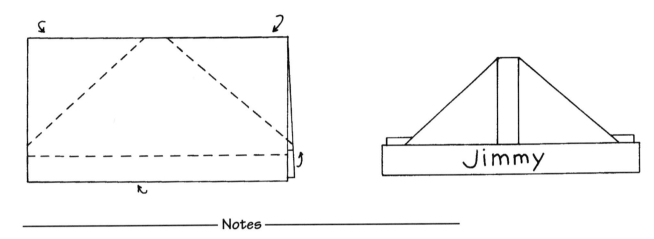

———— Notes ————

Helping

Books

Big Help
ANNA GROSSNICKLE HINES

Clifford's Good Deeds (Also
   in Spanish: *Las Buenas
   Acciones de Clifford*)
NORMAN BRIDWELL

Helping Out
GEORGE ANCONA

I Can Help
TOM COOKE

I Help Mommy
BERNICE CHARDIET

Little Red Hen
PAUL GALDONE

Mother's Helper
HELEN OXENBURY

My Apron
ERIC CARLE

My First Look at Sorting

My Messy Room
MARY PACKARD

Paddington Makes a Mess
MICHAEL BOND

Pizza Party
GRACE MACCARONE

Tidy Titch
PAT HUTCHINS

*Tom & Pippo and the
Washing Machine*
HELEN OXENBURY

What Do I Do?
(English and Spanish)
NORMA SIMON

You and Me, Little Bear
MARTIN WADDELL

Rhythms, Rhymes, and Fingerplays

Clean Up Song   (tune: "Mary Had a Little Lamb")

We can help pick up the toys,
   (mimic the action)
Up the toys, up the toys.
We can help pick up the toys,
To make things nice and neat.

[Repeat with]
   wipe off the chair
   sort the clothes
   dust the house
   sweep the floor
   pick up rug spots (carpet squares)

I Can Help

Push the button
On the elevator door.
   (mimic actions)
Pick up the toys
Lying on the floor.
Feed the dog,
Water the cat.
Take off my shoes,
Put on my hat.
Pour a drink,
Wipe up my mess.
Turn off the light,
Get undressed.
There are lots of ways
Throughout the day
   (hands spread wide)
I help Mommy *(point to self)*
As we work and play.

One, Two, Buckle My Shoe

One, two, buckle my shoe.
   (touch shoe)
Three, four, shut the door.
   (bring hands together)
Five, six, pick up sticks.
   (pretend to pick up objects)
Seven, eight, lay them straight.
   (pretend to lay objects in a row)
Nine, ten, do it again.

[Repeat once]

Parents' Follow-Up Ideas

Make cleaning up and putting away toys into a game by cutting silhouettes of toys or common items out of contact paper (or use pictures from magazines). Apply the pictures to shelves or outsides of drawers where the items should be stored. By putting the correct item in the right place, your child is cleaning up and practicing matching skills at the same time.

Toddlers can pick things up and put them in the trash, put things away, carry light objects, help set the table, wash and dry their own hands, empty a small trash can, sponge off the table, help dust, feed some pets, sort laundry by colors and types of clothes, and put away unbreakable, reachable groceries or dishes.

Have child-sized tools or similar toys (a toy lawn mower will double as a vacuum cleaner) for your toddlers to use and encourage them to mimic you as you do chores. This will improve their physical coordination, observation, and sequencing skills. Talk about the kind of help you need with a job and describe step-by-step how you will do it, using "first we . . . , then we . . ." Keep instructions simple and review them at each step, admiring your child's assistance and progress, as well as the result of a job well-done together. Name all the tools you are using, such as a vacuum cleaner, broom, rake, or wheel barrow, and talk about how you are working, "dust under the table . . . pick up the leaves behind the bush . . ." Keep mock cleaning tools (sponge, bucket, small broom) in the child's play area.

Craft

Refrigerator Magnets

You will need: pictures (cut from magazines, advertising flyers, food labels, or catalogs)

index cards

glue

magnetic strips (available in craft stores)

scissors

clear contact paper (optional)

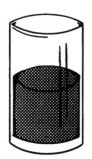

Using pictures of your child's favorite foods, glue them to index cards to make them more durable. (Optional: cover with clear contact paper to make them cleanable.) Cut a piece of magnetic strip and peel the paper from the adhesive side. Attach the magnetic strip to the back of the food picture. They will now stick to any metal appliance.

Let your child use the food magnets to help decide what to have for breakfast or lunch, creating picture menus on the refrigerator. Or play a sorting game naming the food and the food group to which it belongs ("Apple is a fruit"). Help your toddler create a meal plan by suggesting, "pick a vegetable to go with that," or "what fruit do you want for dessert?" Food magnets can also create lists for the grocery store or picnic basket.

Store magnets in a box or can near the refrigerator, or make a magnetic storage box out of a sturdy box (Velveeta cheese), applying long magnetic strips to the back.

Make other refrigerator magnets of people, shapes, objects, animals, and activities. A set of household-chore magnets can be used on the washing machine or dryer to entertain your toddler while you are working or to plan chores you can both do together. Take the magnets on the road using a cookie sheet (with a rim so the magnets don't slide off) or a large coffee can (covering the rim with cloth tape to protect little fingers).

Program Notes

Sign Language

HELP   Lay your left fist in the palm of the right hand and raise them both upward, as though your right hand were giving assistance to the left.

This is a fun theme because toddlers *love* to help. The storytime puppet introduces the theme by announcing it is time to clean something (a small portion of the story space, a table, chair, the flannelboard, or the lap stage). Have several small cleaning tools on hand (cloths, pails, brooms, etc.), and let the children help with pretend cleaning. They can dust, sweep, wipe, and brush the space or object until you or the puppet declares it clean. Make sure to praise them for their assistance and the great job they do.

Throughout the program, make opportunities for children to "help" with the stories or their props, moving pieces on the flannelboard or holding objects. Singing the "Clean Up" song, the storyteller and the children pick up the carpet squares or put books in a box at the end of the program.

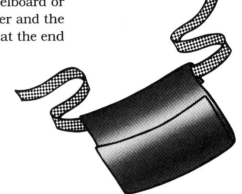

Giveaways are "helper" aprons (similar to nail aprons obtained free or inexpensively from lumber yards). They can be made by folding a pocket into a rectangle of fabric, then folding the upper edge over a ribbon and gluing the edges with fabric glue.

Fingertaster "tastes" condiments, such as ketchup, mustard, chocolate sauce, etc.

Children exit the story space "sweeping" the floor.

——————————— **Notes** ———————————

Homes

Books

At Home
SIAN TUCKER

Building a House
BYRON BARTON

Farm House

Goodbye House
FRANK ASCH

Homes
JAN PIENKOWSKI

A House by the Sea
JOANNE RYDER

Houses and Homes
ANN MORRIS

In a Red House
NANCY TAFURI

Is Anyone Home?
RON MARIS

Moving Day
ROBERT KALAN

Moving from One to Ten
SHARI HALPERN

My First Look at Home

Nicky Upstairs and Down
HARRIET ZIEFERT

Our Garage Sale
ANNE F. ROCKWELL

This Is My House (Also
    in Spanish: *Esta Es
    Mi Casa*)
ARTHUR DORROS

Whose House Is This?
CHARLES REASONER

Rhythms, Rhymes, and Fingerplays

Houses

This is a nest for a bluebird. *(cup hands together)*
This is a hive for a bee. *(close hands together)*
This is the hole for bunny rabbit *(arms form circle)*
And this is a house for me! *(peak fingers over head)*

Do You Know Where I Live?
  (tune: "Did You Ever See a Lassie?")

[Chorus]

Do you know where I live?
Where I live, where I live?
Do you know where I live?
Where I make my home?

I live in a red barn,
A red barn, a red barn.
I live in a red barn,
And I am a cow.

I live in a big tree,
A big tree, a big tree.
I live in a big tree,
And I am a squirrel.

I live in a little hole,
A little hole, a little hole.
I live in a little hole,
And I am a rabbit.

I Shut the Door

I shut the door and lock it tight,
    (clap hands, make locking motion)
And put the key out of sight, *(pretend
    to put "key" in pocket)*
And I played in the bright sunlight.
    (wave hands above head)

I found the key to open the door,
    (pull "key" from pocket)
And turned, and turned, and turned
    some more, *(make turning motions
    as if holding a key)*
And then I opened up the door! *(hands
    together, move one hand away)*

Parents' Follow-Up Ideas

Help your child learn the different names for places where people live: houses, townhouses, duplexes, condos, apartments, mobile homes, travel trailers or motor homes, motels, etc. Point out the various parts of buildings where people live and the names for them: structures (windows, doors, walls, stairs, porches), rooms (kitchens, bathrooms, bedrooms, closets), and furnishings (chairs, sofas, beds). Talk about others' homes you have visited—those of friends and relatives. Do the same with animal homes, encouraging children to be creative: "Do you think a dog would live in a tree?"

Create "homes" for stuffed animals, puppets, or dolls using different sizes of boxes, baskets, grocery sacks, etc. Help children make their own villages by cutting doors and windows for them so the residents can go in and see out. Talk about where different kinds of people or animals might live and why. Even if a toy is "homeless," you can talk about the kind of places it would like to live in.

Homes are where people receive letters, and *all* children love to get mail. Help children "write" to friends or relatives who will correspond with them. Cut the fronts off old greeting cards and use them as postcards (the postage is less expensive). Your children can draw a picture or dictate a message to put on them. Let your children choose colorful stamps at the post office, attach them, and post them through mail slots or mail boxes. Talk about how mail carriers help take messages from one place to another. Make a pretend mailbox at home with a slot and a back door, and set aside all the "junk" mail for your children, giving them stickers for stamps.

Craft

Bird Feeder

You will need: peanut butter

Styrofoam cup

piece of string

bird seed

Tie a knot in one end of the string. Make a small hole in the bottom of the cup and thread the string through the hole with the knot on the inside. Cover the cup, inside and out, with peanut butter and roll it in bird seed until it is well covered. Hang the cup outside near a window so you can watch the birds eat!

Program Notes

Sign Language

HOUSE   Peak your hands over the head, separate hands
and move them sideways and down, like a roofline.

Introduce the theme with the storytime puppet or stuffed animal talking about where it lives: in a closet, in a pocket, etc. If stories about "moving" will predominate, the puppet brings a box and asks the children to help pack some of its stuff (books, hat, clothes, etc.). Follow-up at next week's program with the puppet mentioning its new home and unpacking all its favorite things.

For the song "Do You Know Where I Live?" put different animal pictures on the flannelboard and extend the song into an activity by having the children make animal sounds or move like the animals. Using a shoe box with a slot in the lid, let children "mail" letters to a buddy-puppet or absent friend. Gather unopened "junk" mail, giving one en-velope to each child who then puts it in the mailbox. Distribute your program handouts as "letters" from this same mailbox.

Giveaways are key bookmarks made by copying this page.

Fingertaster "tastes" flavors in the kitchen, such as bread, cheese, peanut butter, etc.

Children exit the story space carrying pretend boxes for the puppet who's moving, which they can "leave" in the children's area.

Notes

Love (Valentine's Day)

Books

Ask Mr. Bear
MARJORIE FLACK

Clifford, We Love You
NORMAN BRIDWELL

Corduroy (Also in Spanish:
    Corduroy: Edicion Espanola)
DON FREEMAN

*Daddy, Would You
Love Me If . . .*
CARLA DIJS

Guess How Much I Love You
SAM MCBRATNEY

Hugs
CYNDY SZEKERES

I Love You as Much . . .
LAURA KRAUSS MELMED

Just For You
MERCER MAYER

*"More, More, More,"
Said the Baby*
VERA WILLIAMS

On Mother's Lap
ANN HERBERT SCOTT

To Baby with Love
JAN ORMEROD

Valentine Friends
ANN SCHWENINGER

*What Is Valentine's Day?
A Lift-the-Flap Book*
HARRIET ZIEFERT

Will There Be a Lap for Me?
DOROTHY COREY

*Word Bird's Valentine
Day Words*
JANE BELK MONCURE

Why Do You Love Me?
MARTIN BAYNTON

Rhythms, Rhymes, and Fingerplays

Skinna-Marinky   (tune: "Skinnamarink")

Skinna-marinky dinky dink, skinna-marinky doo.
    (sway gently)
I *(point to self)* love *(cross arms across chest)* you!
    (point to child)
Skinna-marinky dinky dink, skinna-marinky doo.
I *(point to self)* love *(cross arms across chest)* you!
    (point to child)
I love you in the morning, and in the afternoon.
    (sway side-to-side, arms crossed over chest)
I love you in the evening, and underneath the moon.
    (arms open wide)
Oh, skinna-marinky dinky dink, skinna-marinky doo.
I *(point to self)* love *(cross arms across chest)* you!
    (point to child)

Make a Valentine

Snip, snip, snip the paper. *(slide palms of
    hand up and down like blades of scissors)*
Paste, paste, paste the paper. *(brush
    fingers against palm of other hand)*
Press, press, press the paper.
    (press palms together)
To make a valentine for you!
    (make "giving" motion)

I Have a Little Heart

I have a little heart *(hand over heart)*
And it goes thump, thump, thump
    (pat chest with fingers)
It keeps right on beating
When I jump, jump, jump. *(jump in place)*

I get a special feeling *(hug shoulders)*
When I look at you. *(point to children)*
It makes me want to give you
    (shrug shoulders shyly)
A kiss or two! *(storyteller blows kisses
    to child, parent kisses child on cheek)*

Parents' Follow-Up Ideas

Everyone likes to know they are loved. Tell your children often that
you care. Especially when disciplining them or dealing with stressful
situations, help them understand that you can dislike something
they've done while continuing to love them. Touching is an important
way to show children that they are loved. Make sure your toddlers get
lots of hugs, kisses, and tender touches every day. It makes you feel
good, too.

Hearts are a universal symbol of love. Cut folded heart-shapes
from different colors and textures of paper (sandpaper, tissue paper,
aluminum foil, embossed wallpaper, etc.). Vary the sizes. Let your
children sort them by sizes and colors or line them up with large ones
on one end and small ones on the other. Talk about the different textures and how they look and feel. Make two sets of textured hearts,
putting one set in a box or sack. Your child can hold one heart in his
or her hand and reach into the box to locate the other by feel.

Cut the fronts from old greeting cards and make a colorful book
with them. Punch a hole in the upper left corner and thread the cards
together on ribbon or yarn. Loosely tie a knot in the ribbon so the
"pages" of the book can be easily turned. Make up stories about the
pictures on the cards. Use the card book as a counting book, counting hearts, bears, or any common objects.

Craft

Ribbon Bookmark

You will need: a photograph (that can be cut)

scissors

a 6″ piece of ribbon (or colored paper)

glue

felt-tipped marking pen

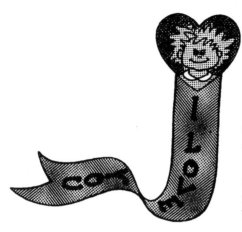

Cut the photograph into the shape of a heart with the person's face in the center of the heart. Glue the heart-photo to one end of the ribbon and let it dry thoroughly.

With a marking pen, write a special message on the bookmark like "I Love You," "Best Grandma," "Big Sister," or the name of the person in the picture or the one receiving the bookmark.

Program Notes

Sign Language

LOVE   Cross your arms over the chest with hands on shoulders, like a hug.

The storytime puppet introduces the theme by bringing a paper heart to the storyteller.

The book *Ask Mr. Bear* works well as a flannelboard story; finish it by having the children give big "bear" hugs to their adults.

Giveaways are construction paper hearts made by folding the paper and cutting an arc along the fold line.

Fingertaster "tastes" sweet things, such as honey, jelly, sugar, etc.

Children exit the story space after giving the fingertaster or storytime puppet a big hug.

————————————— **Notes** —————————————

——— Mealtimes (Thanksgiving) ———

Books

Dinnertime
CLAIRE HENLEY

Eating Out
HELEN OXENBURY

Food
JAN PIENKOWSKI

Happy Thanksgiving!
WENDY CHEYETTE LEWISON

*I Know an Old Lady Who
Swallowed a Fly*
COLIN AND JACQUI HAWKINS

Let's Eat
PATRICK YEE

Let's Eat: Vamos a Comer
ALAN BENJAMIN

Lunch!
DENISE FLEMING

Max's Breakfast
ROSEMARY WELLS

Mealtimes
ZOE DAVENPORT

Sam's Cookie
BARBRO LINDGREN

Very Last First Time
JAN ANDREWS

What a Good Lunch!
SHIGEO WATANABE

*What Is Thanksgiving?
A Lift-the-Flap Book*
HARRIET ZIEFERT

*What's in My Pocket?
A Pop-Up & Peek-In Book*
DAVID CARTER

*Word Bird's Thanksgiving
Words*
JANE BELK MONCURE

Rhythms, Rhymes, and Fingerplays

Yummy Lunch   (tune: "Little Drummer Boy")

I'll have a piece of pizza, Yummy-yum-yum.
Some crunchy carrots, too. Yummy-yum-yum.
Give me a glass of milk, please. Yummy-yum-yum.
And for dessert some grapes. Oh, yummy-yum-yum . . .
Yummy-yum-yum, . . . fill up my tum . . .
With a delicious lunch, . . . yummy-yum-yum.
Yummy-yum-yum.

The Apple Tree

Away up high in the apple tree *(point up)*
Two red apples smiled at me. *(point to self)*
I shook that tree as hard as I could,
    (shaking motion)
And down they came . . . *(point down)*
Mmmmm, they were good! *(rub tummy)*

Doughnut

Here is a doughnut *(form circle with
 thumbs and forefingers)*
Round and fat.
There's a hole in the middle *(hold finger-
 circle up and look through it)*
But you can't eat that!! *(shake head)*

It's Almost Thanksgiving

Run, turkey, run! *(pat knees)*
Run, turkey, run!
It's almost Thanksgiving.
Run, turkey, run!

Roll, pumpkin, roll! *(roll hands)*
Roll, pumpkin, roll!
It's almost Thanksgiving.
Roll, pumpkin, roll!

Grow, corn, grow! *(raise arms above head)*
Grow, corn, grow!
It's almost Thanksgiving.
Grow, corn, grow!

Eat, children, eat! *(make eating motion)*
Eat, children, eat!
It is now Thanksgiving.
Eat, children, eat!

Parents' Follow-Up Ideas

Cut pictures from magazines or labels from cans or boxes. Glue them to index cards to make a matching game. You will need two pictures of each food. Turn all the cards face down on the table or floor. Take turns with your child, turning over two cards at a time. Examine the pictures and name the food. Do the cards match? If so, remove them. If not, turn them face down and put them back in the same place. Talk with your child as you turn over the first card to demonstrate how you identify the picture and remember if you've seen one like it before: "Here is a banana! I remember seeing another banana before. Where was that? You are right! It was in the top row." This game helps toddlers develop their memories and learn more words about foods, colors, shapes, and spatial concepts.

Make a food book by gluing pictures to notebook or typing paper. Start with your child's favorite foods. (*Hint:* Glue sticks are easier for toddlers to handle than bottles of glue.) Staple pages together or put them in a three-ring binder. Group pictures together in larger food groups: vegetables, fruits, breads, meats, etc. Encourage your child to put foods together to make pretend meals or create meal pages.

Gather pictures of foods together on one page for breakfasts, lunches, snacks, and dinners.

Before taking your children to eat in a restaurant, play-act the experience at home. Let them help you make a menu of lunch choices using the food pictures (above). Take turns pretending to be the customer and the wait staff. Unlike home, where children can play until called to a meal that is ready and waiting for them, there are always delays in restaurants. Help your children understand the reasons they (and everybody else) must wait until the meal is served. Plan things you can do at the restaurant while waiting for the food to come.

Craft

Finger-Tasting Sock Puppet

You will need: an old sock with toe and heel intact

needle and thread

notions for features (buttons, pompoms, yarn)

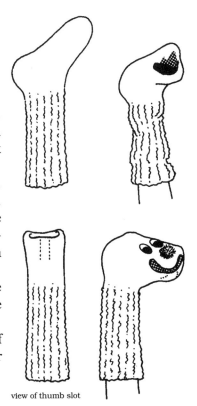

view of thumb slot

Place the sock over your hand with the heel over your knuckles. Open your fingers wide inside the sock and tuck the toe into the palm of your hand. With needle and thread, sew the underside of the sock "mouth," forming a slot into which your thumb can slide.

Sew on eyes, keeping them close to the mouth opening. Add nose, hair, clothes . . . whatever you want to make the puppet real. Please, no teeth, however. Keep the puppet nonthreatening. Features can be made with any scraps or odds and ends you have around. Avoid using materials that cannot be washed. The puppet can be thrown in the laundry with the family clothes.

Sock puppets are very flexible, "make faces" easily, and can be used by either adults or children. Practice moving your fingers inside the puppet to make happy faces, sad faces, and silly faces.

To taste fingers: Have the puppet gently suck or lick the fingers of children with a slurping sound, and then tell each child what his or her finger tasted like. Use flavors with which the children are familiar.

Program Notes

Sign Language

EAT   With the tips of your thumb and fingertips together, tap your mouth twice.

Note: Snacks lend themselves to this theme, but take care since some children have food allergies (milk, flour, sugar, peanuts). Check with adults the previous week, and if there are children who cannot have the planned snack, cancel it or ask the adult for a suitable alternative that will work for all program participants.

Introduce the theme by putting a bib on the storytime puppet who is going out to dinner. Between stories children pretend mealtimes: washing hands, setting the table, eating, drinking, and washing dishes. Use simple felt shapes for a flannelboard table setting, letting children help: large circle = plate, small circle = glass, rectangles = spoon and fork.

A sack puppet version of the song *I Know an Old Lady Who Swallowed a Fly* with a window stomach (pattern in appendix A) is always popular.

Giveaways are place mats made of large pieces of construction paper. Each has a child's name written on it and table setting shapes glued on. The place mats will last longer if they are laminated.

Fingertaster "tastes" restaurant foods, such as French fries, hamburgers, and pizza, or traditional Thanksgiving foods, such as turkey, pumpkin pie, corn on the cob, etc.

———————————————— Notes ————————————————

Monkeys

Books

Baby Monkey
PATRICK YEE

Color Box
DAYLE A. DODDS

Curious George (Also in
    Spanish: *Jorge el Curioso*)
H. A. REY

*Five Little Monkeys
Sitting in a Tree*
EILEEN CHRISTELOW

*Five Little Monkeys
with Nothing to Do*
EILEEN CHRISTELOW

Little Gorilla (Also in
    Spanish: *Gorililita*)
RUTH BORNSTEIN

Monkey Match
KAREN E. LITTLE

Monkey See, Monkey Do
MARC GAVE

The Monkeys and the Pedlar
SUZANNE SUBA

Not a Little Monkey
CHARLOTTE ZOLOTOW

So Say the Little Monkeys
NANCY VAN LAAN

Tom & Pippo's Day
HELEN OXENBURY

Two Little Monkeys
MARC BROWN

*What Do You Say When a
Monkey Acts This Way?*
JANE BELK MONCURE

Who Is Coming?
PATRICIA MCKISSACK

Yellow Umbrella
HENRIK DRESCHER

Rhythms, Rhymes, and Fingerplays

Five Little Monkeys

Five little monkeys *(hold up five fingers)*
Swinging in a tree. *(swing hands over head)*
Teasing Mr. Crocodile *(shake one finger)*
"You can't catch me. *(point to self, shake head)*
You can't catch me!"
Up comes Mr. Crocodile quiet as can be.
    (palms together, move hands upward)
Snap! *(clap hands, sharply)*

[Repeat with]
    Four
    Three
    Two
    One

Pop Goes the Weasel   (traditional song)

All around the mulberry bush *(turn in circle)*
The monkey chased the weasel *(make grabbing motions)*
The monkey thought 'twas all in fun. *(shake one finger)*
Pop! *(clap hands)* goes the weasel.

Monkey See, Monkey Do

When you clap, clap, clap your hands *(clap hands)*
The monkey clap, clap, claps his hands. *(clap hands)*
Monkey see *(shade eyes with hands)*
Monkey do *(repeat first motion)*
Monkey does the same as you. *(point to child)*

[Repeat with]

> stamp, stamp, stamp your feet
> jump, jump, jump up high
> make, make, make a funny face
> turn, turn, turn around

Parents' Follow-Up Ideas

Monkey see, monkey do is a simple version of "Simon Says" that teaches your child to listen and follow directions. Begin with small actions ("touch your nose"; "reach up high"; "clap your hands") and save bigger actions for out-of-doors or places with lots of room ("run fast"; "jump high"; "twirl around").

Inexpensive painting books are available at department stores with the colors imbedded into the pages. When you add water with a paintbrush, the colors come out. These books will not promote artistic ability in your child, but they are good for learning to work with a small tool like a paintbrush.

Another way to paint with water in warm weather is to fill a can with water and let your child "paint" the house, the sidewalk, or driveway. Talk about evaporation as the water dries and becomes invisible.

Craft

Clown-Shape Puzzle

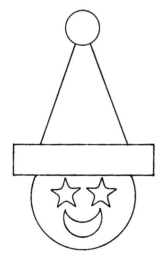

You will need: brightly colored pieces of felt in the following shapes:

> 1 rectangle
> 1 triangle
> 1 large and 1 small circle
> 2 small stars
> 1 crescent (for smile)

For circles, trace around objects (margarine tubs or salt shakers) onto the felt. Use a ruler to draw the rectangle and triangle. Do not worry about pencil marks since the pieces can easily be flipped over when used. Draw the stars and crescent freehand.

Talk with your child about the shapes of these puzzle pieces and their colors. Take turns arranging and rearranging them on a table, sofa cushion, or flannelboard to form a clown's face. Make additional pieces and see what other designs or pictures you can create.

Program Notes

Sign Language

MONKEY   Curl your hands under your arms and make a scratching motion along the sides of the body.

The storytime puppet introduces the theme with a stuffed or toy monkey, teaching children to "chatter" like monkeys.

The "Five Little Monkeys" rhyme works well with flannelboard figures or glove puppets as well as an action rhyme. After all the monkeys have been taken by the crocodile, have the crocodile put them back into the tree again as everyone counts. (This is reassuring to young children, and they love to count.)

Giveaways are paper sack monkey puppets made with lunch sacks, photocopied monkey-faces, and yarn for a tail.

Fingertaster "tastes" things made with bananas, such as banana pudding, banana sandwiches, banana pie, etc.

Children exit the story space chattering like monkeys.

——————————————— Notes ———————————————

Morning

Books

Early Morning in the Barn
NANCY TAFURI

Flip and the Morning
WESLEY DENNIS

Good Morning, Baby
CHERYL WILLIS HUDSON

Good Morning, Chick
MIRRA GINSBURG

Good Morning, Puppy!
CINDY CHANG

Good Morning, Sun
SUZY MCPARTLAND

I Am Eyes: Ni Macho
LEILA WARD

Lucky Morning
SALLY NOLL

Milton, the Early Riser
ROBERT KRAUS

One Morning
CANNA FUNAKOSHI

*Pig, Horse, or Cow,
Don't Wake Me Now*
ARLENE ALDA

Rabbit's Morning
NANCY TAFURI

Wake Up, Baby!
JOANNE OPPENHEIM

Wake Up, Bear
LYNLEY DODD

Wake Up! Sun!
DAVID HARRISON

*When the
Rooster Crowed*
PATRICIA LILLIE

Rhythms, Rhymes, and Fingerplays

Good Morning   (tune: "Good Morning")

Good morning! Good morning! *(sing very slowly,
     as though waking up)*
Wake up and stretch today. *(stretching motion)*
Good morning . . . good morning . . . to you!
     (continue stretching)
Good morning! Good morning! *(say little faster:
     wave hand slowly)*
Wake UP and then we'll say, *(eyes closed,
     then they pop open on* up*)*
Good morning, GOOD MORNING to you.
     (wave slowly)
It's the top of the morning, *(arms sweep over
     head and open wide)*
And I'm here to say, *(point to self)*
We're going to make this *(gesture to group)*
A grand . . . new . . . day! *(clap)*

Good morning! Good morning! *(wave hand
 energetically)*
Jump UP and start the day! *(jump)*
Good morning, good morning to you . . .
 (point to child)
And you . . . and you and you and you.
 (point to different children)
GOOD MORNING! *(call loudly, clapping hands)*

Today   (Clapping Rhyme)

Today is Monday,
 (insert current day of the week)
Today is Monday,
Today is Monday,
What'll we do today?
Wake up, sleepy head.
Wake up, sleepy head.
Wake up, sleepy head.
It's a brand new day!

Looking Out the Window   (tune: "Paw-Paw Patch")

In the morning looking out my window.
In the morning looking out my window.
In the morning looking out my window.
What do I see today?

[Additional verses]

 I see sunshine, looking out my window.
  (insert current weather)
 I see cats and dogs, looking out my window.
 I see people, looking out my window.

Parents' Follow-Up Ideas

A successful way to gently wake sleeping children is to tickle their
ears while softly calling their names. This technique is successfully
used by child care professionals.

For a child who wakes up early, bundle up and go outside (or to an
east-facing window) to watch the sun rise. Once it begins, a sunrise
happens quickly. Talk about the changes happening as the sky gets
lighter and objects go from being invisible to silhouettes to being rec-
ognizable. What other changes can you notice? If you live in the city,
street lights may turn off. Does the wind change? Are there new
sounds? New smells? When the sun is bright enough, dance with
your shadows.

Weather predicting is difficult (even for the experts), but weather
watching is easy. Pick a window through which your toddler can see

the outdoors, and help your child determine what kind of weather is occurring each morning. Talk about obvious signs, such as the sun shining, thunder, or snow on the ground. Also discuss other clues you see: people dressed warmly, flags blowing, or umbrellas. Use weather words and phrases to help your child learn. Keep a weather calendar or weather wheel nearby. Let your toddler mark the calendar with stickers or a simple drawing. When weather changes during the day, talk about how it changed and how you know it changed.

Craft

Weather Wheel

You will need: 2 paper plates

sharp pencil

brass fastener

scissors

washable markers or weather
pictures cut from magazines

Punch a hole in the center of both plates. Divide one plate into six or eight pie-shaped pieces. Draw (or glue) pictures in each section to represent normal weather conditions. Label each picture with descriptive words. Using the other paper plate, cut out a wedge the same size as one of the sections so that the pictures will show through the opening when the plates are placed together. With the cut plate on top, attach both plates together using the brass fastener. The bottom plate will rotate, displaying one weather picture at a time in the window. Let your child make a weather observation each morning and turn the bottom plate until the corresponding weather picture shows. When weather patterns change, encourage your child to change the picture again. To hang the weather wheel, glue or tape a string to the back of the upper plate. To change weather pictures, remove the brass fastener and make a new bottom plate.

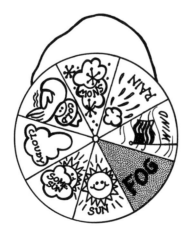

Program Notes

Sign Language

MORNING   With the fingers of the open left hand in the crook of the extended right arm, bring the right palm upward toward the face, like the rising of the sun.

The storytime puppet introduces the theme by arriving very sleepy with a blanket in tow and asking for help waking up. Children can call its name, tickle it under the chin, "ring" like an alarm clock, or come up with their own ideas of how to help the puppet wake. If there is a window nearby, encourage children to look outside to determine the weather so the puppet can get dressed.

Children enjoy making the morning noises of farms, starting with crowing roosters. Make one story a flannelboard farm morning and encourage children to contribute the sounds.

Giveaways are window stickers made by sandwiching a large sticker or magazine picture between two layers of plastic wrap. The wrap sticks to the window and can be easily removed.

Fingertaster "tastes" breakfast foods, such as cereal, toast, pancakes, orange juice, etc.

Children exit the story space singing the "Good Morning" song.

——————————— Notes ———————————

My Body

Books

A, B, C, D, Tummy, Toes,
Hands, Knees
B. G. HENNESSY

All about You
CATHERINE AND LAURENCE ANHOLT

Bright Eyes, Brown Skin
CHERYL WILLIS HUDSON

Faces
JAN PIENKOWSKI

Here Are My Hands
BILL MARTIN AND
JOHN ARCHAMBAULT

How Many Fingers?
A Pop-Up Book
CARLA DIJS

I Hear
HELEN OXENBURY

I Like Me
DEBORAH COKER

I See
RACHEL ISADORA

I Touch
HELEN OXENBURY

Legs
MIKE ARTELL

Like Me and You
RAFFI

My Hands Can
JEAN HOLTZENTHALER

Our Ollie
JAN ORMEROD

Rainbow Is Our Face
LAURA PEGRAM

Where's Your Nose?
DOROTHY ROSE

Rhythms, Rhymes, and Fingerplays

Head and Shoulders   (song)

Head and shoulders, knees and toes.
  (touch each)
Knees and toes, knees and toes.
Head and shoulders, knees and toes.
Eyes and ears and mouth and nose.

[Repeat, starting slowly and getting faster]

I Have a Nose

On my face I have a nose, *(point to nose)*
And way down here I have ten toes. *(point to toes)*
I have two eyes that I can blink. *(blink eyes)*
I have a head to help me think. *(hands on head)*
I have a chin and very near, *(point to chin)*
I have two ears to help me hear. *(hands on ears)*
I have a mouth with which to speak, *(point to mouth)*

And when I run I use my feet. *(tap feet on floor)*
Here are arms to hold up high, *(arms held high)*
And here's a hand to wave good-bye. *(wave)*

We Can Jump

We can jump, jump, jump.
   (follow the actions)
We can hop, hop, hop.
We can clap, clap, clap.
We can stop, stop, stop.
We can nod our heads for "yes,"
We can shake our heads for "no."
We can bend our knees a little bit
And sit . . . down . . . slow.

Parents' Follow-Up Ideas

Toddlers need lots of experience hearing words and language. The more you talk to them, the better their language skills will be. Talk through daily routines ("now we let the water go down the drain"), name *everything:* objects ("here's a hammer, a screwdriver, and pliers"), body parts ("your fingers, nails, knuckles, wrist"), animals ("I see a cricket, a robin, an earthworm"), and vehicles ("that truck is a front-loader, and there's a crane"). If you don't know what something is, say so . . . and go to the library together to find a book about it so you both can learn.

Touching different parts of their bodies with their eyes closed is a challenge for toddlers. This is a game that can be practiced anywhere, even in the car when your child is getting restless. "Close your eyes and touch your knee. Open your eyes to see if you found it."

Trace around your child's hands and feet on posterboard. Use these patterns to create a mobile out of a hanger or small branch, tying on each foot or hand shape with string. Cut another set out of different colors of paper and let your child match them. Trace hands and feet of family members and compare them with each other.

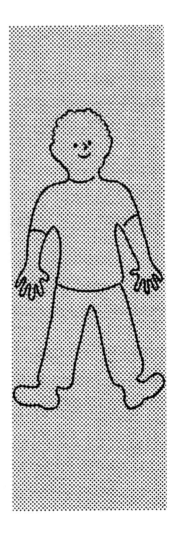

Craft

A Me Picture

You will need: a large grocery sack or wide shelf paper

a pencil

scissors

crayons or washable markers

Cut the bottom from the sack and cut up one side so it will lie flat. Have your child lie down on the sack and quickly trace around him or her. Draw on the features and talk about parts of the body and the clothes that cover them. Color the picture and hang it on a door or the refrigerator or send it as a special card to a grandparent or friend. When you make this activity part of a birthday celebration, you can compare it with last year's picture.

A change of clothes could be made from newspaper or another paper sack and paper-clipped or taped to the picture as situations or weather changes.

Program Notes

Sign Language

ME   Point to yourself with your index finger.

Note: Be sensitive to differences in children with disabilities, pointing out how they are the same as the others, not how they are different.

Introduce the theme by pointing out the facial features on the clown shape puzzle. Make note of the similarities in people's bodies: two hands, two feet, eyes, hair, noses, etc.

Explore the senses using different musical instruments (bells, drums, horn) for sounds, colors for sight, scents (cinnamon, chocolate, banana) for smell, and textures (sandpaper, fur, terry cloth) for touch, giving each child the opportunity to experience each. A flannelboard face with removable features is a good activity. Let children take turns placing eyes, nose, mouth, ears, hair, eyebrows, etc., on the face.

Giveaways are the traced hands. Provide each adult with paper and pencil to trace his or her hand and then their child's hand inside it.

Fingertaster "tastes" foods with strong smells, such as chocolate, banana, oranges, etc.

Children exit the story space clapping their hands.

———————————————— Notes ————————————————

Parades

Books

Animal Parade
JACKI WOOD

Cat Parade!
BETHANY ROBERTS

Crash! Bang! Boom!
PETER SPIER

The Dancing Dragon
MARCIA VAUGHAN

Follow Me
DOROTHY ROSE

Follow the Leader
MIELA FORD

Happy Hedgehog Band
MARTIN WADDELL

I Make Music
ELOISE GREENFIELD

Ocean Parade:
A Counting Book
PATRICIA MACCARTHY

Parade
DONALD CREWS

Parade
HARRIET ZIEFERT

Rat a Tat Tat
SIAN TUCKER

River Parade
ALEXANDRA DAY

Snow Parade
BARBARA BRENNER

Thump, Thump,
Rat-a-Tat-Tat
GENE BAER

Where Does It Go?
MARGARET MILLER

Rhythms, Rhymes, and Fingerplays

Old MacDonald Had a Band   (tune: "Old MacDonald")

Old MacDonald had a band, E-I-E-I-O.
And in that band he had some horns, E-I-E-I-O.
With a toot-toot here,
And a toot-toot there,
Here a toot, there a toot,
Everywhere a toot-toot!
Old MacDonald had a band, E-I-E-I-O.

[Repeat with]
    drums . . . bang, bang
    cymbals . . . crash, crash
    hands . . . clap, clap
    feet . . . stomp, stomp

The Finger Band   (tune: "Mulberry Bush")

The finger band is coming to town,
   *(wiggling fingers, move hands from
   behind back to front)*
Coming to town, coming to town.
The finger band is coming to town,
So early in the morning.

This is the way they wear their hats,
   (hands form pointed hats on heads)
Wear their hats, wear their hats.
This is the way they wear their hats,
So early in the morning.

[Repeat with]

   This is the way they wave their flags
      (hands above head, wave back and forth)
   This is the way they beat their drums
      (beating motion with hands)
   This is the way they blow their horns
      (hands cup mouth like horn)
   This is the way they clash their cymbals
      (clap hands together)
   This is the way they march along *(stand tall,
      march lifting feet high)*

The finger band is going away, *(wiggling fingers,
   move hands from front to behind back)*
Going away, going away.
The finger band is going away,
So early in the morning

Here Comes the Parade!

Clap your hands! *(clap hands)*
Stamp your feet! *(stamp feet)*
The parade is coming down the street.
   (march in place)
Bum, bum, bum, *(motion beating a drum)*
A great big drum.
Root-a-toot-toot, *(hands to mouth like
   blowing a horn)*
A horn and flute.
Bang! Bang! Bang! *(clap hands together)*
Cymbals clang.
Ding-ding-ding, *(small ringing motion)*
Triangles ring.
Clap your hands! *(clap hands)*
Stamp your feet! *(stamp feet)*
The parade is coming down the street.
   (march in place, swinging arms high)

Parents' Follow-Up Ideas

Playing "follow-the-leader" teaches your children to be observant, to copy another's movements, and to be a leader. Tie several pull toys together and let your toddlers lead a parade through the house or the yard. Take turns being the parade leader, starting out by having them simply follow where you go. As your children grasp this concept, add actions to be copied while following your lead . . . and vice versa.

Playing with objects (blocks, toys, or boxes) in a line is a lot of fun for toddlers, and it teaches them about sequencing, an important skill for learning to read. Encourage your children to put the objects in a line. Use phrases such as "first, middle, last, between, in front of, and at the end." Play with other space-related concepts, such as on top of, beside, under, and through, to help your children understand how objects relate to each other.

When you read stories to your children, talk about the sequencing: what has already happened, what is happening now, and "what do you think will happen next?" Putting children down for a nap or to bed at night is the perfect opportunity to "sequence" the events of the day. Remember what you've done together and plan something you will do when your children wake up. Reviewing the day helps children remember things that happened and reinforces new words they might have heard that day.

Craft

Homemade Musical Instruments

Homemade musical instruments are a lot of fun. Many things in the home can be turned into music makers. Use them to create a parade around the house, to accompany television programs, or while listening to the radio or a record.

Drums:	Use empty oatmeal boxes, metal pans, or wooden bowls. Beat them with hands or wooden spoons.
Horns:	Cardboard tubes with holes poked in the sides will produce different notes as children hum or sing through one end to create music.
Tambourine:	Use a ring of keys or metal measuring spoons. Shake them away from the body. Also, tie bells on a small aluminum pie tin for a good effect.
Cymbals:	Use two metal lids or aluminum pie pans. Bang them together.
Shaker:	Use a small container with a tightly fitting lid that is half-filled with beans or macaroni. Tape the lid securely in place to keep small items inside. Shake it fast or slow.
Rhythm sticks:	Use two wooden spoons. Bang them together.

Program Notes

Sign Language

DRUM   Make motions like playing a drum.

The storytime puppet introduces the theme with an oatmeal-container drum and lets children take turns beating it. Between stories children can march around the room acting out the "Finger Band" rhyme. The puppet distributes paper plates, which children put on the floor to use as drums. They follow the puppet's lead in beating their drums fast, slow, loud, and quiet. Between two stories, form children into a parade to march around the story space, waving to adults still seated. Marching slower and slower and more and more quietly will prepare them to sit down for the next story.

Put pictures of musical instruments on the flannelboard. Imitate the sound each instrument makes.

Invite children to make the sounds as you point to the instruments.

Giveaways are parade flags made from straws and paper triangles with children's names printed on them.

Fingertaster "tastes" festive foods, such as hot dogs, cotton candy, nachos, etc.

Children exit the story space marching in their own parade.

───────────────────── Notes ─────────────────────

——— Peek, Peek . . . Hide and Seek ———

Books

Box with Red Wheels
MAUD AND MISKA PETERSHAM

Find the Teddy
STEPHEN CARTWRIGHT
AND CLAUDIA ZEFF

"Fred? Is That You?"
MAVIS SMITH

Hide and Seek Word Bird
JANE BELK MONCURE

Holes and Peeks
ANN JONAS

Moongame
FRANK ASCH

Peekaboo
DOROTHY ROSE

Peekaboo Baby!
DENISE LEWIS PATRICK

The Surprise!
GEORGE SHANNON

We Hide, You Seek
JOSE ARUEGO AND
ARIANE DEWEY

Where Is Clifford?
A Lift-the-Flap Book
NORMAN BRIDWELL

Where Is It?
DEE LILLEGARD

Where, Oh, Where?
ANNA ROSS

Where's My Squishy Ball?
A Lift-and-Touch Book
NOELLE CARTER

Who's at the Door?
JONATHAN ALLEN

Who's There?
CHARLES REASONER

Rhythms, Rhymes, and Fingerplays

Where Are the Baby Mice?

Where are the baby mice? *(make a fist)*
"Squeak, squeak, squeak!"
I cannot see them *(peer into fist)*
Peek! Peek! Peek!
Here they come out from their hole in the wall
1, 2, 3, 4, 5 . . . *(extend fingers as counted)*
And, that's all! *(turn palm up, hand extended)*

Indians Are Creeping

The Indians are creeping *(two fingers*
    tiptoe up forearm)
Shhhhhhhhh! *(raise index finger to lips)*
The Indians are creeping *(repeat above)*
Shhhhhh!

They do not make a sound *(fingers
 tiptoe up arm)*
As their feet touch the ground.
The Indians are creeping *(repeat above)*
Shhhhhhhh!

Who's That Knocking?
(tune: "Who's That Knocking at My Door?")

Who's that knocking at my door?
 (make knocking motion)
Who's that knocking at my door?
Who's that knocking at my door?
Guess who is out there?

[chant] KNOCK, KNOCK! *(chant and clap in rhythm)*
 WHO'S THERE?
 MEOW!
 MEOW WHO?
 IT'S A CAT!

[Repeat with other animals, singing the song between
the chants and prompting children for the answer to
the riddle.]

Parents' Follow-Up Ideas

Look out a window with your children and ask, "What do you see?"
Help your children talk about the weather: sunny, snowy, raining.
Are there birds or animals or people? What are they doing? Are there
trucks, bicycles, cars, airplanes? Do the same thing at night, looking
for dark places, lights (stationary, moving, or blinking), the moon,
and the stars. Window watching helps your children become more
observant and increases vocabulary.

Play hide-and-seek using a stuffed animal or a toy. Hide the toy
(not too well) someplace in the house, keeping it within range of your
children's eyesight and reach. Give hints such as, "Look by the lamp
where Daddy likes to sit." Once the toy is found, have your children
hide it and you search. Ask for a hint, even though it may be in plain
sight. The important thing is to have fun and help your children learn
to follow (and give) directions.

Children like having a "hide out" as a pretending place or just to
get away from things once in a while. Inside the house, drape a blanket over a small table or over two chairs facing away from each other,
or screen a corner of a room with kitchen chairs and a sheet. Outside,
a blanket over a clothesline or a sturdy bush creates a tent. Appliance
boxes are usually large enough for a door to be cut in them.
Encourage children to make their hide outs large enough for a friend
(or you) to visit, and stay aware of what they're doing by peeking in
occasionally.

Craft

Touch Box

You will need: cardboard box with flaps or lid
that closes it completely

an old sock

glue

scissors or box cutter

straight pins

contact paper or paint

Cut a hole in one side of the box (not the side that opens). The hole must be large enough to insert your hand. Cover the box with contact paper or paint.

Cut the ribbed edge (top) off the sock and glue one end around the hole on the *inside* of the box. Pin with straight pins to hold the sock in place until the glue dries thoroughly, then remove the pins.

Put an object in the box and close the lid. As the children reach through the sock, they feel the object. Ask the children to name the object or describe what it feels like, rather than trying to pull it out of the hole. Ask questions: "Is it soft or hard? little or big? warm or cold?" and so on. This activity is good for language development.

Open the lid and take out the object, naming it and describing the way it looks or feels. Children learn to discriminate between objects by the way they feel and look based on descriptions learned from others. Put the same object back in the box or use a different object. Also let the children put something in the box for you to feel.

Program Notes

Sign Language

SURPRISE   Place your hands at the temples in loose fists, palms facing each other. Quickly flick index fingers and thumbs open as the hands are pulled away from the temples and the eyes open wide in surprise.

Introduce the theme by playing "peek-a-boo" while putting name tags on children. Bring a touch box to the program and put something familiar to the children inside. Show them how to reach inside to feel what is there, but remind them not to pull the object out. *Note:* Don't let children be pushed into putting their hands in the touch box. When everyone who wants to participate has had a turn, open the top of the box and let them peek inside to see what's there.

The book *The Surprise!* works well as a flannelboard story, and children enjoy the present-inside-present idea.

Giveaways are turn-around faces made of two plastic cups nested together. The outer cup has an opening cut in it, and the inner cup has faces on opposite sides that are visible through the outer opening when the inner cup is turned. Secure them together with a brass fastener through the cup bottoms.

Fingertaster "tastes" crunchy foods, such as carrots, celery, pretzels, etc.

Children exit the story space playing peek-a-boo.

——————————————————————— Notes ———————————

Picnics

Books

Annabell and the Big Slide
RITA POCOCK

Claude Has a Picnic
DICK GACKENBACH

Come Out, Little Mouse
BERNICE CHARDIET

Hugo at the Park
ANNE F. ROCKWELL

Maisy Goes to the Playground
LUCY COUSINS

Mr. Bear's Picnic
DEBI GLIORI

Nicky's Picnic
HARRIET ZIEFERT

Paddington Goes on a Picnic
MICHAEL BOND

The Picnic
RUTH BROWN

Spot Goes to the Park (Also in Spanish: *Spot Va al Parque*)
ERIC HILL

Spot's First Picnic
ERIC HILL

Teddy Bear's Picnic
JOHN W. BRATTON

Tom & Pippo and the Dog
HELEN OXENBURY

A Tree Is Nice
JANICE UDRY

Up the Steps, Down the Slide
JONATHAN ALLEN

Winter Picnic
ROBERT WELBER

Rhythms, Rhymes, and Fingerplays

On a Picnic   (tune: "London Bridge")

On a picnic, spread the blanket,
Spread the blanket, spread the blanket.
On a picnic, spread the blanket.
It's a picnic in the park.

[Repeat with]
    open the basket
    eat the sandwich
    drink the juice
    run and play
    pack it up
    walk on home

Picnic Baskets

Five picnic baskets,
Waiting by the door.
One went to the park,
And then there were four.

[Additional verses]

 Four . . . As full as they can be,
  One went to the lake . . . three.

 Three . . . Yellow, red and blue;
  One went to the backyard . . . two.

 Two . . . Sitting in the sun, One's for
  Bobby who's sick today . . . one.

One picnic basket.
I think it should be
Taken on a picnic,
By you and me!

Picnic Basket   (tune: "A Tisket, a Tasket")

A tisket, a tasket,
A green and yellow basket.
I packed a picnic for my friend,
And on the way I lost it . . .
I lost it, I lost it.
And on the way I lost it.
I packed a picnic for my friend,
And on the way I lost it.

Parents' Follow-Up Ideas

On a cold or rainy day, have a picnic inside the house with your children. Pack a picnic lunch of small sandwiches or finger foods (cheese cubes, crackers, grapes, carrot or celery sticks, apple slices, animal crackers, etc.) into a small basket or grocery bag. Add a wet washcloth in a plastic bag, napkins, a favorite book, and something to drink. Dress in special "picnic clothes": summer hats, sunglasses, and sandals. Carrying a blanket, search the house with your toddlers for a good "picnic spot." Spread the blanket on the floor, sit on it, and unpack the lunch together. Put sandwiches on napkins or paper plates or give your children a paper cup filled with finger foods. Eat your lunches on the blanket and talk about picnics you have taken together in the past or plan one for the future. Talk about some things you may see on your next outdoor picnic: other children, playground equipment, a lake, insects, or animals. After eating, clean up your lunch debris, returning it to the basket or sack. Wipe sticky fingers on the washcloth and curl up together to read a book. Then play some picnic games on the blanket or in the surrounding area. Practicing picnic activities will help your toddlers know what to expect before encountering the excitement of a real outdoor picnic in the park.

Look for interesting places for picnics around your community. If you live in the city, keep your eyes open for a park or a small plaza far enough from pedestrians where you can sit on the ground. Also consider picnicking on the steps of the library or a museum. Ask the managers inside if they have any objections. Other good picnic places are zoos, botanical gardens, school yards (when school is not in session), or in the backyard. While warm weather is preferred for picnics, pack a picnic and go for a rainy-day walk in the spring, finding a sheltered place, or have a quick snow picnic in the winter.

Craft

Mini Picnic Basket

You will need: plastic or wire berry basket (quart)

strips of fabric, ribbons, or yarn

masking tape

Wash and dry a berry basket. To make weaving easier, wrap one end of the fabric strip, ribbon, or yarn with masking tape. At one corner of the basket, tie one end of the fabric strip through the top square. At a neighboring corner, thread the fabric strip through the top square of the basket, leaving a loop large enough for a handle, and tie it off. Repeat with the remaining corners so that you make two handles on opposite sides of the basket.

Weave the sides of the basket by tying another strip to a bottom corner of the basket. Show your children how to weave the ribbon in, out, and around the sides of the basket. When your children reach the end of the strip, tie on another ribbon (with the knot on the inside) and let them continue. Your toddlers may need help weaving over the fabric ends where handles attach to the top row. When complete, tie the end securely to the basket and weave the fabric tail into the basket on the inside. To make the basket more sturdy, weave across the bottom.

Line the basket with a washcloth or paper towel, and let your children pack it with a juice box, plastic spoon or fork wrapped in a napkin, yogurt, fruit, and a sandwich or finger foods in zipping plastic bags or a paper cup. Help them balance the load so it doesn't spill when they pick up the basket.

Program Notes

Sign Language

PICNIC   Use both hands, left hand behind right, with all fingers pointing at the mouth. Move your hands toward the mouth twice, as though pushing a lot of food in your mouth.

If possible bring a picnic basket or a basket with a napkin cover to the program. Inside have a paper plate for each child with food pictures glued to it or let them pretend the food is there. The storytime puppet invites children to have a picnic with it, and children help spread out a blanket (pretend or not) so they can all sit together to listen to stories and have their picnic. After eating, pass a paper plate with animal stickers on it and invite each child to take a pretend "animal cracker" for dessert.

The flannelboard rectangle becomes the inside of a picnic basket. Let children help "pack" the basket with flannelboard picnic item figures. The rhyme "Picnic Basket" makes a good flannelboard activity too.

Between-story activities can include pretending to play on playground equipment found in parks.

Giveaways are a plastic spoon and fork wrapped in a napkin and sealed with a colorful sticker.

Fingertaster "tastes" picnic foods, such as peanut butter sandwiches, apples, raisins, cookies, etc.

Children exit the story space pretending to swing a picnic basket.

—————————————— Notes ——————————————

Playing

Books

All Fall Down!
HELEN OXENBURY

Corduroy's Toys
LYDIA FREEMAN

*Five Little Monkeys
Jumping on the Bed*
EILEEN CHRISTELOW

I Am an Explorer
AMY MOSES

I Play in My Room
ANNE F. AND HARLOW ROCKWELL

Let's Play: Vamos a Jugar
ALAN BENJAMIN

My Doll Keshia
ELOISE GREENFIELD

My New Sandbox
DONNA JAKOB

Pig, Pig Rides
DAVID MCPHAIL

Play with Me
MARIE HALL ETS

Playing
HELEN OXENBURY

Playtime
CLAIRE HENLEY

Sam's Ball
BARBRO LINDGREN

Spot at Play
ERIC HILL

When We Play Together
NICK BUTTERWORTH

You Push, I Ride
ABBY LEVINE

Rhythms, Rhymes, and Fingerplays

Playing   (tune: "Mulberry Bush")

Let's throw a ball to play today,
Play today, play today.
Let's throw a ball to play today.
Inside and outside, we play.

[Repeat with]

> do a puzzle to play today
> ride a bike
> paint a picture
> build a castle
> play with puppets

Bounce the Ball

I bounce the ball to Billy.* *(make bouncing motion)*
He bounces it back to me. *(make catching motion)*
I bounce the ball to Tran. *(bouncing motion)*
She bounces it back to me. *(catching motion)*
Bounce the ball, bounce the ball, *(bouncing motions)*
We are bouncing the ball.

[*insert children's names]

Five Little Monkeys

Five little monkeys *(hold up five fingers)*
Jumping on the bed. *(jump in place)*
One fell off and bumped his head. *(pat head)*
Mama called the doctor *(motion talking
    into a phone)*
And the doctor said, *(nod head)*
"No more monkeys jumping on the bed!"
    (shake finger as though scolding)

[Repeat with four, three, two, one]

Parents' Follow-Up Ideas

Storing toys in a jumbled toy box is a mess, and things are always getting broken. Keep similar toys together in smaller, more manageable containers, and your children can use their sorting skills while keeping their toys neat. Put little cars in a shoe box, snap beads in a tin can with taped edges, etc. Store small containers of toys on a closet shelf (put seldom-used toys on top shelf), in a dresser drawer, or in a cardboard filing cabinet (light enough to take on a trip or to a friend's house).

Children often receive several toys on birthdays or holidays. They may play with them briefly, then set them aside. Put away some of the ignored toys, and bring one out again in a few weeks. It will appear new to your child, who can better enjoy the toy when it is not lost amid many others. "New-again" toys can be brought out as a special treat when children are left with a babysitter or when they go to visit relatives.

Small toys, like little cars or blocks, seem to multiply as you pick them up to put away. Buy a plastic dust pan and your children can scoop those little toys into a storage container. You can make a scoop by cutting the top off a milk or fabric softener bottle. Cut it at an angle, with the handle on top. Scooping up toys is fast and easy. Best of all, your toddler will enjoy doing this activity alone.

Craft

Clothespin Bird Toss: A game played by Eskimo children.

You will need: wooden clothespins (not the clip kind)

lightweight cardboard, cut into wing shapes

washable marking pen

2 colors of poster paint

Paint one side of the wings one color and the other side a different color. Let the paint dry, then slightly bend the wings in the middle so they form a wide *V* shape. Bend them so that the same color is on the inside of them all. Slide the cardboard wings into the slot of the

clothespin as shown. If the wings are loose and slide too easily, glue another strip of cardboard to the center of the wings. With a marking pen, draw a beak and eyes on the head of the clothespin. Toss the bird into the air to see it fly.

Toddlers will enjoy making the birds fly. They can toss them at a laundry basket or empty wading pool trying to make them land inside. The game played by Eskimo children counts the number of times the bird lands up (wings angled toward ground) and down (wings angled toward sky). When some of the novelty of making the bird fly wears off, encourage your child to keep track of what color is facing upward when the bird lands. If the birds are painted red and yellow, get one red cup and one yellow cup. Each time the bird lands, the child drops a pebble or bean into the appropriate cup. When the game is finished, count the pebbles to see which color appeared most often.

Program Notes

Sign Language

PLAY   Use both hands and have palms facing up. Fold the middle fingers into the palms, leaving the thumbs and little fingers extended. Rotate the hands so the palms face downward, a couple of times.

The storytime puppet introduces the theme by inviting everyone to play.

Between stories, say "Let's play!" introducing the action rhymes. Use a pretend ball for the rhyme "Bounce the Ball."

"Five Little Monkeys" works well on a flannelboard, and it can be used as an action rhyme too.

Giveaways are paper airplanes folded from typing paper.

Fingertaster "tastes" fun foods, such as pudding, popcorn, cookies, raisins, etc.

As children are getting ready to leave, the storytime puppet can ask them how they are going to play the rest of the day.

Children exit the story space jumping.

─────────────── Notes ───────────────

Rabbits

Books

Bunnies Love
LISA MCCUE

Bunny Fun
LENA ANDERSON

The Bunny Hop
TEDDY SLATER

Busy Bunnies
ALAN BENJAMIN

Good Night, Little Rabbit
J. P. MILLER

Little Rabbits
PETER SPIER

Little Rabbit's First Word Book
ALAN BAKER

Mr. Rabbit and the Lovely Present
CHARLOTTE ZOLOTOW

Playtime with Rosie Rabbit
PATRICK YEE

Pop-Up Baby Bunny
PEGGY TAGEL

Rabbits and Raindrops
JIM ARNOSKY

Runaway Bunny (Also in Spanish: *El Conejito Andarín*)
MARGARET WISE BROWN

Stop That Rabbit
SHARON PETERS

Walk Rabbit Walk
COLIN MCNAUGHTON AND ELIZABETH ATTENBOROUGH

What Can Rabbit See?
LUCY COUSINS

Where Is It?
TANA HOBAN

Rhythms, Rhymes, and Fingerplays

Little Rabbit

I saw a little rabbit go hop, hop, hop.
  (hop in place)
I saw his long ears go flop, flop, flop.
  (hands above head, "flop" wrists over and back)
I saw his little eyes go wink, wink, wink.
  (blink eyes)
I saw his little nose go twink, twink, twink.
  (wiggle nose)
I said, "Little Rabbit, won't you stay?"
  (make beckoning motion)
He looked at me and . . . hopped away!
  (hop quickly)

Hop, Hop, Hoppy   (tune: "Peter Cottontail")

Hop, Hop, Hoppy cannot wait, *(bounce in place)*
Jumping near my garden gate.
Hippity, hoppity,
Carrots on his mind. *(pretend to eat carrot
   with little noises)*
Floppy ears are flipping high, *(hands alternately
   flip-flop on top of head)*
Big feet jumping. My, oh my! *(lift one foot and
   then the other)*
Hippity, hoppity, *(bounce in place)*
No carrots left behind. *(shake head sadly)*

Here Is a Bunny

Here is a bunny with ears so funny. *(hands
   above head to make ears, flop wrists)*
Here is his hole in the ground. *(arms create
   circle in front of body)*
When a noise he hears, *(clap hands sharply)*
He pricks up his ears *(hands above head,
   held straight up)*
And jumps in his hole in the ground. *(jump
   into a crouching position)*

Parents' Follow-Up Ideas

Animal riddles are good for times when you are waiting for things to happen (such as being called into the doctor's office). Try these:

I eat grass.	I gallop.	I have feathers.
I say moo.	I trot.	I peck and peck.
What am I?	My hooves go	I say cluck, cluck.
	clip, clop.	What am I?
	What am I?	

Plant a "rabbit garden," even in the middle of winter, by cutting pictures from magazines, food labels, and advertising of garden vegetables: carrots, lettuce, beans, corn, etc. Tape each picture to one end of a coffee stirring stick or paper straw. Insert the opposite end of the stick into a Styrofoam block or an empty box. Arrange them in a line, as though they were growing in the garden. You be the farmer, and let your child be a hungry bunny, sneaking into your garden to eat the goodies there. When the bunny gets caught (only occasionally), the farmer gets to tickle it and hug it, and together you "replant" the garden. Ask your "bunny" to help you choose which vegetables to serve for lunch or dinner.

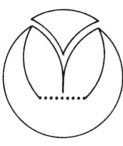

Craft

Rabbit Cup Puppet

You will need: a paper cup   a straw   tape

a picture of a rabbit small enough to fit inside the cup (draw one or cut from magazine or greeting card)

Poke a hole in the bottom of the cup large enough so that a straw can easily slide through. Tape the rabbit picture to one end of the straw and slide the other end of the straw down through the hole in the bottom of the cup. Operate the puppet by sliding the straw up and down. While reciting the rhyme "Here Is a Bunny" (above), let your child operate the rabbit puppet, making it appear and disappear at the proper times.

Program Notes

Sign Language

RABBIT   Cross your hands at the wrists, palms facing away from each other. Extend your index and middle fingers of each hand (fingers kept together) and quickly bend the fingers twice, like a rabbit's ears twitching.

Introduce the theme with a toy rabbit, rabbit puppet, or storytime puppet wearing rabbit ears. Invite children to hop around the story space before settling in their rabbit holes (rug spots).

Use a basket and artificial fruit for *Mr. Rabbit and the Lovely Present.* Give children the opportunity to touch the fruit when the story is finished, inviting them to "hop" up to the basket. Between other stories children can hop fast and slow, crouch down to hide, and hop quickly home (to their adults).

Giveaways are bunny ears made from a paper plate: cut, folded, and stapled and ready to be tied on children's heads.

Fingertaster "tastes" carrot flavors, such as carrot cake, carrot soup, carrot milkshakes, etc.

Children exit the story space hopping like bunnies.

—————————————————— Notes ——————————————————

Rain

Books

Amy Loves the Rain
JULIA HOBAN

Hi, Clouds
CAROL GREENE

In the Rain with Baby Duck
AMY HEST

It Looked Like Spilt Milk
CHARLES SHAW

It's Raining, It's Pouring
KIM EAGLE

James and the Rain
KARLA KUSKIN

Just a Rainy Day
MERCER MAYER

Listen to the Rain
BILL MARTIN AND
JOHN ARCHAMBAULT

Mushroom in the Rain
MIRRA GINSBURG

My Red Umbrella
ROBERT BRIGHT

Outside, Inside
CAROLINE CRIMI

Rain
ROBERT KALAN

Rain Feet
ANGELA JOHNSON

Rainbow of My Own
DON FREEMAN

Skyfire
FRANK ASCH

Umbrella
TARO YASHIMA

Rhythms, Rhymes, and Fingerplays

Walking in the Rain   (tune: "London Bridge")

Let's go walking in the rain,
In the rain, in the rain.
Let's go walking in the rain,
Early in the morning.

[Repeat with]
    jump puddles in our boots
    walk under my umbrella
    feel the raindrops, splash, splash, splash
    see the rainbow, shining bright

Eency Weency Spider   (traditional song)

Eency weency spider went up the water spout.
(wiggle fingers upward in front of body)
Down came the rain and washed the spider out.
(sweep arms down and to one side)
Out came the sun and dried up all the rain,
(arms form circle over head)
And the eency weency spider went up the spout again.
(wiggle fingers upward again)

Busy Windshield Wipers

*(hold arms up in front of body and
move them from side to side)*
Busy windshield wipers go
A-dash, a-dash, a-dash.
Wiping all the drops away
Splash, splash, splash.

Parents' Follow-Up Ideas

Playing in water is educational for toddlers. Stay close by and play with your children whenever they are near even a small amount of water. Help them learn safety rules (stay away from hot water; don't throw water; keep objects out of the mouth). The kitchen sink, a bathtub, or a wading pool are good places for water play. When clean-up time comes, toddlers can be good helpers.

Good water toys are sponges, plastic containers (some with holes), measuring cups, eye droppers, funnels, jar lids, or anything unbreakable. Add interest with a squirt of shaving cream or food coloring.

This is a great language-building time. "Pour, spill, sprinkle, splash, spurt, squirt, dribble, flow, flood, trickle, and spray" all describe different ways that water behaves. Each word sounds like what it describes. Use these words to increase your children's vocabulary and the way they think about water.

Pry the ball off an empty roll-on deodorant jar and wash the bottle out. Fill it with tempera paint and push the ball back on. Presto: you have a giant ball-point pen that paints. Cover a table with newspaper and let your children create pictures on shelf paper or paper sacks.

Craft

A Rainbow

You will need:

a paper plate	a craft stick
colored paper streamers	tape or a stapler
scissors	a marker

Cut a pie-shaped wedge from the paper plate and draw a face near the outer edge. Attach colored streamers along the outer edge, and staple the inner edge to the stick. When your child holds the stick, the rainbow colors will move over and around him or her like a flexible rainbow!

Program Notes

Sign Language

RAIN   Place your hands at the shoulders, palms facing outward and fingers curved slightly. Bend your wrists twice, like rain falling.

Introduce the theme with an umbrella (if you are not superstitious, an open one). Let each child come to sit or stand under the umbrella with you.

It Looked Like Spilt Milk is good for flannelboard sharing. Use "Eency Weency Spider" as an action rhyme, standing and stretching high as the spider climbs and sweeping hands to the floor when it rains. Repeat it more than once, saying it loudly with lots of action, and then again with smaller actions and quiet voices. The rhyme can also be used as a flannelboard presentation.

Giveaways are paper rain hats or fluttering rainbows (see craft).

Fingertaster "tastes" colorful foods, such as green peppers, red cherries, oranges, purple plums, etc.

Children exit the story space wearing their rain hats or waving their rainbows over their heads.

——————————— Notes ———————————

Read to Me!

Books

Baa, Baa, Black Sheep
MOIRA KEMP

Chinese Mother Goose Rhymes
ROBERT WYNDHAM

Country Mouse and City Mouse
PATRICIA AND FREDERICK MCKISSACK

Hey Diddle, Diddle and Other Mother Goose Rhymes
TOMIE DEPAOLA

Hickory, Dickory, Dock
MARILYN JANORITZ

Humpty Dumpty
TRACEY MORONEY

Jaha & Jamil Went Down the Hill: An African Mother Goose
VIRGINIA KROLL

Little Red Hen (Also in Spanish: *La Gallinita Roja*)
PATRICIA AND FREDERICK MCKISSACK

Mary Had a Little Lamb
SARA J. HALE

Meet Peter Rabbit
BEATRIX POTTER

Molly at the Library
RUTH RADLAUER

Mother Goose Rhymes: Print-Braille Edition

My Book
RON MARIS

Reading
JAN ORMEROD

Three Bears
BYRON BARTON

Tom & Pippo Read a Story
HELEN OXENBURY

Rhythms, Rhymes, and Fingerplays

Hickory Dickory Dock

Hickory, dickory, dock . . . tick, tock. *(swing arms in front of body like pendulum)*
The mouse ran up the clock. *(make climbing motion)*
The clock struck one, *(clap hands once)*
The mouse ran down. *(reverse climbing motion)*
Hickory, dickory, dock . . . tick, tock. *(repeat first motion)*
Hickory, dickory, dock.

Mary Had a Little Lamb   (song)

Mary had a little lamb,
Little lamb, little lamb.
Mary had a little lamb,
Its fleece was white as snow.

And everywhere that Mary went,
Mary went, Mary went.
Everywhere that Mary went,
That lamb was sure to go.

Jack and Jill   (chant)

Jack and Jill went up the hill *(clap in rhythm,
    four times each line)*
To fetch a pail of wa-ter.
Jack fell down and broke his crown,
And Jill came tumbling af-ter.

<u>Jack,</u> <u>Jack,</u> <u>Jack</u> and <u>Jill,</u> <u>Jill,</u> <u>Jill,</u> *(clap on
    underlined words)*
Went <u>up,</u> <u>up,</u> <u>up</u> the <u>hill,</u> <u>hill,</u> <u>hill.</u>
Up the hill, went Jack and Jill, *(clap in rhythm)*
To fetch a pail of water.
<u>Jack,</u> <u>Jack,</u> <u>Jack</u> fell <u>down,</u> <u>down,</u> <u>down,</u> *(clap on
    underlined words)*
And <u>broke,</u> <u>broke,</u> <u>broke</u> his <u>crown,</u> <u>crown,</u> <u>crown.</u>
Jack fell down and broke his crown *(clap in rhythm)*
And Jill came tumbling after.

[The strong rhythm in this rhyme makes it a fun one
to play with. Changing the cadence and repetitions
creates a new chant. Try it with: Jack, Jack (pause)
Jack-Jack.]

Parents' Follow-Up Ideas

Read to your children every day. Change your voice as you read, from
high to low, fast to slow, soft to loud. Keep the story interesting and
be prepared to read favorites over and over again. If your children will
not sit still for an entire book, the book may be too long or their listening skills are still too limited. Instead of reading the words in the
book, try "reading" a few pictures at a time. Here are some questions
you might ask about a picture to encourage discussion with your
child:

1. What do you see in the picture? (Children need to know
   the names of objects as well as people and animals.)
2. What is happening?
3. What are the people (animals) doing?
4. Do you see something funny (sad, silly, dangerous, and so
   on) in this picture? What do you think will happen next?

5. Do you see someone who is angry (happy, sad, frightened) in this picture? Why do you think he or she is feeling that way?
6. How many _____ do you see? (Children enjoy counting objects in pictures.)
7. What is over (under, beside, behind) the _____ in this picture?
8. I see something that is red (or any color). What do you see that is red in this picture? (or) What color is the boy's shirt?
9. What shapes can you find in this picture? (circles, squares, stars)
10. What do you see that is big? Little?
11. What do you think the girl is saying?
12. What sounds could you hear if you were in this picture? (or) What sound does this cat make?

Reading pictures acquaints children with books, demonstrating how the story progresses from beginning (front of the book) to end. They also learn that there is a pattern of reading left-to-right as they look at the pages of a book and you slide your finger under the words while reading.

Reading pictures allows greater flexibility for using books with children of all ages. The story can change with each encounter as new things are discovered in the illustrations. Children become an active part of the story by helping to create it.

Listening skills are learned, and it takes time. To help your toddlers lengthen their attention spans, start with short sessions and take your cues from your children. When they get restless, stop.

When you read a book or tell stories to your children, sit close enough so you are touching. Touching children as you read (an arm around the shoulders, sitting on your lap, and stroking or patting their arms) increases brain activity and helps the children learn more and remember better. Besides, it is another gesture of how much your toddlers mean to you. Remember, when you hear, "Read it again," your children are asking for more than hearing the words another time. Your time and attention are very valuable to them.

A good way to teach values is through stories, but they should not be heavy-handed with the ending "And the moral to that story is. . . ." Even young children can tell right from wrong when presented in a story form. When children are struggling with an issue (like jealousy, sharing, or biting), it helps enormously for them to listen to a story about characters with similar problems. Ask your librarian to help you find appropriate books, or simply start with "Once upon a time . . ." and create your own story using a favorite toy as the main character. Encourage your children to help you tell the story and to find solutions for the character's problem.

Craft

Zipping-Bag Books

You will need: reclosable plastic bags (sandwich size)

poster board pages, cut to fit easily inside
the bags; one page per bag

magazine pictures, photographs, or childrens'
artwork

permanent marker (optional)

hole punch

yarn

Decide what kind of book you will make. You can make theme
books (things with wheels, red things, favorite foods, animals), books
about family members, counting pages with stickers, or make up stories with randomly chosen pictures. Select enough pictures or photographs so there will be one picture on each side of the poster board
page. Glue pictures to both sides of the poster board and let them dry
thoroughly. If you wish, label under each picture with a permanent
marker.

Slide one page into each bag and close the zipping seal, getting the
extra air out of the bag. Stack the bags on top of each other with the
resealing edge at the top. Punch two holes in the left side of each bag
and tie them together with yarn. Encourage your child to "read" the
pictures. These books can be used over and over again. Wipe them off
with a damp cloth when they become sticky and change the pictures
inside when you are both ready for something new.

Program Notes

Sign Language

BOOK   Put your palms together with fingers pointing forward; open your hands, keeping the little fingers together, as though opening a book.

This is a great time to introduce children's classics and nursery rhymes to toddlers and their parents. If your library does not have an age requirement for library cards, encourage parents to get cards for their toddlers at this program. The storytime puppet can produce its own library card and bring favorite books to the storyteller to be shared with everyone. Share at least one story about the library to reinforce where you are. Nursery rhymes work well when they are introduced as flannelboard activities followed by chanting them as the group claps or marches in a circle.

Giveaways are book bags. If your library does not have access to "real" book bags, collect enough plastic grocery bags and tie colorful ribbons to the handles.

Fingertaster "tastes" dinnertime foods, such as meatloaf, green beans, catfish, etc.

Children exit the story space chanting "Jack and Jill."

―――――――――――――――― Notes ――――――――――――――――

————— Sizes and Shapes —————

Books

All Shapes and Sizes
SHIRLEY HUGHES

Big Dog, Little Dog (Also in
    Spanish: *Perro Grande,
    Perro Pequeño*)
P. D. EASTMAN

Big Long Animal Song (Also in
    Spanish: *Gran Canción de
    los Animales*)
MIKE ARTELL

Blue Sea
ROBERT KALAN

Brown Rabbit's Shape Book
ALAN BAKER

*Catching: A Book for Blind and
Sighted Children with Pictures
to Feel as Well as to See*
VIRGINIA JENSEN

*My First Book of
Shapes and Colors*
IAN WINTON

My First Look at Sizes

*Roly Goes Exploring: A Book
for Blind and Sighted Children*
PHILIP NEWTH

Shapes
JAN PIENKOWSKI

Shapes, Shapes, Shapes
TANA HOBAN

Sizes
JAN PIENKOWSKI

Spot Looks at Shapes
ERIC HILL

*The Tiny, Tiny Boy and
the Big, Big Cow*
NANCY VAN LAAN

Titch
PAT HUTCHINS

Word Bird's Shapes
JANE BELK MONCURE

Rhythms, Rhymes, and Fingerplays

Where Is Thumbkin?

Where is Thumbkin? *(hands behind back)*
Where is Thumbkin?
Here I am! *(right thumb extended in front)*
Here I am! *(left thumb extended)*
How are you this morning? *(wiggle right thumb)*
Very well, I thank you. *(wiggle left thumb)*
Run and play. *(right hand behind back)*
Run and play. *(left hand behind back)*

[Repeat with]

Pointer *(index finger)*
Tall-one *(middle finger)*
Ring-one *(ring finger)*
Baby *(little finger)*
Everyone *(all fingers)*

Do You Know Shapes?   (tune: "Muffin Man")

Do you know a circle shape? *(hands draw
    large circles in air)*
A circle shape? A circle shape?
Round and round and round it goes,
To make a circle shape.

Do you know a triangle shape? *(hands draw
    triangles in air)*
A triangle shape? A triangle shape?
Three pointy corners and three straight sides
Make a triangle shape.

Do you know a rectangle shape? *(hands draw
    rectangle in air)*
A rectangle shape? A rectangle shape?
Two long sides and two short sides,
Make a rectangle shape.

Sometimes I Am Tall

Sometimes I am tall. *(stretch up on toes)*
Sometimes I am small. *(crouch down low)*
Sometimes I am very, very tall. *(stretch
    and reach up hands)*
Sometimes I am very, very small.
    (crouch low to floor)
Sometimes tall . . . *(stretch up)*
Sometimes small . . . *(crouch low)*
See how I am now. *(stand normally)*

Parents' Follow-Up Ideas

On a trip to a department or grocery store, look for items that have different shapes. Some shapes (such as rectangles) are easier to find than others (triangles), but it can be done. Help your children look for shapes on product labels and see how they are arranged on the shelves.

Use size-related words often when reading to your children, looking at magazines, watching TV, or taking a walk. Reinforce common words such as tall, short, big, and small with less-common words that describe size: fat, skinny, huge, tiny, wide, narrow. Remember when comparing the sizes of two objects, look at them from your children's point of view. Objects look different when seen from a different perspective.

Go on a rock-collecting walk, taking along an empty milk bottle to help carry rocks back home. Encourage your children to look for rocks that are different sizes and shapes. Can they find rocks that are round or flat? When finding a new rock, compare it with others already gathered. Have your children arrange the rocks by size to see where the new rock will fit in line. Keep the rocks in an egg carton when you get home, and when the egg carton gets full, find a good place to create a rock garden outside or on a windowsill.

Craft

Flannelboard

You will need: a piece of flat, heavy cardboard

a piece of flannel or felt, 1″ larger than the dimensions of the cardboard piece

scrap pieces of materials with naps (felt, flannel, velvet, corduroy) or sandpaper

glue

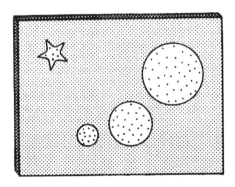
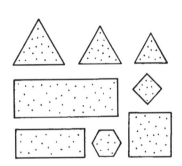

Wipe the cardboard with a clean cloth to remove dust. Spread glue over all the surface on one side of the cardboard. Put the flannel over the glue and smooth it flat. Let it dry thoroughly. Overlap the edges of the flannel over the cardboard and glue it to the other side. Weight or pin edges so they will dry flat. Let it dry thoroughly.

Cut out the shapes from the material scraps. Make basic shapes (circles, triangles, and so forth), animal shapes, people shapes, or crazy shapes. Use pictures from magazines or coloring books for patterns or glue these pictures to the material for ready-made flannel pieces. Vary the shapes in size: small, medium, and large. Pictures glued onto the smooth side of sandpaper will also stick to a flannelboard (and cutting sandpaper sharpens scissors!).

Show your child how the pieces will stick to the flannelboard; then let the child play with them alone or arrange the pieces together to tell a story, make a picture, or teach about sizes.

Program Notes

Sign Language

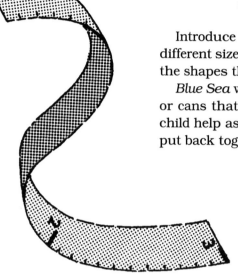

LITTLE With index fingers extended, move your hands toward each other.

BIG With hands open and palms facing, move your hands away from each other.

Introduce the theme with the clown shape puzzle emphasizing the different sizes (stars are smaller than the large circle or rectangle) and the shapes themselves.

Blue Sea works well on a flannelboard. Follow it with nesting dolls or cans that fit inside each other to further explore sizes. Let each child help as the dolls are taken apart, lined up to be compared, and put back together again.

Giveaways are measuring strips made from 36″ paper or fabric by marking inches and feet with a yard stick. The strip can be attached to a child's bedroom door to measure height.

Fingertaster "tastes" flat foods, such as bread, pancakes, toast, pita bread, etc.

Children exit the story space drawing circles in the air with their fingers.

——————————————— **Notes** ———————————————

Sounds

Books

Are You My Mommy?
CARLA DIJS

"Buzz" Said the Bee
WENDY CHEYETTE LEWISON

Clifford's Noisy Day
NORMAN BRIDWELL

Fiddle-I-Fee: A Noisy Nursery Rhyme
JACKI WOOD

"Hi, Pizza Man!"
VIRGINIA WALTER

Hoot, Howl, Hiss
MICHELLE KOCH

I Hear
RACHEL ISADORA

Listen to Me (Also in Spanish: *Escúchame*)
BARBARA J. NEASI

Listening Walk
PAUL SHOWERS

Moo, Baa, La-La-La!
SANDRA BOYNTON

Mr. Brown Can Moo! Can You? A Book of Wonderful Sounds
DR. SEUSS

Noisy Nora (Also in Spanish: *Julieta Está Quieta*)
ROSEMARY WELLS

Polar Bear, Polar Bear, What Do You Hear?
BILL MARTIN

Q Is for Duck
MARY ELTING AND MICHAEL FOLSOM

Shhh! A Lift-the-Flap Book
SALLY GRINDLEY

Splish Splash, Bang Crash!
KAREN GUNDERSHEIMER

Rhythms, Rhymes, and Fingerplays

Boom! Bang!

Boom, bang, boom, bang! *(beat one fist in other palm)*
Rumpety, lumpety, bump! *(slap hands on knees)*
Zoom, zam, zoom, zam! *(shoot hands across front of body)*
Clippety, clappety, clump! *(nod head from side to side)*
Rustles and bustles *(hug hands to shoulders)*
And swishes and zings, *(lean side to side)*
What wonderful noises *(throw hands over head)*
A thunderstorm brings!! *(clap hands together)*

Plink, Plank, Plunk   (tune: "Three Blind Mice")

Plink, plank, plunk. *(pretend to play banjo)*
Plink, plank, plunk.
Strum, tickle-tickle, strum.
Strum, tickle-tickle, strum.

I make music
On my banjo.
I play fast,
And I play slow.
Fingers running to and fro,
Plink, plank, plunk.

Pound Goes the Hammer

Pound, pound, pound-pound-pound
  (pound one fist into other palm)
Goes the hammer.
Pound-pound-pound.

Bzz, bzz, bzz-bzz-bzz, *(hand open,*
  thumb up, make sawing motion)
Goes the saw.
Bzz-bzz-bzz.

Chop, chop, chop-chop-chop, *(hand*
  open, chop into other palm)
Goes the axe.
Chop-chop-chop.

Parents' Follow-Up Ideas

Talk to your toddler about sounds you hear. Ask some of these questions:

1. Close your eyes and listen. What sounds do you hear? Cars? Horns? Running water? Radio or television? What else?
2. Lightly put your fingers on your throat when singing or talking. Do you feel your throat tingle?
3. While talking, gently pat your chest or your mouth to make the sound change. Can you do that while singing?
4. (Put different-sized items in small covered containers and shake.) Does macaroni sound different from raisins? cereal?
5. Practice talking in a loud voice . . . now a normal voice . . . now a whisper. Can you be perfectly still? Can you hear more sounds when you are still?

Craft

Paper Plate Banjo

You will need: 2 paper plates   glue

scissors   4 rubber bands

a paint stirrer

Cut a hole in the middle of one plate. Glue the rims of the plates together with the insides facing. Let dry. Glue the paint stirrer to the plate with the hole (but not covering the hole). After the glue dries, stretch the rubber bands, two on each side of the stirrer, over the hole in the plate. Tape the rubber bands to prevent their sliding off plate. Strum gently to make music!

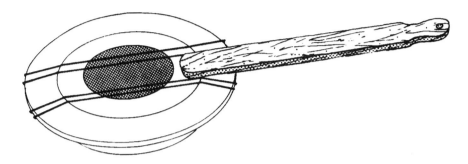

Program Notes

Sign Language

LISTEN   Cup your right hand to the ear, as if trying to hear.

Introduce the theme with different sound makers: whistle, toy piano, crumpling paper, clapping hands. Ask the children to close their eyes while you make the sound and see if they can guess the source. Always name the source of the sound and describe the sound itself (loud, soft, shrill). Encourage children to mimic the sounds in all the stories you share.

Use different noisemakers to make the sounds in the stories you share. *Polar Bear, Polar Bear, What Do You Hear?* makes a good flannelboard story.

Giveaways are pie-tin tambourines made by punching three evenly spaced holes in a small aluminum pie tin and tying a small bell into each one.

Fingertaster "tastes" foods that make noise, such as Rice Krispies, celery, potato chips, popcorn, etc.

Children exit the story space making quiet noises (humming, whispering, shhhh-ing).

—————— Notes ——————

Spring (Spring Holidays)

Books

Clifford's Springtime
NORMAN BRIDWELL

Danny and the Easter Egg
EDITH KUNHARDT

Did You Hear the Wind Sing Your Name? An Oneida Song of Spring
SANDRA DE COTEAU ORIE

Happy Easter, Grandma!
HARRIET ZIEFERT

Honey Rabbit
MARGO HOPKINS

Oh, Bother! It's the Easter Bunny
NANCY PARENT

Max's Chocolate Chicken
ROSEMARY WELLS

Mrs. Sato's Hens
LAURA MIN

My First Passover
TOMIE DEPAOLA

My Spring Robin
ANNE ROCKWELL

Sammy Spider's First Passover
SYLVIA A. ROUSS

Spot's First Easter
ERIC HILL

Spring Is Here
TARO GOMI

Wake Me in the Spring
JAMES PRELLER

Who's Hatching?
CHARLES REASONER

Word Bird's Spring Words
JANE BELK MONCURE

Rhythms, Rhymes, and Fingerplays

Eggs   (chant)

Eggs in the tree tops.
Eggs on the ground.
Eggs in the water.
Eggs all around!

[Chorus]

Eggs. Eggs. Lots of eggs.
"Who's inside?" the little one begs.

This one hatches, and
I see a smile.
It's a toothy crocodile.

Here's an egg
Way in back,
Out comes a baby duck,
Quack, quack, quack.

Inside this egg,
Who does dwell?
A tiny turtle in its shell.

Eggs in the water.
Make a wish.
When they pop open, there'll be fish.

Of all the eggs,
I like best
The robin's eggs in her nest.

Easter Bunnies

Five Easter bunnies *(five fingers)*
Sleeping on the floor.
One hopped away, *(hopping motion)*
And then there were four. *(four fingers)*

[Repeat with]

> Four . . . hiding near a tree . . . three.
> Three . . . sniffing at my shoe . . . two.
> Two . . . sitting in the sun . . . one.
> One . . . doesn't know what to do.
>   Back hops another . . . two.
> Two . . . what do you think they see?
>   . . . three.
> Three . . . by the garden door . . . four.
> Four . . . glad to be alive. Here comes the
>   last one . . . five.

Little Flower   (tune: "I'm a Little Teapot")

I'm a little flower, *(cupped hands held close
    to the body)*
In the ground.
When the sun shines warmly *(wiggle shoulders
    and body)*
I wiggle all around.
This way and that way *(hands move left and right,
    raising slowly)*
I push to the top. *(hands come to rest near chin)*
I reach out my green leaves, *(extend fingers)*
And then I POP! *(fingers spring outward like
    flower petals)*

Parents' Follow-Up Ideas

Gather plastic eggs of different sizes. Cut holes of varying sizes in the
lid of a box, making certain the eggs can pass through. Talk with your
children about the differences in sizes and have them drop the eggs

one at a time into the box. Can they anticipate which eggs will fit into which holes? Collect small objects and pieces of clothing (socks, handkerchiefs) to see which fit inside which eggs.

Other plastic-egg activities include: sorting the eggs by color or size, counting them, and filling them with small snacks (raisins, carrot rounds) and hiding them for an egg-hunting picnic. To store plastic eggs, nest them (open) inside an egg carton.

Spring is an excellent time to look and listen for birds because they are more visible then, gathering nesting materials on the ground and perching in trees with bare branches. Talk about how birds fly, eat, carry things, and move on the ground (walking or hopping). Discuss how baby birds hatch from eggs. Find pictures in magazines and advertising flyers of different sizes and colors of birds. Listen for bird sounds. Can your toddlers hear a difference? Borrow a bird book from the library and help your children learn the names of birds seen most often around your home.

Eat a "flower" for lunch. Make individual pizzas, using one half of a toasted English muffin. Evenly spread pizza sauce on top and sprinkle with mozzarella cheese. Arrange toppings into a flower shape with some ingredients becoming petals and some the center: pepperoni slices, chopped green pepper, olive slices, mushroom chunks. Bake at 425° for 10 minutes. For a no-cook flower, use a rice cake, peanut butter, raisins, banana slices, pineapple pieces, or coconut.

Craft

Chinese Lantern Tree

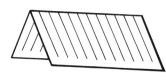

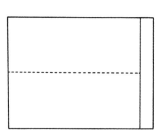

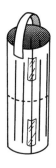

You will need: a coffee can filled with sand (or a tall flower vase with marbles in it)

a bare branch with several smaller twigs

rectangular pieces of construction paper

scissors

tape

colorful ribbons or yarn (optional)

Insert the base of the tree branch securely into the coffee can or vase so that the smaller twigs become the branches of a little tree. Start with a full-sized piece of construction paper to make a large lantern, since it is easier to follow directions on a larger project. For future lanterns, cut construction paper in half (or into smaller rectangles) making lanterns the appropriate size for your tree.

Cut a strip from the paper to make a handle for the lantern. Fold the remaining construction paper in half lengthwise. With the folded edge facing you, make several cuts in the paper, being careful not to cut completely across it. Unfold the paper and bring the short ends together, curling it into a cylinder and taping the edges. Gently push the ends of the cylinder together to cause the lantern cuts to open outward, and tape the handle strip to the top. The large lantern will probably be too big for your lantern tree, so hang it from a ceiling fixture. Fill the branches of your tree with colorful small lanterns, and add bows of ribbons or yarn. The lantern tree can be made in honor of Teng Chieh, the Chinese Lantern Festival, celebrated in the spring of each year.

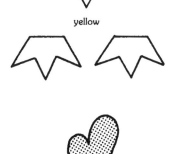

Program Notes

Sign Language

SPRING   Your left hand cups your right hand, which has the fingertips together and pointing upward. Slowly move the right hand upward, opening the fingers at the same time, like a flower emerging from the ground and blooming.

Introduce the theme with a pompom chick hidden in a plastic egg or the storytime puppet dressed as a bunny or a spring flower.

Use the "Easter Bunnies" rhyme as a flannelboard presentation or change it to "Little Bunnies." Use the "Eggs" rhyme with a flannelboard or with plastic eggs in a nest (basket) with the animals (pictures or toys) inside. Hide plastic eggs around the story space and encourage each child to find *one*, calling on each by name to search (adult can help) while the others watch.

Giveaways are pompom chicks made by gluing two small pompoms together and adding a felt beak, feet, and a comb and tiny wiggly eyes. Let children "find" them in the egg hunt.

Fingertaster "tastes" springtime foods, such as strawberries, lettuce, etc., or Easter treats (chocolate bunnies, jelly beans, etc.)

Children exit the story space "peeping" like baby chicks.

--- **Notes** ---

yellow

red

Summer

Books

Amy Loves the Sun
JULIA HOBAN

At the Beach
ANNE ROCKWELL

Beach Day
HELEN OXENBURY

In the Ocean
CLAIRE HENLEY

Joe's Pool
CLAIRE HENLEY

Joshua by the Sea
ANGELA JOHNSON

Maisy Goes Swimming
LUCY COUSINS

On Our Vacation
ANNE F. ROCKWELL

Our Puppy's Vacation
RUTH BROWN

Spot Goes to the Beach
ERIC HILL

Summer Day
DOUGLAS FLORIAN

Sun, Sand, Sea, Sail
NICKI WEISS

Sunshine
JAN ORMEROD

Swim
EVE RICE

Tom & Pippo on the Beach
HELEN OXENBURY

Word Bird's Summer Words
JANE BELK MONCURE

Rhythms, Rhymes, and Fingerplays

Digging in the Sand   (tune: "Farmer in the Dell")

We're digging in the sand,
   (follow the actions)
We're digging in the sand,
Hi-ho-the derrio.
We're digging in the sand.

[Repeat with]

   filling up the pail
   pouring out the sand
   making roads in sand

Inchy Pinchy Crab   (tune: "Eency Weency Spider")

Inchy pinchy crab *(wiggle fingers, moving
   hands sideways)*
Scurrying down the beach
Up comes a big wave *(sweep arms right to left)*
And carries him out to sea. *(sweep them
   back again)*

Swimming and swimming, *(swimming motion)*
He gets back to shore.
And inchy pinchy crab *(wiggle fingers, moving*
    hands sideways)
Goes up the beach once more.

By the Sea   (tune: "By the Beautiful Sea")

By the sea, by the sea, *(sway gently,*
    side to side)
By the beautiful sea.
You and me, you and me, *(point to*
    children and then to self)
Oh, how happy we'll be.

Splashing water and digging sand
    (mimic actions)
Watching seagulls, catching balls, and
Having fun, having fun, *(sway)*
By the beautiful sea.
You and me, you and me, *(point to*
    children and then to self)
By the sea!

Parents' Follow-Up Ideas

For ice cream cones with less mess, here are a couple of suggestions
to make them more sturdy and absorb some of the drips. For pointed
cones, tuck a wedge of marshmallow inside the cone before adding
the ice cream. For flat-bottom cones, put a small vanilla cookie in the
bottom of the cone. These tips make getting to the bottom of the treat
even more fun.

Outside summer fun can include art projects:

1. Sidewalk chalk can decorate walks, driveways, and fences and
   will wash away with rain or a garden hose.
2. Let your child "paint" with water on fences, sidewalks, or drives.
   A bucket of water and a small paintbrush or roller can create
   wet pictures (the water darkens the surface) that then evapo-
   rate completely.
3. Put children in old bathing suits and let them paint each other
   with body paints made from no-tears shampoo and a little food
   coloring. When the works of art are finished, simply rinse them
   off with a hose or a bucket of warm water. (Food coloring may
   stain some fabrics, so you will want to test the "paint" on an inside seam first.)

Traveling with small children on vacation can be a challenge. Pack
a busy bag with several favorite tapes, books, nesting containers, and

a coffee can filled with toy animals and magnets. Sing favorite songs together and play with nursery rhyme chants. Look out the windows for different kinds of vehicles, colors, shapes, or unusual objects. Point out familiar signs: traffic signs; billboards; hospital or library signs; gas stations; and restaurant, discount, and grocery store chains. Even the youngest toddlers can recognize symbols and understand that they have meaning. This is the first step of reading preparation. Plan to stop often so all can stretch their legs and enjoy the scenery.

Craft

Water Lens

You will need: a clear, plastic, two-liter soda bottle

craft knife or scissors

cloth or duct tape (water-resistant)

A water lens will allow your child to look at objects underwater in a wading pool, bath tub, or at the beach. Cut the top from a plastic soda bottle. Carefully remove the black bottom, leaving a clear, curved container. (One-piece, clear soda bottles have molded bottoms that can distort the view of objects.) Cover the rim with tape and cut two small slits, opposite each other, near the top, making handles. Tape the edges of hand slits.

Show your child how to put the curved end of the lens into the water (not so deep that water spills inside), and how to look inside to see objects, fish, plants, and toys beneath the waves or below bath bubbles.

Safety tip: Never leave your child unattended near water, no matter how shallow. Also, do not allow your child to put his or her face completely inside the water lens.

The container can also be used to carry small loads of beach toys to and from the pool or shore.

Program Notes

Sign Language

SUMMER   Drag the side of the right index finger across the forehead, curling the finger into your fist at the other side as though you were wiping sweat from your brow.

The storytime puppet introduces the theme wearing sunglasses and a summer hat.

"Joe's Pool" is a good flannelboard story. Between stories encourage children to mimic summer activities, like swimming, sandbox play, or playing with a beach ball.

Giveaways are visors made with poster board and yarn, letting the children decorate them at home.

Fingertaster "tastes" summer treats, such as watermelon, ice cream cones, frozen juice, etc.

Children exit the story space pretending to walk barefooted in tickly grass (tiptoeing).

— Notes —

Trains and Planes

Books

The Airplane Book
EDITH KUNHARDT

Airport
BYRON BARTON

Don't Spill It Again, James
ROSEMARY WELLS

Flying
DONALD CREWS

Freight Train
DONALD CREWS

Happy Birthday, Thomas
W. AWDRY

I Want to Be an Astronaut
BYRON BARTON

*Little Choo-Choo: Sounds,
Sights, and Opposites*
SUZANNE GREEN

The Little Engine That Could
WATTY PIPER

Locomotive
JOANNE BARKAN

1, 2, 3 to the Zoo
ERIC CARLE

Planes
ANNE F. ROCKWELL

Short Train, Long Train
FRANK ASCH

Train
CHRIS L. DEMAREST

Trains
ANNE ROCKWELL

Up, Up in a Plane
DOROTHY STOTT

Rhythms, Rhymes, and Fingerplays

Flying, Flying   (tune: "Sailing, Sailing")

Flying, flying, *(soaring with arms outstretched,
    lean side-to-side)*
Up in the sky so high.
In my plane I zip and zoom *(duck head on
    "zip" and "zoom")*
As I go flying by.

Fly high, fly low, *(arms up, then down)*
And loop-di-loop the sky. *(arms create circles)*
In my plane I'm like a bird *(return to soaring)*
As I go flying by.

Here Comes the Choo-Choo Train

Here comes the choo-choo train *(elbows slide along
    sides, arms make forward circles)*
Puffing down the track.
Now it's going forward . . .
Now it's going back. *(reverse circles)*

Hear the bell a-ringing. *(one hand above head, make bell-ringing motion)*
Ding . . . Ding . . . Ding . . . Ding
Hear the whistle blow. *(cup hands around mouth)*
Whooooo-Whoooooo!
Chug, chug, chug, chug *(make side circles slowly, then pick up speed)*
ch . . . ch . . . ch . . . ch . . . ch . . . ch . . . ch . . .
Shhhhhh . . . *(fold hands in lap)*
Everywhere it goes.

Parents' Follow-Up Ideas

Sounds of all kinds fascinate small children, and they love to imitate them. Make up a guessing game involving sounds of living things (cats, dogs, cows) and familiar nonliving things (cars, trains, clocks, sirens). You make the sound and let your children guess. Then let your children try to stump you.

Make a pull-toy train for your children by tying several small boxes together with shoestrings or twine. Shoeboxes without the lids are perfect for small toys or stuffed animals to ride inside. Talk about the different cars on a train and where they are in the line: first, middle, last. When stopped at a train crossing, sing a train song ("Down by the Station" or "I've Been Working on the Railroad") and try to guess what the cargo might be in different cars (people, food stuffs, and animals—real and make believe).

Visit an airport so your children can watch the activity as airplanes land and take off. Go inside the airport to watch as planes taxi to the gate, unload and load passengers and luggage, and taxi away again. Let your toddlers imitate the actions of the workers on the ground. Watch luggage on a carousel and try to guess what's inside the bags.

Safety tip: Be very careful around the luggage carousel. Children view it as a flat merry-go-round and want to climb on it or put their hands on the moving belt, both of which are dangerous. Also, large crowds of people sweep through airports in waves. Keep an eye on your children so you do not become separated.

Craft

Train Stick Puppets

You will need: construction paper, cut in 3″×5″ rectangles

black construction paper (for engine and wheels)

scissors

crayons or washable markers

glue and tape

craft sticks

Make various train cars in the following manner:

Engine: 3″×5″ black construction paper

1″ square black paper (smoke stack)

2″ square black paper, with window (cab)

triangle of black paper (scoop)

2 wheels

1 craft stick

Train cars: 3″×5″ construction paper (various colors for each car)

2 wheels for each car

1 craft stick

(Decorate the train cars with doors, slats, and windows.)

Attach pieces of each train car together with glue, and tape the car to a craft stick. Stand the train up along the back of a sofa with the sticks between the cushions or have a train parade when friends visit. This is also a good opportunity to talk about colors, shapes, first-middle-last, and other kinds of vehicles with your child.

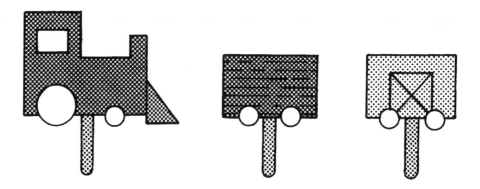

Program Notes

Sign Language

TRAIN   Extend your index and middle fingers of both hands, palms down. The fingers of the right hand lay across the fingers of the left hand and move back and forth over the backs of the left fingers, showing the cross-ties on a railroad track.

Introduce the theme as you enter the story space by making "chugging" noises like a train.

Freight Train works well both on the flannelboard and as an activity using stick puppets. Give each child a train stick puppet (keeping the engine for yourself), and ask them to follow you around the story space: chug-chugging, ringing bells, blowing whistles, and waving at still-seated adults. Vary the "speed" at which the train moves: fast, slow, stop, etc. Move in straight and winding lines. Have them "park" their train cars at the station to get the stick puppets back from them, and put the puppets out of sight.

Giveaways are train bookmarks made by photocopying this page for the pattern.

Fingertaster "tastes" foods that go together, peanut butter and jelly, ham and eggs, etc.

Children exit the story space chugging like a train.

———————— Notes ————————

Trucks, Cars, and Buses

Books

An Auto Mechanic
DOUGLAS FLORIAN

Bumper to Bumper
JACKI WOOD

The Car Trip
HELEN OXENBURY

Cars
ANNE ROCKWELL

Corduroy on the Go
LISA MCCUE

Dig, Drill, Dump, Fill
TANA HOBAN

*How Many Trucks Can
a Tow Truck Tow?*
CHARLOTTE POMERANTZ

Joshua James Likes Trucks
   (Also in Spanish: *A Pedro
   Perez le Gustan los
   Camiones*)
CATHERINE PETRIE

Just Us Women
JEANNETTE CAINES

Machines at Work
BYRON BARTON

My Little Red Car
CHRIS L. DEMAREST

Stop! Go! Word Bird
JANE BELK MONCURE

Truck
DONALD CREWS

*Wheels of the Bus, with
Pictures That Move*
PAUL ZELINSKY

Who Drives This?
CHARLES REASONER

Zoom, Car, Zoom
SUZY MCPARTLAND

Rhythms, Rhymes, and Fingerplays

Wheels on the Bus   (song)

The wheels on the bus go round and round,
   (roll hands over each other)
Round and round, round and round.
The wheels on the bus go round and round,
As it goes down the street.

[Additional verses]

The people on the bus bounce up
   and down *(bounce in place)*

The doors on the bus go open/shut *(move
   hands away from each other and back)*

The babies on the bus go "Wah! Wah!
   Wah!" *(make crying motions)*

The mommies on the bus go "Shhh!
Shhh! Shhh!" *(make shhhh-ing motion)*
The driver on the bus says "Move on
back!" *(motion behind over the shoulder)*

Auto, Auto

Auto, auto, may I have a ride? *(point to self)*
Yes, yes, yes, yes. Step inside. *(nod head,
motion toward you)*
Pour in the water, *(pouring motion with right hand)*
Pump in the gas. *(pouring motion with left hand)*
Chug-away, chug-away, but not too fast!
(steering motion)

If I Were . . .

If I were an airplane *(spread arms wide like wings)*
I would fly up in the sky. *(arms still out, lean left and right)*
If I were a tricycle *(pump legs as if peddling)*
I would wave as I went by. *(wave)*
If I were a dump truck *(elbow bent, hand on shoulder)*
I would dump my heavy load. *(let hand fall)*
But if I were a car or bus
I'd roll on down the road. *(roll hands over each other)*
If I were a choo-choo train *(hands close to sides)*
Along the tracks I'd chug. *(push-pull alternately with arms)*
And if I were a steam shovel *(hands near knees, palms up)*
I would have a big hole dug. *(scooping motion with hands)*
If I were a whirlybird *(whirl hands over head)*
I'd sing a whirly tune. *(make whirrrring noise)*
But if I were a rocket ship *(palms together close to chest)*
I'd blast off to the moon! *(shoot hands upward)*

Parents' Follow-Up Ideas

Toddlers enjoy learning the names of different kinds of vehicles.
Name them for your children.

trucks: semitrailer, tow, dump, and pickups

cars: station wagons, vans, convertibles, limousines

tractors

buses

trains

trolleys

airplanes

boats

Get a book from the library and see how many types of vehicles there are. Play matching or counting games, saying "I see a pickup truck. Can you see one, too?" Do the same with colors.

When traveling with small children, take along a busy box. Fill a small box with objects that your children can play with alone: blocks and foam balls, covered containers with snap-off lids, magnets and a small cookie sheet, a piece of cardboard covered with aluminum foil (a mirror), and a mesh bag from the produce department and yarn with tape around one end for weaving. Include a tape player and tapes of stories and music. Keep the busy box just for trips, to make sure it remains a special treat. Let your children add one or two favorite toys to take along each time.

Create an easy car-bingo game for your children by drawing nine squares on a piece of cardboard. Put one picture in each square, using things that are plentiful on your journey so your toddlers will have several opportunities to see them. Draw simple pictures or cut them from magazines and glue them in the squares. Make bingo games with colors (red things), shapes (circles, triangles), familiar places (McDonalds, playgrounds, gas stations), vehicles (big trucks, school bus, trains), nature (clouds, trees, animals), etc. Each time your children find something on the bingo cards, give them a sticker to put on those squares. Make several different cards for long trips and cover them with clear contact paper to make them reusable.

Safety tip: Never leave children alone in a car. Toddlers are very observant, and even when strapped in a car seat, they can get into trouble "driving like Mom!"

Craft

Pretend Steering Wheel

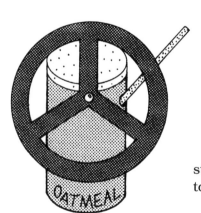

You will need: cardboard

an oatmeal box

a brass fastener

a narrow cardboard tube
    (from pants hanger)

scissors

hole punch

Cut out a 9″ circle from cardboard and cut spaces in it to create a steering wheel. Punch a hole in the side of the oatmeal box near the top, and attach the steering wheel with the brass fastener.

Poke a hole to the right of the steering wheel and push the cardboard tube into it creating a gear shift lever. The tube should fit loosely enough to be moved up and down. Place the cereal box between your child's knees, leaving hands free to "steer and change gears."

Program Notes

Sign Language

CAR   Make the motion of holding a steering wheel, moving hands slightly (in opposition to each other), as if driving a car.

Introduce the theme by "driving" into the story space, inviting children to "park" themselves on a rug spot. Use the traffic light from the colors theme. Invite the children to drive with you: go fast, go slow, stop, turning this way and that, waving at the seated adults, and finally parking their cars back in their rug-spot "garages" and putting the keys in their pockets.

Giveaways are paper-plate steering wheels made by folding the plate into quarters and cutting four wedges from it.

Fingertaster "tastes" foods from drive-in restaurants, such as hamburgers, French fries, Tater Tots, etc.

Children exit the story space "driving" their cars.

—————————————— Notes ——————————————

Walking

Books

Going on a Lion Hunt
HARRIET ZIEFERT

Gramma's Walk
ANNA GROSSNICKLE HINES

I Can Take a Walk!
SHIGEO WATANABE

I Walk and Read
TANA HOBAN

I Went Walking (Also in
   Spanish: *Sali de Paseo*)
SUE WILLIAMS

*Let's Go Home,
Little Bear*
MARTIN WADDELL

*Let's Take a Walk:
Vamos a Caminar*
ALAN BENJAMIN

Lily Takes a Walk
SATOSHI KITAMURA

Molly Goes Hiking
RUTH RADLAUER

Mooses Come Walking
ARLO GUTHRIE

Nicky's Walk
CATHRYN FALWELL

Sheep Take a Hike
NANCY SHAW

Spot's Walk in the Woods
   (Also in Spanish: *Spot
   Pasease por el Bosque*)
ERIC HILL

Tom & Pippo Go for a Walk
HELEN OXENBURY

Trek (Also in Spanish:
   El Trayecto)
ANN JONAS

Walking through the Jungle
JULIE LANCOME

Rhythms, Rhymes, and Fingerplays

As I Was Walking   (tune: "Rig-a-Jig-Jig")

As I was walking down the street, *(march in place)*
Down the street, down the street,
As I was walking down the street,
Hi, ho! Hi, ho! Hi, ho! *(clap hands and march)*

Max and his mom I chanced to meet.
   (wave at child and adult)
Chanced to meet, chanced to meet.
Max and his mom I chanced to meet.
Hi, ho! Hi, ho! Hi, ho! *(clap hands)*

A rig-a-jig-jig and away we go, *(clapping
   hands, walk in a small circle)*
Away we go, away we go.
A rig-a-jig-jig and away we go. *(return
   back to your starting place)*
Hi, ho! Hi, ho! Hi, ho!

[Repeat, greeting other children and adults]

Walking

One foot, *(raise one leg)*
Now the other, *(raise other leg)*
We walk down the street. *(march in place)*
Walking fast . . . *(march fast)*
Walking slow . . . *(march slow)*
We walk on two feet. *(march in place)*

[Continue with]

> Dogs walk down the street. *(add arms
>   to marching motion)* . . . four feet
> Spiders . . . *(add wiggling fingers)* . . .
>   eight feet

Here We Go   (tune: "Looby Loo")

Here we go walking slow, *(march in place, slowly)*
Here we go walking fast, *(march quickly)*
Here we go walking round and round, *(march in circle)*
Round the block and back. *(back to original position)*

[Additional verses]

> We hold hands walking slow . . . *(swing hands)*
> We climb steps so slow . . . *(climbing stairs motion)*
> We watch for cars going slow . . . *(look left and right)*

[Repeat first verse]

Parents' Follow-Up Ideas

Take a discovery walk of your neighborhood or a favorite park. Children love to bring home souvenirs to remind them of the things they've seen, but be selective about the types of remembrances you choose. Remind children not to pick living plants without permission; it's better to look and smell but leave plants intact. Explain that bird feathers can have small insects living in them. *Safety tip:* Watch that your children do not put their hands in their mouths after handling "found" objects.

To bring souvenirs home, put a loop of masking tape around the child's wrist, sticky side out. Small treasures can be safely attached for the return walk. Once home, examine the treasures and recall where or how they were found. Put a sticker on your walk map (see the "Craft" section) to mark the treasure, and then keep the souvenir in a "discovery" box . . . use it to make a mobile or art collage or return it to the outdoors.

Keep walks with your children short so they do not get overly tired. Taking walks together is good exercise, but wearing your children out leaves a cranky, unhappy memory of the activity. Introduce them to new or potentially frightening experiences gently. Young children can become overwhelmed by the presence of many people or by excited pets. Be a buffer when your children need it, but let them explore with you close by when they want.

Be sensitive to the world from your children's point of view. Many things adults find interesting are blocked from toddlers' vision by low bushes, bodies, or cars. Try to get close enough that they can see interesting things without being lifted to your height. Squat down to examine things from their perspective. You may discover the world in a brand new way, and you will send a message to your children that being small is okay—they don't have to be tall to see the "good stuff."

Craft

Walk Map

You will need: 2 pieces of cardboard the same size

pencil

clear packing tape

cloth tape

washable markers, paints, or crayons

pictures cut from magazines or photographs

clear contact paper (optional)

Create a foldup map of your neighborhood or a park where you walk most often with your toddler. Start by taking a short walk together along your most common walking route. Draw a quick sketch of the route, noting the landmarks and objects that interest your child. To make the map, tape together two pieces of cardboard on the back side. Lay out a *very* simple map of your route that starts and ends at your

house, including only a few of your child's landmarks. Paint or color the map simply, green for grass, blue for water, etc. Draw landmarks with markers or glue to the map photographs or pictures from magazines to mark points of interest. When the paint and glue are dry, tape the fold on the front of the map with clear tape so that it will not tear. Cover the edges with cloth tape. (Optional: To further protect the surface, laminate or cover on both sides with clear contact paper.)

Take the map with you on your next walk, pointing to landmarks and showing how to use the map to get home. Let your child use the map to plan a walk before you take it, deciding which direction you will walk and what you will see. Encourage your child to play with the map, building houses with boxes and blocks or driving cars down the streets. The map can be folded for storage, and stickers can be added when new landmarks become important or as reminders of special memories. Make other simple maps of favorite places like the zoo, the park, the playground, grandma's yard, etc.

Program Notes

Sign Language

WALK Have your hands in front, palms down, with fingers pointed away from the body. Alternately swing hands down, palms facing body, and pull each arm back to the body, in a motion like the legs walking.

The storyteller introduces the theme by inviting children to "go for a walk" as they enter the story space. Walk around the rug spots, pointing out things of interest at toddlers' eye levels: a picture on the wall, drinking fountain, elevator button, etc.

Storytime puppet leads the song, "As I Was Walking," waving and greeting each child or shaking hands, if they will. If you have a group that works well independently, let the first child and adult become the greeters as everyone sings, claps, and marches in place: "As Max and his mom walked down the street . . . Keisha and her dad they chanced to meet," and so on.

Giveaways can be simple, hand-drawn maps of the library or the library grounds, with three or four "landmarks" of interest to toddlers. Encourage the adults to point them out as they leave.

Fingertaster "tastes" foods from other places, such as tacos, spaghetti, fried rice, pineapple, etc.

Children exit the story space as explorers, looking for something specific (red or a smiling face or a bird).

 Notes

Wind

Books

Amy Loves the Wind
JULIA HOBAN

Away Went the Farmer's Hat
JANE BELK MONCURE

Barney's Big Balloon
MARK BERNTHAL

Benjamin's Balloon
ALAN BAKER

Clifford Counts Bubbles
NORMAN BRIDWELL

Gilberto and the Wind (Also in
    Spanish: *Gilberto y el Viento*)
MARIE HALL ETS

How the Wind Plays
MICHAEL LIPSON

Kite Flier
DENNIS HASELEY

Kite in the Park
LUCY COUSINS

Please Wind?
CAROL GREENE

The Same Wind
BETTE KILLION

Too Many Balloons (Also in
    Spanish: *Demasiados Globos*)
CATHERINE MATTHIAS

When the Wind Stops
CHARLOTTE ZOLOTOW

The Wind Blew
PAT HUTCHINS

Wind Says Good Night
KATY RYDELL

Windy Day
LAURA PEGRAM

Rhythms, Rhymes, and Fingerplays

Five Bright Kites   (tune: "Three Blind Mice")

Five bright kites. *(show five fingers)*
Five bright kites.
See how they fly *(sway arms over head)*
Up in the sky.
One dives low *(arms swing down)*
And one swoops high. *(arms swing high)*
Two get tangled *(arms cross)*
And the last floats by. *(move one hand slowly)*
I love to watch my kites in the sky. *(shade eyes
    and peer upward)*
Five bright kites. *(show five fingers)*

Wind Tricks

The wind is full of tricks today; *(shake index finger)*
It blew my daddy's hat away. *(hand on head)*
It chased our paper down the street *(reach down,
    to one side)*

And almost blew us off our feet. *(jump up and down)*
It makes the trees and bushes dance. *(wave arms)*
Just listen to it howl and prance. *(cup hand to ear)*
Whoooooooooo-oooooooooo.

Five Winds

(point to fingers one at a time with each line)
This little wind blows rain.
This little wind drifts snow.
This little wind whistles a tune. *(whistle)*
This little wind whispers low. *(whisper)*
And this little wind rocks baby birds
To and fro, to and fro, to and fro.
(hands together, rock back and forth)

Parents' Follow-Up Ideas

Make a paper fan by pleating a piece of paper and folding it in half. Show your children how to make "wind" by moving the fan. See if your children can make enough wind to blow a piece of paper off a table. How about a feather? Or a button? Talk about the differences in weight and how the wind can move some things but not others.

Observe the weather each day and talk with your toddlers about the changes. "Yesterday was sunny, but today is raining." Mark on the calendar with stickers or crayons the days that are sunny, snowy, rainy, cloudy, or windy.

To help your children understand that air is all around us, point out things moving in the wind, such as flags, leaves, or stray pieces of paper. Help your toddlers notice birds flying and air blowing from heating or cooling vents in the house. Walk against the wind, blow bubbles, or drop confetti from your hand into an air current. Give your children a light scarf or several crepe paper streamers to dance outside with the wind or with air currents inside the house.

Craft

A Shape Kite

You will need: construction paper in bright colors

scissors

tape

string

a small stick or unsharpened pencil

Cut a circle, a triangle, a rectangle, a star, and a crescent shape from the construction paper, keeping them all about the same size. Lay the shapes in a line on a flat surface leaving 1″ between them.

Tie one end of the string to the stick and lay the stick down in front of the line of shapes, leaving 1″ between the stick and the first shape. Stretch the string across the shapes and tape it securely to the back of each one.

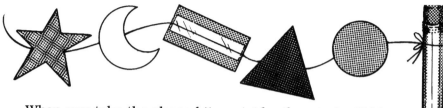

When you take the shape kite outside, the wind will blow the shapes. If there is no wind, hold the stick up high and walk with it. The shape kite will float behind you like a banner.

By cutting shapes out of plastic container lids and painting them, you can create another version of a shape kite to attach outside. Punch holes on opposite edges of each shape and assemble them in a line by tying them together with string. Attach this to a tree or pole that is visible from a window, and your child can tell you if the wind is blowing outside without leaving the house.

Program Notes

Sign Language

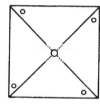

WIND   With the fingers of both hands extended and spread wide, palms facing each other, move hands simultaneously to the right and then left, as if they were blowing in the wind.

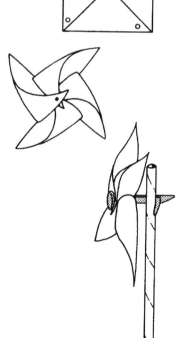

Introduce the theme using a pinwheel and letting each child blow to make it turn. If a child cannot blow hard enough, the storyteller should help.

Who Took the Farmer's Hat? can be shared with a real straw hat to show the various positions of the hat in the story and to help children understand why the animals thought it was something else. *The Wind Blew* makes a good flannelboard story, shortening the number of items if necessary. Also use a flannelboard with the rhyme "Five Bright Kites."

Giveaways are pinwheels made from a square of paper clipped on the diagonals with corners folded to the center. Attach it to the end of a straw with a brass fastener.

Fingertaster "tastes" foods that are light enough to blow in the wind, such as marshmallows, coconut, bread, corn chips, etc.

Children exit the story space flying like kites or making their pinwheels spin.

─────────────────────── Notes ───────────────────────

Winter

Books

Amy Loves the Snow
JULIA HOBAN

Dear Rebecca, Winter Is Here
JEAN CRAIGHEAD GEORGE

First Snow!
WENDY CHEYETTE LEWISON

First Snowfall
ANNE F. AND HARLOW ROCKWELL

Ice Is . . . Whee!
CAROL GREENE

It's Snowing, Little Rabbit
MARIE WABBES

Just a Snowy Day
MERCER MAYER

The Mitten
ALVIN TRESSELT

Snow Lambs
DEBI GLIORI

Snowballs
LOIS EHLERT

The Snowman Touch & Feel Book
RAYMOND BRIGGS

Snowy Day (Also in Spanish: *Un Día de Nieve*)
EZRA JACK KEATS

Tom & Pippo in the Snow
HELEN OXENBURY

Winter Day
DOUGLAS FLORIAN

Winter Rabbit
PATRICK YEE

Word Bird's Winter Words
JANE BELK MONCURE

Rhythms, Rhymes, and Fingerplays

It's Snowing   (tune: "A Tisket, a Tasket")

It's snowing! It's snowing!
The winter wind is blowing
Snowflakes swirling round and round
And covering the ground.
The ground, the ground.
Snowflakes all around,
Snow is falling from the sky
And covering the ground.

Snowman

Here's a jolly snowman *(form chubby tummy with hands)*
He has a carrot nose *(touch nose)*
Along came a bunny *(hop)*
Looking for some lunch *(look around)*
He ate that snowman's carrot nose *(touch nose)*
Nibble *(hop)*, Nibble *(hop)*, Crunch! *(sit down)*

Five Little Snowmen

Five little snowmen all in a row *(hold up five fingers)*
Each with a hat *(pat top of head)*
And a big red bow. *(pull at neck like fixing a bow tie)*
Out came the sun *(arms form big circle over head)*
And it stayed all day. *(lean to the left)*
And one of those snowmen melted away! *(put down one finger)*

[Repeat with]

> Four
> Three
> Two
> One

Parents' Follow-Up Ideas

During quiet time look through a photo album and let your toddler identify the people he or she knows. Children like seeing pictures of themselves and acknowledging how much they are growing.

Children love to see things go in one end of a cardboard tube and come out the other end. The longer the tube the better! Talk about what will fit in the tube and what is too big for it. Put two things in and see which comes out first.

Trace your toddler's hands onto a paper sack for a mitten pattern. Cut two mittens from several kinds of materials (paper, cloth, sandpaper, cardboard). Put one of each kind on a table and the others in a paper sack. Have your child pull one mitten from the sack and match it with its mate. This matching game will work with socks, towels, shoes, or any paired items in the home.

Craft

Five Little Snowmen

You will need: white, black, and red felt

scissors

glue

pen or washable marker

a flannelboard

Draw five snowmen (three circles on top of each other) on the white felt. Make them all different sizes and shapes. Draw five different-sized hats on the black and bows on the red felt. Cut them out. Turn the pencil marks to the back and assemble each snowman by gluing the hat and bow in place. Draw a face on each one.

Line the snowmen up on the flannelboard or a sofa cushion and recite the "Five Little Snowmen" rhyme. Remove one snowman as each melts. Your child will soon take over the task of "melting" the snowmen. Use the snowmen to talk about size and placement in line: "Let's melt the big one," or "The one in the middle is going to melt next."

Program Notes

Sign Language

SNOW Hold hands high with palms facing down. Wiggle your fingers gently and slowly move them down like snow gently falling.

Introduce the theme with the storytime puppet bundled up for cold weather with a scarf and hat.

After using *The Snowy Day,* invite the children to pretend to dress warm enough to go out in the snow. Let them pretend to scoot their feet, knock snow from a tree branch with it landing on their heads, build a snowman, make a snow angel, and put a snowball in their pockets. Flannelboard presentations for this program can include the rhyme "Five Little Snowmen" and *The Mitten* (use only the first five animals and the cricket for the story and make the mitten in two pieces so the animals can get inside).

Giveaways are paper snowflakes cut from paper lace doilies with their edges shaped like snowflakes.

Fingertaster "tastes" cold foods, such as ice cream, frozen juice, snow cones, etc.

Children exit the story space "walking fat" like snowmen.

———————————— Notes ————————————

Zoos

Books

At the Zoo
CLAIRE HENLEY

Bobby's Zoo
CAROLYN LUNN

But Not the Hippopotamus
SANDRA BOYNTON

Count-a-Round Zoo

Dear Zoo
ROD CAMPBELL

Goodnight Gorilla
PEGGY RATHMAN

My Zoo
JANE CONTEH-MORGAN

Petting Zoo
JACK HANNA

Sam, Who Never Forgets
EVE RICE

*When We Went
to the Zoo*
JAN ORMEROD

*Who Sees You?
At the Zoo*
CARLA DIJS

Zoo
JAN PIENKOWSKI

Zoo Animals
BYRON BARTON

The Zoo Book
JAN PFLOOG

Zoo Doings
ALAN BENJAMIN

Zoo Looking
MEM FOX

Rhythms, Rhymes, and Fingerplays

Zoo Animals   (tune: "If You're Happy")

If you want to be a monkey, jump up high. *(jump)*
If you want to be a monkey, jump up high.
If you want to be a monkey, if you want to be a monkey,
If you want to be a monkey, jump up high.

[Repeat with]

　　eagle . . . flap your wings
　　elephant . . . swing your trunk
　　crab . . . walk like this *(sideways)*
　　lion . . . roar out loud
　　giraffe . . . stand up tall
　　snake . . . slither slow

Horse in Striped Pajamas   (chanting rhyme)

Look, Daddy, look! *(clap hands with
    the rhythm of the chant)*
Do you see?
There's a horse
In striped pajamas.

No, no, no!
That's not what it is.
That's an animal
People call a zebra.

[Repeat with]

> cat with polka-dots on . . .
>   leopard
> bird in its tuxedo . . .
>   penguin

At the Zoo

At the zoo, we saw a bear *(shade eyes, then
    look surprised)*
With great big paws and shaggy hair.
    (raise hands like claws, then touch hair)
At the zoo, a zebra we found *(shade eyes, then
    look surprised)*
With black and white stripes all around.
    (hands criss-cross in front of body)
At the zoo, a giraffe so tall *(reach arms overhead)*
It could look right over the top of the wall.
    *(hands at eye level, lower them under chin
    as though peeking over a wall)*
At the zoo, the monkeys run *(run in place)*
And jump and swing having lots of fun.
    (jump, swing arms)

Parents' Follow-Up Ideas

Much has changed in zoos. Where once animals paced in small, barred cages, modern zoos have exhibits that present the natural habitat of animals as much as possible. There's a lot of glass and very few bars. Make opportunities to visit a zoo often with your children. Exploring all the exhibits may take several trips. Talk about the different kinds of animals and how they are related to each other (cats, bears, birds). Encourage your toddlers to compare and contrast animals (which is taller? fatter?) or to put them into categories by color, size, number of legs, where they live (water, trees, rocks), and if they have feathers or fur. Help your children learn the animals' names and collect pictures from magazines and zoo brochures to make a zoo book of favorites. Stop by the zoo gift shop and look for inexpensive toy animals to play with at home, now that your children have seen them, heard them, and watched them move. Explore "adopt-an-animal" programs at your local zoo. After the zoo visit, help your children remember which were the biggest, smallest, tallest, or loudest animals you saw that day.

Most zoos have a petting zoo where younger children can touch, pet, and feed domestic animals. Stay close to your child in petting areas, since eager animals can frighten young children especially when being fed by visitors. Help your children learn the names of different kinds of animals and see the similarities and differences between them. If your zoo has opportunities to meet exotic animals first hand, find out how old children need to be to participate. For many children this is the only opportunity they will have to touch animals most people see only in books or on television.

Craft

Zoo Animals

You will need: animal pictures cut from
                        magazines or brochures

index cards

scissors

glue

craft sticks

To make the pictures more sturdy, glue them to index cards. When the glue dries, cut out the animals and glue them to the bottom of a craft stick, as shown. Animals can be made to "walk" by moving the stick.

Help your toddler build a zoo out of blocks, rocks, plastic containers, etc. He or she can act out stories or re-create zoo exhibits with these stick puppets. They can also be used in matching games (find another bird, an animal with stripes, or another of same color) or can be sorted by where they live (water, trees) or how they move (crawl, slither, fly, run).

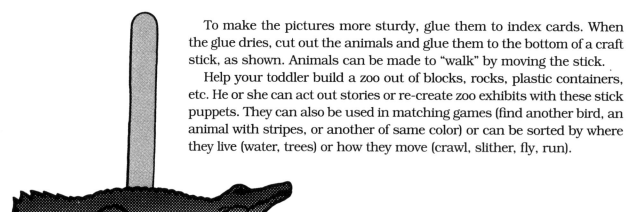

Program Notes

Sign Language

ZOO Extend the fingers of your left hand and fold your thumb into the palm, palm outward. Your right index finger makes a "Z" starting at the left index finger and ending along the top of the thumb.

The storytime puppet introduces the zoo theme with toy animals or brings books to the storyteller.

The storyteller and puppet chant "Horse in Striped Pajamas" using toy animals or flannelboard pictures. Change "Daddy" in the chant to the storyteller's name, and the puppet takes the child's part. *Sam, Who Never Forgets* works well as a flannelboard story using animal pictures glued to felt to create a flannelboard zoo. Let children imitate the actions (swinging elephant's trunk, galloping zebras) or the sounds (roaring lions, hissing snakes) of the animals in the zoo.

Giveaways can be brochures from the local zoo or animal posters gathered from children's magazines or publishers.

Fingertaster "tastes" silly zoo foods, such as kangaroo bread, monkey pudding, zebra Jello, etc.

Children exit the story space walking like a zoo animal.

———————————————— **Notes** ————————————————

APPENDIX A

Construction of Storytime Materials

There are several items that are used in many, if not all, programs. The following instructions will assist the storyteller in the construction of these materials.

Lap Stage

Used with puppets and lap-board presentations

You will need: a cardboard box (at least 10″×13″×16″)

contact paper, burlap, or paint

box cutter or craft knife

glue

Velcro strips

spring clothespins (optional)

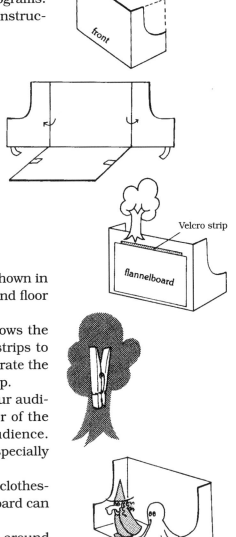

Cut the top and back off the box and cut the two sides as shown in the illustration. The remaining whole sides will be the front and floor of the stage.

Separate the sides and the stage floor as shown. This allows the stage to fold flat for storage or transportation. Glue Velcro strips to the sides and floor to stabilize the lap stage during use. Decorate the stage by painting it or covering it with contact paper or burlap.

To use the stage, set it on your lap with the front facing your audience. Puppets, props, or a script can lie inside on the floor of the stage, easily accessible to you but out of sight of your audience. Finger puppets, rod puppets, or small hand puppets are especially suitable for use with a lap stage.

Scenery can be attached to the stage by gluing it to spring clothespins that are clipped to the top of the stage. A small flannelboard can be attached to the front of the stage with Velcro strips.

The stage can also be used as a lap board (simply turn it around with the floor facing your audience). Standup figures, toys, or props can be manipulated across the stage floor as a story is told.

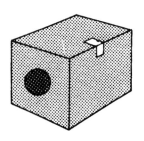

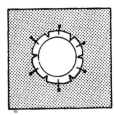

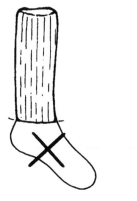

Touch Box

Used for touch-box activities and storage during programs

You will need: a cardboard box (all sides intact and
a lid that opens)

box cutter or craft knife

contact paper, material, or paint

ribbed top from a sock

glue

straight pins

Velcro strips

Cut a circular hole in one side of the box, large enough for your hand to easily pass through. Cover the box with contact paper, material, or paint.

Insert one end of the sock-top into the hole and glue it on the *inside* of the box. Stretch and clip the sock edges to make it fit. Pin the sock in place until the glue dries thoroughly. Remove the pins. Glue the Velcro strips to the lid of the box so that it closes securely.

To use, put an object inside the box and close the lid. Demonstrate to the children how your hand can go into the box through the sock. Instruct them to feel what is inside the box (but *not* to pull it out through the sock). Encourage them to talk about what they feel: "Is it soft or hard? little or big? warm or cold? Do you know what it is?"

When each child has had a turn, remove the object through the lid of the box. Give them time to see and touch it a second time if they want. Describe the object (color, texture, size, and so on) as they examine it; always name the object (balloon, ball, banana, and so on).

By using the touch box to keep storytime props, giveaway items, and puppets out of view until they are needed in the program, you make it a familiar part of your storytime. Children will participate more fully in touch-box activities when they see the box often. They like to put things into containers and will readily return storytime props (musical instruments, rod puppets, and so on) to the touch box when you finish with them.

Generic Glove Puppet

Used with finger plays and glove-puppet stories

You will need: a plain cotton gardening glove

Velcro tabs

needle and thread

pompoms or felt figures

Sew Velcro tabs to the front and back of each fingertip of the glove. Sew a strip of Velcro to the palm of the glove for scenery or props.

Make figures to use with the glove from pompoms or felt as shown. Sew a tab of Velcro to the figures so they will adhere to the tabs on the glove.

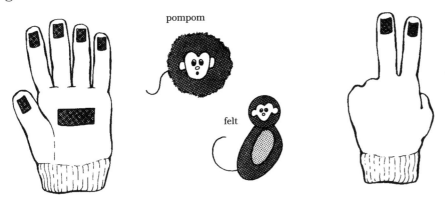

Scenery or props set the stage for a glove-puppet story. They can be made from felt or cardboard and attached to the palm of the glove with Velcro strips.

For counting rhymes, use the Velcro tabs on the back of the glove fingers. Objects can appear or disappear completely as fingers are folded into the fist.

Sock Puppet Fingertaster

Used for tasting fingers and saying goodbye

You will need: a knee sock

notions for facial features
(buttons, pompoms, yarn)

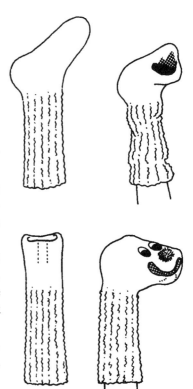

Place your hand inside the sock with the tips of your fingers near the toe and the heel across your knuckles as shown.

Open your hand wide inside the sock and tuck the toe into the palm of your hand to form the mouth. Sew a slot through both thicknesses of fabric into the bottom of the mouth for your thumb to slide into. This secures the mouth.

Sew on eyes (buttons), keeping them close to the mouth. This makes the puppet less threatening to young children. Add a nose (pompom), hair (yarn) . . . whatever other features or clothing you want to make the puppet special. No teeth, please. Avoid using materials that cannot be washed (like felt)—this puppet gets a lot of "loving."

Sock puppets are very flexible and they "make faces" easily. Practice moving your fingers inside the puppet to make it smile, frown, or turn into a silly face.

Practice "talking" by using the puppet in front of a mirror.

To taste fingers, the puppet asks the children if they want their fingers tasted. If so, the puppet sucks or licks the offered finger with a slurping sound. The puppet then tells each child what his or her finger tasted like. Use flavors with which children are familiar: fruit, soft drinks, dinner items. If children return for additional "tasting," the puppet can oblige but does not need to remember what flavor individuals were. Often the child simply wants to be touched again.

Clown Shape Puzzle

Used in opening routine

You will need: brightly colored felt in the following shapes:

　　　　1 1″×4″ rectangle

　　　　1 triangle (base 3″; height 4½″)

　　　　2 circles (1 large, 1 small)

　　　　2 small stars

　　　　1 crescent (for a smile)

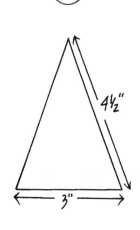

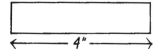

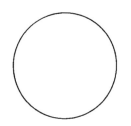

Use bright colors of felt that contrast with each other in basic hues: yellow, orange or pink, red, purple, blue, green. Toddlers can easily distinguish these colors from each other.

Trace around objects such as water glasses or salt shakers to obtain patterns for the circles, keeping them in the proportions as shown.

Cut the shapes from felt and place them at random on the flannelboard. As they are rearranged into a clown, name each shape and its relationship to the others. For instance: "This is a triangle. I will put it on top of the big circle . . . put the little circle at the top of the triangle."

As your group becomes familiar with the shapes and their place in the puzzle, put a piece in the wrong place (rectangle at the top of the triangle) and ask them if it looks right. The children will enjoy the surprise and helping you to "get it right."

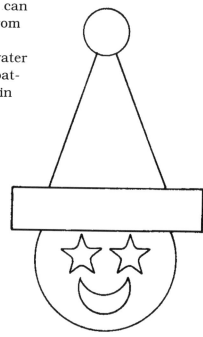

Clown Name Tag

Used to identify children by name

You will need: construction paper in basic colors
 (pink, green, blue, yellow, orange,
 red, tan, purple)

 scissors

 glue

 gummed stars

 clear contact paper

 yarn

 hole punch

 safety pins (optional)

Cut the shapes shown from various colors of construction paper and assemble them into the clown's face. Cut twice as many rectangles and crescents as you need. Glue the shapes together, adding the gummed stars as eyes. Glue a second rectangle and second face to the back of each name tag in the same position as the first. Print each child's name on *both* sides of the name tag. Laminate or cover each name tag with clear contact paper.

Punch a hole in the circle pompom and thread it with yarn. Use enough yarn to slip the name tag over each child's head or cut it shorter and attach a small safety pin to be pinned to the child's clothing.

Parents' name tags are squares or rectangles of construction paper with both their first and last names printed on them. Punch a hole in the top and add yarn and a safety pin to attach to the parents' clothing. Keep the name tags of child and parent paper-clipped together between programs.

I Know an Old Lady Sack Puppet

Used during the song in Mealtimes and for presentation of shapes and colors

You will need: 2 grocery sacks

 scissors

 stapler

 tape

 8½″×11″ piece of clear acetate
 (book report cover)

 cardboard face, hands, and feet

 material scraps

 glue

 poster board

Cut a window (7″×10″) in one sack as shown. Cut a slot under the flap of the sack and another slot along the side fold.

Tape the edges of the window and the slots to reinforce them. Glue the clear acetate on the inside of the sack so that it covers the window.

Insert the second sack into the one with the holes making all corners and edges fit exactly. Staple both sacks across the front just under the window. This keeps the figures from sliding down too far to be seen in the window.

Cover the sack with material, leaving open the slots and window. Glue material securely. Glue on face, hands, and feet.

Insert your hand inside the sack so that the fingers make the flap move up and down. When the Old Lady "swallows" something, the flap moves upward and objects are dropped into the slot under it. They then appear in the window. They can be removed through the slot in the sack's side.

Make the objects to be swallowed from felt or heavy poster board. If felt is used, it must be weighted with fishing or drapery weights so that they drop into the window. Poster board slides down easily.

Create the animals in the song (fly, spider, and so on) and as the song is sung, drop each animal into the window where it can be seen by the children. Also use this puppet to introduce colors, shapes, and alphabet letters. There is no end to the things the Old Lady can eat.

Caterpillar and Butterfly Sock Puppets

Used with *The Very Hungry Caterpillar* in Bugs and Caterpillars

You will need: brightly colored or striped sock

white sock, same size as colored sock

a finger from an old glove

felt in the same colors as the sock puppet

glue

buttons and craft eyes

For the caterpillar, insert the white sock into the colored one. Construct the mouth as described for the sock puppet, sewing through both socks to secure the mouth. Add buttons near the mouth for the puppet's eyes.

For the butterfly, make and decorate felt wings. Glue craft eyes to the finger from the old glove to make the butterfly's body. Glue the wings to the body.

To use the puppets, fold the butterfly's wings over its body and flatten. Slide the butterfly between the white and colored socks. The caterpillar sock puppet stays on the hand for most of the story. To spin a cocoon, turn both socks inside out as you pull the puppet off your hand. The butterfly then emerges from its hidden pocket.

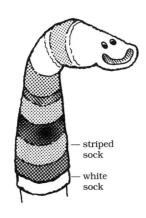

— striped sock

— white sock

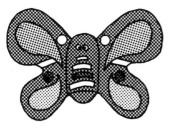

detail of finger puppet

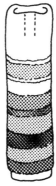

socks inside out

cocoon

Clip Art

This clip art figure can be copied and enlarged for a coloring page giveaway, or it can be used as a logo for toddler storytime programs in library handouts and publicity. It can also become a T-shirt transfer using fabric crayons.

Professional Bibliography

Program Planning and Program Resources

Association for Library Services to Children. *Programming for Very Young Children: Birth through Age Five.* Chicago: ALA, 1996.

Baby Names, Toddler Games, & Parent Strain: Public Library Services to Young Families, recorded at the Public Library Association National Conference held March 20–23, 1991, in San Diego, California. Audio cassette.

Bauer, Caroline Feller. *The New Handbook for Storytellers.* Chicago: ALA, 1995.

Brennan, Jan. *Treasured Time with Your Toddler: A Monthly Guide to Activities.* Little Rock, Ark.: August House, 1991.

Briggs, Diane. *52 Programs for Preschoolers: The Librarian's Year-Round Planner.* Chicago: ALA, 1997.

Catlin, Cynthia. *Toddlers Together: The Complete Planning Guide for a Toddler Curriculum.* Illus. by Karen Theusen. Beltsville, Md.: Gryphon, 1994.

———. *More Toddlers Together: The Complete Planning Guide for a Toddler Curriculum.* Vol. II. Illus. by Joan Waites. Beltsville, Md.: Gryphon, 1996.

DeSalvo, Nancy N. *Beginning with Books: Library Programming for Infants, Toddlers and Preschoolers.* Hamden, Conn.: Library Professional Publ., 1993.

Fleming, Bonnie Mack, and Darlene Softley Hamilton. *Resources for Creative Teaching in Early Childhood Education.* Songs and parodies by JoAnne Deal Hicks. New York: Harcourt, 1977.

Gates, Frieda. *Glove, Mitten and Sock Puppets.* New York: Walker, 1978.

Greene, Ellin. *Books, Babies, and Libraries: Serving Infants, Toddlers, Their Parents and Caregivers.* Chicago: ALA, 1991.

Hunt, Tamara, and Nancy Renfro. *Puppetry in Early Childhood Education.* Austin, Tex.: Nancy Renfro Studios, 1982.

I Saw a Purple Cow and 100 Other Recipes for Learning. Boston: Little, Brown, 1972.

Jeffrey, Debby Ann. *Literate Beginnings: Programs for Babies and Toddlers.* Chicago: ALA, 1995.

Lima, Carolyn W. *A to Zoo: Subject Access to Children's Picture Books.* 4th ed. New York: Bowker, 1993.

McKinnon, Elizabeth, and Gayle Bittinger. *Busy Bees Spring (Fall, and Winter): Fun for Two's and Three's.* Illus. by Barb Tourtillotte. Everett, Wash.: Warren, 1994.

———. *Busy Bees Summer: Fun for Two's and Three's.* Illus. by Barb Tourtillotte. Everett, Wash.: Warren, 1995.

1001 Teaching Props: Simple Props to Make for Working with Young Children. Everett, Wash.: Warren, 1992.

Richey, Virginia H., and Katharyn E. Puckett. *Wordless/Almost Wordless Picture Books: A Guide.* Englewood, Colo.: Libraries Unltd., 1992.

Ross, Laura. *Finger Puppets.* New York: Lothrop, 1971.

Sierra, Judy, and Robert Kaminski. *Multicultural Folktales: Stories to Tell Young Children.* Selected trans. by Adela Artola Allen. Phoenix, Ariz.: Oryx, 1991.

Signed English Dictionary for Preschool and Elementary Levels. Edited by Harry Bornstein and others. Washington, D.C.: Gallaudet College Pr., 1975.

Start Early for an Early Start. Edited by Ferne Johnson. Chicago: ALA, 1976.

Warren, Jean. *Cut and Tell Stories for Fall (Winter and Spring).* Everett, Wash.: Totline Pr., 1984.

———. *Toddler Theme-a-Saurus: The Great Big Book of Toddler Teaching Themes.* Illus. by Judy Shimono. Totline Publications, a division of Frank Schaffer Publications, 23740 Hawthorne Blvd., Torrance, CA 90505, 1991.

Wilmes, Liz, and Dick Wilmes. *2's Experience Felt Board Fun.* Illus. by Janet McDonnell. Elgin, Ill.: Building Blocks, 1994.

Wilson, LaVisa Cam. *Infants & Toddlers: Curriculum and Teaching.* 2d ed. Albany, N.Y.: Delmar, 1990.

Martin, Elaine. *Baby Games: The Joyful Guide to Child's Play from Birth to Three Years.* Rev. and updated. Philadelphia: Running Pr., 1988.

Miller, Karen. *Things to Do with Toddlers and Twos.* Marshfield, Mass.: Telshare, 1984.

Razzi, James. *Easy Does It!* New York: Parents, 1969.

Renfro, Nancy. *Bags Are Big! Paper Bag Craft Book.* Austin, Tex.: Nancy Renfro Studios, 1986.

Sattler, Helen Roney. *Recipes for Art and Craft Materials.* New York: Lothrop, 1973.

Silberg, Jackie. *Games to Play with Toddlers.* Illus. by Linda Greigg. Mt. Rainier, Md.: Gryphon, 1993.

———. *Games to Play with Two Year Olds.* Illus. by Linda Greigg. Beltsville, Md.: Gryphon, 1994.

———. *More Games to Play with Toddlers.* Illus. by Cheryl Kirk Noll. Beltsville, Md.: Gryphon, 1996.

Supraner, Robyn. *Rainy Day Surprises You Can Make.* Mahwah, N.J.: Troll, 1981.

Wilmes, Liz, and Dick Wilmes. *2's Experience Art.* Illus. by Janet McDonnell. Elgin, Ill.: Building Blocks, 1995.

———. *2's Experience Dramatic Play.* Illus. by Janet McDonnell. Elgin, Ill.: Building Blocks, 1995.

——— Activities and Crafts ———

Bean, Cheryl A., and Sandra D. Albertson. *Just in Time with Nursery Rhymes.* Longview, Wash.: Just In Time, 1980.

Chernoff, Goldie Taub. *Easy Costumes You Don't Have to Sew.* New York: Four Winds, 1984.

Cole, Ann, and Carolyn Haas. *Purple Cow to the Rescue.* Boston: Little, Brown, 1982.

Gates, Frieda. *Easy-to-Make Costumes.* Englewood Cliffs, N.J.: Prentice-Hall, 1981.

———. *Easy-to-Make Puppets.* Englewood Cliffs, N.J.: Prentice-Hall, 1981.

Haas, Carolyn Buhai. *Look at Me: Creative Activities for Babies and Toddlers.* Chicago: Chicago Review, 1987.

Hagstrom, Julie. *Games Toddlers Play.* Illus. by Christiane Stalland. New York: Pocket, 1986.

———. *Let's Pretend: Games of Fantasy for Babies and Young Children.* New York: A & W Visual Libr., 1982.

Honig, Alice S. *Playtime Learning Games for Young Children.* Syracuse, N.Y.: Syracuse Univ. Pr., 1982.

Lally, John Ronald, and Ira J. Gordon. *Learning Games for Infants and Toddlers: A Playtime Handbook.* Illus. by Bill Finch. Syracuse, N.Y.: New Readers, 1977.

Lopshire, Robert. *How to Make Snop Snappers and Other Fine Things.* New York: Greenwillow, 1977.

——— Fingerplays and Music ———

Cole, Joanna, and Stephanie Calmenson, comps. *The Eentsy, Weentsy Spider: Fingerplays and Action Rhymes.* Illus. by Alan Tiegreen. New York: Mulberry, 1991.

Defty, Jeff. *Creative Fingerplays & Action Rhymes: An Index and Guide to Their Use.* Illus. by Ellen Kae Hester. Phoenix, Ariz.: Oryx, 1992.

Dowell, Ruth I. *Move over Mother Goose: Fingerplays, Activity Verses, and Funny Rhymes.* Illus. by Concetta C. Scott. Beltsville, Md.: Gryphon, 1994.

Glazer, Tom. *Music for Ones and Twos: Songs and Games for the Very Young Child.* Garden City, N.Y.: Doubleday, 1983.

Grayson, Marion F. *Let's Do Fingerplays.* Washington, D.C.: Robert B. Luce, 1962.

Hammett, Carol, and Elaine Bueffel. *It's Toddler Time.* Long Branch, N.J.: Kimbo Educational, 1982. Audio cassette.

———. *Toddlers on Parade: Musical Exercises for Infants and Toddlers.* Long Branch, N.J.: Kimbo Educational, 1985. Audio cassette.

Johnson, Laura T. *Fun Activities for Toddlers.* Long Branch, N.J.: Kimbo Educational, 1982. Audio cassette.

Keefe, Betty. *Fingerpuppets, Fingerplays and Holidays.* Omaha, Nebr.: Special Literature Pr., 1984.

McGrath, Bob, and Katharine Smithrim. *Songs and Games for Toddlers.* Toronto, Ont.: Kids' Records, 1985. Audio cassette.

Nursery Rhymes from Mother Goose in Signed English. Washington, D.C.: Gallaudet College Pr., 1972.

Roberts, Lynda. *Mitt Magic: Finger Plays for Finger Puppets.* Illus. by James Morris. Beltsville, Md.: Gryphon, 1985.

Stewart, Georgiana Liccione. *My Teddy Bear and Me: Musical Play Activities for Infants and Toddlers.* Long Branch, N.J.: Kimbo Educational, 1984. Audio cassette.

Touch, Teach & Hug a Toddler. Long Branch, N.J.: Kimbo Educational, 1985. Audio cassette.

Warren, Jean. *Piggyback Songs for Infants and Toddlers.* Illus. by Marion Hopping Ekberg. Chorded by Barbara Robinson. Everett, Wash.: Warren, 1985.

Wilmes, Liz, and Dick Wilmes. *2's Experience Fingerplays.* Illus. by Janet McDonnell. Elgin, Ill.: Building Blocks, 1994.

Wirth, Marian, and others. *Musical Games, Fingerplays, and Rhythmic Activities for Early Childhood.* West Nyack, N.Y.: Parker, 1983.

Wiseman, Ann. *Making Musical Things.* New York: Scribner, 1979.

Toddler Characteristics ——— and Parenting Books ———

Albi, Linda. *Mothering Twins: From Hearing the News to Beyond the Terrible Twos.* New York: Simon & Schuster, 1993.

Alvino, James, and the editors of Gifted Children Monthly. *Parents' Guide to Raising a Gifted Toddler: Recognizing and Developing the Potential of Your Child from Birth to Five Years.* Boston: Little, Brown, 1989.

Badger, Earladeen. *Infant/Toddler: Introducing Your Child to the Joy of Learning.* New York: Instructo McGraw-Hill, 1981.

Beebe, Brooke M. *Tips for Toddlers.* Illus. by Denise Cavalieri Fike. New York: Dell, 1983.

Bell, T. H. *Your Child's Intellect: A Guide to Home-Based Preschool Education.* Salt Lake City: Olympus, 1972.

Brown, Laurene Krasny. *Toddler Time: A Book to Share with Your Toddler.* Boston: Little, Brown, 1990.

Butler, Dorothy. *Babies Need Books.* New York: Atheneum, 1980.

Crary, Elizabeth. *Without Spanking or Spoiling: A Practical Approach to Toddler and Preschool Guidance.* Seattle, Wash.: Parenting Pr., 1979.

Cryer, Debby, Thelma Harms, and Beth Bourland. *Active Learning for Twos.* Menlo Park, Calif.: Addison-Wesley, 1988.

Devine, Monica. *Baby Talk: The Art of Communicating with Infants and Toddlers.* New York: Plenum, 1991.

Dexter, Sandi. *Joyful Play with Toddlers: Recipes for Fun with Odds and Ends.* Illus. by Karen Pew. Seattle, Wash.: Parenting Pr., 1995.

Eisenberg, Arlene, Heidi E. Murkoff, and Sandee E. Hathaway. *What to Expect: The Toddler Years.* New York: Workman, 1994.

Fisher, John J. *Toys to Grow with: Infants & Toddlers: Endless Play Ideas That Make Learning Fun.* New York: Putnam, 1986.

Green, Christopher. *Toddler Taming: A Survival Guide for Parents.* Illus. by Roger Roberts. New York: Fawcett Columbine, 1985.

Kimmel, Martha, and David Kimmel. *Mommy Made, and Daddy Too: Home Cooking for a Healthy Baby and Toddler.* New York: Bantam, 1990.

Lieberman, Alicia F. *The Emotional Life of the Toddler.* New York: Maxwell Macmillan Intnl., 1993.

Lindsay, Jeanne Warren. *The Challenge of Toddlers: Parenting Your Child from One to Three.* Buena Park, Calif.: Morning Glory, 1991.

Marzollo, Jean. *Supertot: Creative Learning Activities for Children from 1 to 3.* New York: Harper, 1977.

Marzollo, Jean, and Janice Lloyd. *Learning through Play.* New York: Harper, 1972.

Munger, Evelyn M., and Susan Jane Bowden. *Beyond Peek-a-Boo and Pat-a-Cake: Activities for Baby's First 24 Months.* 3d ed. Clinton, N.J.: New Win, 1993.

Pagnoni, Mario. *Computers and Small Fries: A Computer-Readiness Guide for Parents of Tots, Toddlers, and Other Minors.* Wayne, N.J.: Avery, 1986.

Parentmaking: A Practical Handbook for Teaching Parent Classes about Babies and Toddlers. Rev. ed. Menlo Park, Calif.: Banster, 1995.

Popper, Adrienne. *Parents Book for the Toddler Years.* New York: Ballantine, 1986.

Rosemond, John K. *Making the "Terrible" Twos Terrific!* Kansas City, Mo.: Andrews and McMeel, 1993.

Schrank, Rita. *Toddlers Learn by Doing: Toddler Activities and Parent/Teacher Activity Log.* Atlanta, Ga.: Humanics, 1984.

Shimm, Patricia H., and Kate Ballen. *Parenting Your Toddler: The Expert's Guide to the Tough and Tender Years.* Reading, Mass.: Addison-Wesley, 1995.

Sparling, Joseph, and Isabelle Lewis. *Learning Games for the First 3 Years: A Guide to Parent-Child Play.* New York: Walker, 1979.

Under Three: A Comprehensive Guide to Caring for Your Baby and Toddler. Edited by John S. O'Shea. New York: Van Nostrand Reinhold, 1988.

Van der Zande, Irene. *1, 2, 3—the Toddler Years: A Practical Guide for Parents & Caregivers.* 2d ed. Santa Cruz, Calif.: The Center, 1993.

Varni, James W., and Donna G. Corwin. *Time-Out for Toddlers: Positive Solutions to Typical Problems in Children.* New York: Berkley, 1991.

Warren, Paul. *My Toddler: The Beginning of Independence.* Stepping-Stones Series for Christian Parents. Nashville, Tenn.: Thomas Nelson, 1994.

White, Burton L. *Educating the Infant and Toddler.* Lexington, Mass.: Lexington, 1988.

Zweiback, Meg. *Keys to Parenting Your Two-Year-Old.* Hauppauge, N.Y.: Barron's, 1993.

Periodical Resources

Baar-Lindsay, Christopher. "Library Programming for Toddlers." *Public Libraries* 22 (1983): 111–13.

Dowd, Frances Smardo, and Judith Dixon. "Successful Toddler Storytimes Based on Child Development Principles." *Public Libraries* 35 (1996): 374–80.

Kidstuff: A Treasury of Early Childhood Enrichment Materials. Guidelines Press, 1307 S. Killian Dr., Lake Park, FL 33403. Published monthly.

Richardson, Selma K. *Magazines for Children: A Guide for Parents, Teachers, and Librarians.* Chicago: ALA, 1991.

Totline Newsletter. Totline Press, P.O. Box 2255, Everett, WA 98203. Published monthly.

Walsh, Joseph A. "Parenting Programs in Libraries." *School Library Journal* 29 (1983): 32–5.

Weissbourd, Bernice. "As They Grow/Two-Year-Olds." *Parents Magazine.* Regular monthly column.

Bibliography of Titles Used in Programs

Alda, Arlene. *Pig, Horse, or Cow, Don't Wake Me Now.* Doubleday, 1994. Morning

———. *Sheep, Sheep, Sheep: Help Me Fall Asleep.* Doubleday, 1992. Bedtime

Alexander, Sue. *Who Goes Out on Halloween?* Illus. by G. Brian Karas. Bantam, 1990. Autumn

Allen, Jonathan. *Purple Sock, Pink Sock.* Morrow, 1992. (Board book) Getting Dressed

———. *Up the Steps, Down the Slide.* Morrow, 1992. (Board book) Picnics

———. *Who's at the Door?* Morrow, 1993. (Board book) Peek

Allen, Pamela. *Bertie and the Bear.* Coward, 1984. Dancing

———. *Who Sank the Boat?* Putnam, 1990. Boats

Ancona, George. *Helping Out.* Houghton, 1991. Helping

Anderson, Lena. *Bunny Fun.* Farrar, 1991. Rabbits

Anderson, Peggy Perry. *To the Tub.* Houghton, 1996. Frogs and Turtles

Andrews, Jan. *Very Last First Time.* Illus. by Ian Wallace. Simon & Schuster, 1986. Mealtimes

Anholt, Catherine, and Laurence Anholt. *All about You.* Viking, 1992. My Body

———. *Twins: Two by Two.* Candlewick, 1992. Family

Anholt, Laurence. *The New Puppy.* Illus. by Catherine Anholt. Western, 1995. Dogs

Animals, Animals in the Circus. National Geographic, 1993. Circus

Arnold, Tedd. *No More Water in the Tub!* Dial, 1995. Bath Time

Arnosky, Jim. *Rabbits & Raindrops.* Putnam, 1997. Rabbits

Artell, Mike. *Big Long Animal Song.* Goodyear, 1994. Also in Spanish: *Gran Canción de los Animales.* Goodyear, 1995. Sizes and Shapes

———. *Legs.* Simon & Schuster, 1996. My Body

Aruego, Jose, and Ariane Dewey. *We Hide, You Seek.* Greenwillow, 1979. Peek

Asch, Frank. *Goodbye House.* Simon & Schuster, 1989. Homes

———. *Just Like Daddy.* Simon & Schuster, 1984. Family

———. *Moon Bear.* Simon & Schuster, 1993. Bears

———. *Moon Bear's Canoe.* Simon & Schuster, 1993. Boats

———. *Moondance.* Simon & Schuster, 1993. Dancing

———. *Moongame.* Simon & Schuster, 1984. Peek

———. *Short Train, Long Train.* Scholastic, 1992. (Board book) Trains and Planes

———. *Skyfire.* Simon & Schuster, 1988. Rain

Astley, Judy. *When One Cat Woke Up: A Cat Counting Book.* Dial, 1990. Cats

Awdry, W. *Happy Birthday, Thomas!* Illus. by Owain Bell. Random, 1990. Trains and Planes

Aylesworth, Jim. *One Crow: A Counting Rhyme.* Illus. by Ruth Young. Harper, 1990. Counting

Baer, Gene. *Thump, Thump, Rat-a-Tat-Tat.* Harper, 1989. Also in big book format, Harper Trophy, 1992. Parades

Baker, Alan. *Benjamin's Balloon.* Lothrop, 1990. Wind

———. *Brown Rabbit's Shape Book.* Kingfisher, 1994. (Board book) Sizes and Shapes

———. *Little Rabbit's First Word Book.* Kingfisher, 1996. (Board book) Rabbits

———. *White Rabbit's Color Book.* Kingfisher, 1994. (Board book) Colors

Balian, Lorna. *Humbug Witch.* Humbug, 1992. Autumn

Bang, Molly. *One Fall Day.* Greenwillow, 1994. Autumn

_____. *Ten, Nine, Eight.* Greenwillow, 1983. Also in print Braille edition, National Braille Press, 1991. Bedtime

Barkan, Joanne. *Binyah, Binyah Hide & Seek.* Simon & Schuster, 1996. (Lift-the-flap book) Frogs and Turtles

_____. *Clown Caboose.* Illus. by Christina Ong. Simon & Schuster, 1993. (Board book) Circus

_____. *Locomotive.* Illus. by Richard Walz. Simon & Schuster, 1992. (Board book) Trains and Planes

Barton, Byron. *Airport.* Harper, 1982. Trains and Planes

_____. *Boats.* Harper, 1986. Boats

_____. *Building a House.* Hampton Brown, 1992. Homes

_____. *Buzz! Buzz! Buzz!* Simon & Schuster, 1995. Bugs and Caterpillars

_____. *I Want to Be an Astronaut.* Harper, 1988. Trains and Planes

_____. *Machines at Work.* Harper, 1987. Trucks, Cars, and Buses

_____. *Three Bears.* HarperCollins, 1991. Also in big book format, HarperCollins, 1994. Read to Me

_____. *Where's Al?* Clarion, 1989. Dogs

_____. *Zoo Animals.* HarperCollins, 1995. (Board book) Zoos

Battles, Edith. *What Does the Rooster Say, Yoshio?* Illus. by Toni Hormann. Albert Whitman, 1978. Birds

Baynton, Martin. *Why Do You Love Me?* Greenwillow, 1990. Love

Benjamin, Alan. *Busy Bunnies.* Illus. by Christopher Santoro. Simon & Schuster, 1988. Rabbits

_____. *Dear Santa.* Simon & Schuster, 1993. (Board book) December

_____. *Hanukkah.* Simon & Schuster, 1993. (Board book) December

_____. *Let's Eat: Vamos a Comer.* (English and Spanish.) Simon & Schuster, 1992. (Board book) Mealtimes

_____. *Let's Play: Vamos a Jugar.* (English and Spanish.) Simon & Schuster, 1992. (Board book) Playing

_____. *Let's Take a Walk: Vamos a Caminar.* (English and Spanish.) Simon & Schuster, 1992. (Board book) Walking

_____. *What Color? ¿Qué Color?* (English and Spanish.) Simon & Schuster, 1992. (Board book) Colors

_____. *Zoo Doings.* Simon & Schuster, 1994. Zoos

Berends, Polly. *I Heard Said the Bird.* Illus. by Brad Sneed. Dial, 1995. Babies

Berenstain, Stan, and Jan Berenstein. *He Bear, She Bear.* Random, 1974. Bears

_____. *Old Hat, New Hat.* Random, 1970. Hats

Bernhard, Durga. *What's Maggie Up To?* Holiday, 1992. Cats

Bernthal, Mark. *Barney's Big Balloon.* Illus. by Chris Sharp and David McGlothlin. Barney, 1995. Wind

Berry, Holly. *Old Macdonald Had a Farm.* North-South, 1994. Farms

Big Bird's Color Game. Western, 1989. (Board book) Colors

Blocksma, Mary. *Best Dressed Bear.* Illus. by Sandra Cox Kalthoff. Childrens, 1984. Also in Spanish: *El Oso Más Elegante.* Childrens, 1986. Dancing

_____. *Rub-A-Dub-Dub: What's in the Tub?* Illus. by Sandra Cox Kalthoff. Childrens, 1984. Bath Time

_____. *Where's That Duck?* Illus. by Sandra Cox Kalthoff. Childrens, 1985. Also in Spanish: *Dónde Está el Pato?* Childrens, 1990. Birds

Blos, Joan W. *Martin's Hats.* Illus. by Marc Simont. Morrow, 1984. Hats

Bond, Michael. *Paddington at the Circus.* Illus. by John Lobban. HarperCollins, 1992. Circus

_____. *Paddington Goes on a Picnic.* Illus. by Nick Ward. HarperCollins, 1994. (Board book) Picnics

_____. *Paddington Makes a Mess.* Illus. by Nick Ward. HarperCollins, 1994. (Board book) Helping

_____. *Paddington Takes a Bath.* Illus. by John Lobban. HarperCollins, 1992. Bath Time

_____. *Paddington's Colors.* Illus. by John Lobban. Viking, 1991. Colors

_____. *Paddington's Garden.* Illus. by John Lobban. HarperCollins, 1993. Gardens

_____. *Paddington's 1 2 3.* Illus. by John Lobban. Viking, 1991. Counting

_____. *Paddington's Things I Feel.* Illus. by John Lobban. HarperCollins, 1994. Feelings

Boo, Marcial. *Butterfly Kiss.* Illus. by Tim Vyner. Harcourt, 1995. Bugs and Caterpillars

Bornstein, Ruth. *Little Gorilla.* Houghton, 1979. Also in Spanish: *Gorililita.* Scholastic, 1993. Monkeys

Boynton, Sandra. *A Is for Angry: An Animal and Adjective Alphabet.* Workman, 1987. Feelings

_____. *Barnyard Dance.* Workman, 1993. (Board book) Dancing

_____. *Birthday Monsters.* Workman, 1993. (Board book) Birthdays

_____. *Blue Hat, Green Hat.* Simon & Schuster, 1995. (Board book) Hats

_____. *But Not the Hippopotamus.* Simon & Schuster, 1995. (Board book) Zoos

_____. *Doggies.* Simon & Schuster, 1995. (Board book) Dogs

_____. *Going to Bed.* Simon & Schuster, 1995. (Board book) Bedtime

_____. *Moo, Baa, La-La-La!* Simon & Schuster, 1995. (Board book) Sounds

Brannon, Tom. *Monster Faces.* Random, 1996. (Board book) Feelings

Bratton, John W. *Teddy Bear's Picnic.* Illus. by Renate Kozikowski. Simon & Schuster, 1990. Picnics

Brenner, Barbara. *Snow Parade.* Illus. by Mary Tara O'Keefe. Crown, 1984. Parades

Bridwell, Norman. *Clifford at the Circus.* Scholastic, 1985. Circus

_____. *Clifford Counts Bubbles.* Scholastic, 1992. (Board book) Wind

_____. *Clifford the Firehouse Dog.* Scholastic, 1994. Firefighters

_____. *Clifford, We Love You.* Scholastic, 1994. Love

_____. *Clifford's Animal Sounds.* Scholastic, 1991. (Board book) Farms

_____. *Clifford's Bathtime.* Scholastic, 1991. (Board book) Bath Time

_____. *Clifford's Bedtime.* Scholastic, 1991. (Board book) Bedtime

_____. *Clifford's Family.* Scholastic, 1984. Also in Spanish: *La Familia de Clifford.* Scholastic, 1989. Family

_____. *Clifford's First Christmas.* Scholastic, 1994. December

_____. *Clifford's First Halloween.* Scholastic, 1995. Autumn

_____. *Clifford's Good Deeds.* Scholastic, 1985. Also in Spanish: *Las Buenas Acciones de Clifford.* Trans. by Argentina Palacios. Scholastic, 1989. Helping

_____. *Clifford's Noisy Day.* Scholastic, 1992. (Board book) Sounds

_____. *Clifford's Springtime.* Scholastic, 1994. Spring

_____. *Where Is Clifford? A Lift-the-Flap Book.* Scholastic, 1989. Peek

Briggs, Raymond. *The Snowman Touch & Feel Book.* Random, 1994. (Texture book) Winter

Bright, Robert. *Georgie.* Doubleday, 1944. Also in Spanish: *Jorgito.* Trans. by Argentina Palacios. Scholastic, 1991. Autumn

_____. *My Red Umbrella.* Morrow, 1985. Rain

Brown, Marc. *Two Little Monkeys.* Dutton, 1989. (Board book) Monkeys

Brown, Margaret Wise. *Big Red Barn.* HarperCollins, 1991. Also in Spanish: *El Gran Granero Rojo.* Harper Arco Iris, 1996; and big book format, HarperCollins, 1989. Farms

_____. *Goodnight, Moon.* Illus. by Clement Hurd. Harper, 1947. Also in Spanish: *Buenas Noches, Luna.* Harper Arco Iris, 1995; and pop-up book: *Goodnight Moon Room: A Pop-Up Book.* Harper & Row, 1985. Bedtime

_____. *Little Fireman.* Illus. by Esphyr Slobodkina. HarperCollins, 1952. Firefighters

_____. *Runaway Bunny.* Illus. by Clement Hurd. Harper, 1942. Also in Spanish: *El Conejito Andarín.* Trans. by E. Aida. Harper Arco Iris, 1995. Rabbits

Brown, Ruth. *A Dark, Dark Tale.* Dial, 1981. Also in big book format, Dial, 1991. Autumn

_____. *Ladybug, Ladybug.* Puffin, 1992. Bugs and Caterpillars

_____. *Our Puppy's Vacation.* Dutton, 1987. Summer

_____. *The Picnic.* Dutton, 1993. Picnics

Brown, Tricia. *Hello, Amigos!* Photos by Fran Ortiz. Holt, 1986. Birthdays

Brunhoff, Laurent de. *Babar's Bath Book.* Random, 1992. (Vinyl book) Bath Time

Bunting, Eve. *Flower Garden.* Illus. by Kathryn Hewitt. Harcourt, 1994. Gardens

Burningham, John. *Mr. Gumpy's Outing.* Holt, 1995. Boats

Butler, Dorothy. *My Brown Bear Barney.* Illus. by Elizabeth Fuller. Greenwillow, 1989. Bears

Butterworth, Nick. *Making Faces.* Candlewick, 1993. Feelings

_____. *When It's Time for Bed.* Little, Brown, 1995. (Board book) Bedtime

_____. *When We Play Together.* Little, Brown, 1995. (Board book) Playing

Caines, Jeannette. *Abby.* Illus. by Steven Kellogg. Harper & Row, 1973. Family

_____. *Just Us Women.* Illus. by Pat Cummings. Harper & Row, 1982. Trucks, Cars, and Buses

Campbell, Rod. *Dear Zoo.* Simon & Schuster, 1982. (Lift-the-flap book) Zoos

_____. *Pop-Up Farm Animals.* Simon & Schuster, 1995. Farms

_____. *Pop-Up Garden Friends.* Simon & Schuster, 1993. Gardens

Carle, Eric. *Do You Want to Be My Friend?* Crowell, 1971. Friends

_____. *Have You Seen My Cat?* Simon & Schuster, 1991. Cats

———. *My Apron.* Putnam, 1994. (Book and apron) Helping

———. *My Very First Book of Colors.* Crowell, 1985. Colors

———. *1, 2, 3 to the Zoo.* Putnam, 1990. (Board book) Trains and Planes

———. *The Secret Birthday Message.* Crowell, 1972. Birthdays

———. *The Very Hungry Caterpillar.* Putnam, 1981. Also in French: *La Chenille Affamée.* Putnam, 1992; in Spanish: *La Oruga Muy Hambrienta.* Putnam, 1989; and in Vietnamese: *Chú Sâu Rọm Quá Đói.* Mantra, 1992. Bugs and Caterpillars

———. *The Very Quiet Cricket.* Putnam, 1990. Bugs and Caterpillars

Carter, David. *What's in My Pocket? A Pop-Up & Peek-In Book.* Putnam, 1989. Mealtimes

Carter, Noelle. *Where's My Christmas Stocking? A Lift-and-Touch Book.* Scholastic, 1995. (Texture book) December

———. *Where's My Fuzzy Blanket? A Lift-and-Touch Book.* Scholastic, 1991. (Texture book) Cats

———. *Where's My Squishy Ball? A Lift-and-Touch Book.* Scholastic, 1993. (Texture book) Peek

Cartwright, Stephen, and Claudia Zeff. *Find the Kitten.* Usborne, 1984. (Board book) Cats

———. *Find the Teddy.* Usborne, 1984. (Board book) Peek

Castañeda, Omar. *Abuela's Weave.* Illus. by Enrique O. Sanchez. Lee & Low, 1993. Also in Spanish: *El Tapiz de Abuela.* Trans. by E. Aida. Lee & Low, 1994. Family

Chang, Cindy. *Good Morning, Puppy!* Illus. by Deborah Borgo. Price Stern Sloan, 1994. (Board book) Morning

Chardiet, Bernice. *Come Out, Little Mouse.* Illus. by Jeffrey Dinardo. Puffin, 1994. (Lift-the-flap book) Picnics

———. *I Help Mommy.* Illus. by Pamela Cote. Puffin, 1994. (Lift-the-flap book) Helping

———. *Let's Trim the Tree.* Illus. by Megan Halsey. Puffin, 1994. December

Charles, Donald. *Calico Cat's Year.* Childrens, 1984. Also in Spanish: *El Año del Gato Galano.* Trans. by Lada Kratky. Childrens, 1986. Cats

———. *Count on Calico Cat.* Childrens, 1974. Also in Spanish: *Cuenta con Gato Galano.* Trans. by Lada Kratky. Childrens, 1984. Counting

———. *Ugly Bug.* Dial, 1994. Bugs and Caterpillars

Charlip, Remy. *Handtalk Birthday.* Photos by George Ancona. Simon & Schuster, 1987. Birthdays

Chlad, Dorothy. *When There Is a Fire, Go Outside.* Illus. by Lydia Halverson. Childrens, 1982. Also in Spanish: *Cuando Hay un Incendio Sal para Fuera.* Childrens, 1984. Firefighters

Chocolate, Deborah M. *Kente Colors.* Walker, 1996. December

———. *My First Kwanzaa Book.* Scholastic, 1992. (Board book) December

Christelow, Eileen. *Five Little Monkeys Jumping on the Bed.* Houghton, 1993. Playing

———. *Five Little Monkeys Sitting in a Tree.* Houghton, 1991. Monkeys

———. *Five Little Monkeys with Nothing to Do.* Houghton, 1996. Monkeys

Clark, Emma Chichester. *Catch That Hat!* Little, Brown, 1990. Hats

Clements, Andrew. *Who Owns the Cow?* Houghton, 1995. Farms

Coker, Deborah. *I Like Me.* Western, 1995. My Body

Come to the Circus. Simon & Schuster, 1980. (Board book) Circus

Conteh-Morgan, Jane. *My Family.* Bantam, 1995. (Board book) Family

———. *My Farm.* Bantam, 1995. (Board book) Farms

———. *My Garden.* Bantam, 1995. (Board book) Gardens

———. *My Zoo.* Bantam, 1995. (Board book) Zoos

Cooke, Tom. *I Can Help.* Western, 1994. Helping

Corey, Dorothy. *Will It Ever Be My Birthday?* Illus. by Eileen Christelow. Albert Whitman, 1986. Birthdays

———. *Will There Be a Lap for Me?* Illus. by Nancy Poydar. Albert Whitman, 1992. Love

———. *You Go Away.* Illus. Caroline Rubin and Lois Axeman. Albert Whitman, 1976. Growing Up Safe

Count-a-Round Zoo. Joshua Morris, 1990. (Board book) Zoos

Cousins, Lucy. *Flower in the Garden.* Candlewick, 1992. (Board book) Gardens

———. *Kite in the Park.* Candlewick, 1992. (Board book) Wind

———. *Maisy Goes Swimming.* Little, Brown, 1990. Summer

———. *Maisy Goes to the Playground.* Candlewick, 1992. (Board book) Picnics

———. *Noah's Ark.* Candlewick, 1993. Boats

———. *What Can Rabbit See?* Morrow, 1991. Rabbits

Cowen-Fletcher, Jane. *Mama Zooms.* Scholastic, 1993. Family

Crews, Donald. *Carousel.* Greenwillow, 1982. Circus

_____. *Flying.* Greenwillow, 1986. Trains and Planes

_____. *Freight Train.* Greenwillow, 1978. Also in big book format, Mulberry, 1993. Trains and Planes

_____. *Harbor.* Greenwillow, 1982. Boats

_____. *Parade.* Greenwillow, 1983. Parades

_____. *Sail Away.* Greenwillow, 1995. Boats

_____. *Truck.* Greenwillow, 1980. Trucks, Cars, and Buses

Crimi, Caroline. *Outside, Inside.* Simon & Schuster, 1995. Rain

Dabcovich, Lydia. *Sleepy Bear.* Dutton, 1982. Also in big book format, Dutton, 1993. Bears

Davenport, Zoe. *Mealtimes.* Ticknor & Fields, 1995. Mealtimes

Day, Alexandra. *Good Dog, Carl.* Simon & Schuster, 1991. Dogs

_____. *River Parade.* Puffin, 1992. Parades

De Coteau Orie, Sandra. *Did You Hear the Wind Sing Your Name? An Oneida Song of Spring.* Walker, 1995. Spring

Demarest, Chris L. *My Blue Boat.* Harcourt, 1995. (Board book) Boats

_____. *My Little Red Car.* Boyds Mills, 1992. Trucks, Cars, and Buses

_____. *Ship.* Harcourt, 1995. (Board book) Boats

_____. *Train.* Harcourt, 1996. (Board book) Trains and Planes

Dennis, Wesley. *Flip and the Morning.* Puffin, 1977. Morning

DePaola, Tomie. *Hey Diddle Diddle and Other Mother Goose Rhymes; Print-Braille Edition.* Putnam, 1988. Read to Me

_____. *My First Passover.* Putnam, 1991. Spring

Dijs, Carla. *Are You My Mommy?* Simon & Schuster, 1990. (Pop-up book) Sounds

_____. *Daddy, Would You Love Me If . . .* Simon & Schuster, 1996. (Pop-up book) Love

_____. *How Many Fingers? A Pop-Up Book.* Random, 1994. My Body

_____. *Who Sees You? At the Zoo.* Putnam, 1987. (Pop-up book) Zoos

_____. *Who Sees You? On the Farm.* Putnam, 1987. (Pop-up book) Farms

_____. *Who's Afraid?* Holt, 1996. (Pop-up book) Counting

Dodd, Lynley. *Apple Tree.* Gareth Stevens, 1985. Gardens

_____. *Wake Up, Bear.* Gareth Stevens, 1988. Morning

Dodds, Dayle A. *Color Box.* Illus. by Giles Laroche. Little, Brown, 1992. Monkeys

Dorros, Arthur. *This Is My House.* Scholastic, 1992. Also in Spanish: *Esta Es Mi Casa.* Scholastic, 1995. Homes

Drescher, Henrik. *Yellow Umbrella.* Simon & Schuster, 1987. Monkeys

Dudko, Mary Ann, and Margie Larsen. *Barney's Hats.* Photos by Dennis Full. Barney, 1993. Hats

Dunn, Judy. *Little Kitten.* Photos by Phoebe Dunn. Random, 1983. Cats

Dyer, Jane. *Goldilocks and the Three Bears.* Putnam, 1984. Bears

Eagle, Kin. *It's Raining, It's Pouring.* Whispering Coyote, 1994. Rain

Eastman, P. D. *Big Dog, Little Dog.* Random, 1973. Also in Spanish: *Perro Grande, Perro Pequeño.* Trans. by Pilar de Cuenca and Ines Alvarez. Random, 1982. Sizes and Shapes

Edelman, Elaine. *Boom-De-Boom.* Illus. by Karen Gundersheimer. Pantheon, 1980. Dancing

Ehlert, Lois. *Fish Eyes: A Book You Can Count on.* Harcourt, 1990. Counting

_____. *Growing Vegetable Soup.* Harcourt, 1987. Also in Spanish: *A Sembrar Sopa de Vegetales.* Trans. by Alma Flor Ada and F. Isabel Campoy. Libros Viajeros, 1996; and in big book format, Harcourt, 1987. Gardens

_____. *Red Leaf, Yellow Leaf.* Harcourt, 1991. Autumn

_____. *Snowballs.* Harcourt, 1995. Winter

Elliott, Dan. *A Visit to the Sesame Street Firehouse.* Illus. by Joe Mathieu. Random, 1983. Also in Spanish: *Una Visita a la Estación de Bomberos de Sesame Street.* Trans. by Norma S. Miro and Paola B. Saunders. Random, 1992. Firefighters

Elting, Mary, and Michael Folsom. *Q Is for Duck.* Illus. by Jack Kent. Houghton, 1980. Sounds

Emberley, Ed. *Go Away, Big Green Monster.* Little, Brown, 1993. (Pop-up book) Autumn

Emergency. Dorling Kindersley, 1995. (Board book) Firefighters

Ets, Marie Hall. *Gilberto and the Wind.* Viking, 1963. Also in Spanish: *Gilberto y el Viento.* Trans. by Teresa Mlawer. Lectorum, 1995. Wind

_____. *Play with Me.* Viking, 1955. Playing

Falwell, Cathryn. *Nicky's Walk.* Houghton, 1991. Walking

_____. *We Have a Baby.* Houghton, 1993. Babies

Farm House. Illus. by Zokeisha. Simon & Schuster, 1983. Homes

Fast Rolling Fire Trucks. Illus. by Carolyn Bracken. Grosset, 1984. (Board book) Firefighters

Feelings, Muriel. *Jambo Means Hello: Swahili Alphabet Book.* Illus. by Tom Feelings. Dial, 1985. Friends

Flack, Marjorie. *Ask Mr. Bear.* Simon & Schuster, 1968. Love

Fleming, Denise. *Lunch!* Holt, 1992. Mealtimes

Florian, Douglas. *An Auto Mechanic.* Greenwillow, 1991. Trucks, Cars, and Buses

———. *Summer Day.* Greenwillow, 1988. Summer

———. *Turtle Day.* HarperCollins, 1989. Frogs and Turtles

———. *Winter Day.* Greenwillow, 1987. Winter

Ford, Miela. *Follow the Leader.* Greenwillow, 1996. Parades

———. *Sunflower.* Illus. by Sally Noll. Greenwillow, 1995. Gardens

Fox, Mem. *Zoo Looking.* Mondo, 1996. Zoos

Freeman, Don. *Bearymore.* Viking, 1976. Circus

———. *Corduroy.* Viking, 1968. Also in Spanish: *Corduroy: Edicion Espanola.* Viking, 1988; and in print-Braille edition, National Braille, 1984. Love

———. *Dandelion.* Viking, 1964. Birthdays

———. *Pocket for Corduroy.* Viking, 1978. Also in Spanish: *Un Bolsillo para Corduroy.* Viking, 1992. Getting Dressed

———. *Rainbow of My Own.* Viking, 1966. Rain

Freeman, Lydia. *Corduroy's Day.* Illus. Lisa McCue. Viking, 1985. (Board book) Counting

———. *Corduroy's Party.* Illus. by Lisa McCue. Viking, 1985. (Board book) Birthdays

———. *Corduroy's Toys.* Illus. by Lisa McCue. Viking, 1985. (Board book) Playing

Funakoshi, Canna. *One Morning.* Illus. by Yohji Izawa. Simon & Schuster, 1991. Morning

Gackenbach, Dick. *Claude Has a Picnic.* Houghton, 1993. Picnics

———. *Claude, the Dog.* Houghton, 1979. December

———. *What's Claude Doing?* Houghton, 1986. Growing Up Safe

Galdone, Paul. *Little Red Hen.* Seabury, 1973. Helping

———. *The Three Little Kittens.* Houghton, 1988. Cats

Gallwey, Kay. *Dancing Daisy.* Trafalgar, 1995. Dancing

Garne, S. T. *One White Sail: A Caribbean Counting Book.* Illus. by Lisa Etre. Simon & Schuster, 1992. Counting

Gave, Marc. *Monkey See, Monkey Do.* Illus. by Jacqueline Rogers. Scholastic, 1993. Monkeys

George, Jean Craighead. *Dear Rebecca, Winter Is Here.* HarperCollins, 1993. Winter

Ginsburg, Mirra. *The Chick and the Duckling.* Illus. by Jose Aruego and Ariane Dewey. Simon & Schuster, 1972. Birds

———. *Four Brave Sailors.* Illus. by Lynn Tafuri. Greenwillow, 1987. Boats

———. *Good Morning, Chick.* Illus. by Byron Barton. Greenwillow, 1980. Morning

———. *Mushroom in the Rain.* Illus. by Jose Aruego and Ariane Dewey. Simon & Schuster, 1987. Rain

Gliori, Debi. *Mr. Bear's Picnic.* Western, 1995. Picnics

———. *Snow Lambs.* Scholastic, 1995. Winter

Goennel, Heidi. *Colors.* Little, Brown, 1990. Colors

Gomi, Taro. *Spring Is Here.* Chronicle, 1989. Spring

Gorbaty, Norman. *Fire Engine.* Putnam, 1993. (Board book) Firefighters

———. *Turtle Count.* Simon & Schuster, 1991. Frogs and Turtles

Green, Suzanne. *Little Choo-Choo: Sounds, Sights, and Opposites.* Illus. by Miho Fujita. Doubleday, 1988. Trains and Planes

Greene, Carol. *Hi, Clouds.* Illus. by Gene Sharp. Childrens, 1983. Rain

———. *Ice Is . . . Whee!* Illus. by Paul Sharp. Childrens, 1983. Winter

———. *Please, Wind?* Illus. by Gene Sharp. Childrens, 1982. Wind

Greenfield, Eloise. *Big Friend, Little Friend.* Illus. by Jan Gilchrist. Black Butterfly, 1991. (Board book) Friends

———. *I Make Music.* Illus. by Jan Gilchrist. Black Butterfly, 1991. (Board book) Parades

———. *My Doll Keshia.* Illus. by Jan Gilchrist. Black Butterfly, 1991. (Board book) Playing

———. *On My Horse.* Illus. by Jan Gilchrist. HarperCollins, 1994. Farms

———. *Sweet Baby Coming.* Illus. by Jan Gilchrist. HarperCollins, 1994. Babies

Gretz, Susanna. *Frog in the Middle.* Simon & Schuster, 1991. Frogs and Turtles

Greydanus, Rose. *Big Red Fire Engine.* Illus. by Paul Harvey. Troll, 1980. Also in Spanish: *Un Carro de Bomberos Grande y Rojo.* Troll, 1981. Firefighters

Grindley, Sally. *Shhh! A Lift-the-Flap Book.* Illus. by Peter Utton. Little, Brown, 1992. Sounds

Gundersheimer, Karen. *Splish Splash, Bang Crash!* Scholastic, 1995. Sounds

Guthrie, Arlo. *Mooses Come Walking.* Illus. by Alice Brock. Chronicle, 1995. Walking

Guy, Ginger Foglesong. *Black Crow, Black Crow.* Illus. by Nancy Winslow Parker. Greenwillow, 1991. Birds

Hague, Kathleen. *Numbears: A Counting Book.* Holt, 1986. Bears

Hale, Sarah J. *Mary Had a Little Lamb.* Illus. by Bruce McMillan. Scholastic, 1990. Farms

_____. *Mary Had a Little Lamb.* Illus. by Tomie DePaola. Holiday, 1984. Read to Me

Hall, Kirsten. *At the Carnival.* Scholastic, 1996. Circus

Hall, Zoe. *It's Pumpkin Time!* Illus. by Shari Halpern. Scholastic, 1994. Autumn

Halpern, Shari. *Moving from One to Ten.* Simon & Schuster, 1993. Homes

Hamsa, Bobbie. *Dirty Larry.* Childrens, 1983. Bath Time

Hanna, Jack. *Petting Zoo.* Doubleday, 1992. (Texture book) Zoos

Harper, Isabelle. *My Cats, Nick & Nora.* Illus. by Barry Moser. Scholastic, 1995. Cats

_____. *My Dog Rosie.* Illus. by Barry Moser. Scholastic, 1994. Dogs

Harrison, David. *Wake Up! Sun!* Illus. by Hans Wilhelm. Random, 1986. Morning

Haseley, Dennis. *Kite Flier.* Illus. by David Wiesner. Simon & Schuster, 1993. Wind

Havill, Juanita. *Jamaica and Brianna.* Illus. by Anne S. O'Brien. Houghton, 1993. Getting Dressed

Hawkins, Colin, and Jacqui Hawkins. *I Know an Old Lady Who Swallowed a Fly.* Putnam, 1987. Mealtimes

Hayes, Sarah. *Eat Up, Gemma.* Illus. by Jan Ormerod. Lothrop, 1988. Growing Up Safe

_____. *Happy Christmas, Gemma.* Illus. by Jan Ormerod. Lothrop, 1986. December

_____. *Stamp Your Feet.* Illus. by Jan Ormerod. Lothrop, 1988. Dancing

_____. *This Is the Bear.* Illus. by Helen Craig. Candlewick, 1993. Bears

_____. *This Is the Bear and the Scary Night.* Illus. by Helen Craig. Little, Brown, 1992. Feelings

Hazen, Barbara Shook. *Goodbye Hello.* Simon & Schuster, 1994. Also in Spanish: *Adiós! Hola!* Simon & Schuster, 1994. Friends

Hendrickson, Karen. *Baby and I Can Play Together.* Parents, 1990. Babies

Henley, Claire. *At the Zoo.* Hyperion, 1992. Zoos

_____. *Dinnertime.* Putnam, 1994. (Board book) Mealtimes

_____. *In the Ocean.* Hyperion, 1992. Summer

_____. *Joe's Pool.* Hyperion, 1994. Summer

_____. *Playtime.* Putnam, 1994. (Board book) Playing

Hennessy, B. G. *A, B, C, D, Tummy, Toes, Hands, Knees.* Illus. by Wendy Watson. Viking, 1989. My Body

_____. *Corduroy's Christmas: A Lift-the-Flap Book.* Illus. by Lisa McCue. Viking, 1992. December

_____. *Corduroy's Halloween: A Lift-the-Flap Book.* Illus. by Lisa McCue. Viking, 1995. Autumn

Herman, Gail. *What a Hungry Puppy!* Illus. by Norman Gorbaty. Putnam, 1993. Dogs

Hest, Amy. *In the Rain with Baby Duck.* Candlewick, 1995. Rain

Hill, Eric. *Spot At Play.* Putnam, 1985. Playing

_____. *Spot Counts 1 to 10.* Putnam, 1989. (Board book) Counting

_____. *Spot Goes Splash!* Putnam, 1984. Bath Time

_____. *Spot Goes to a Party.* Putnam, 1992. Also in Spanish: *Spot Va a una Fiesta.* Putnam, 1995. Birthdays

_____. *Spot Goes to the Beach.* Putnam, 1985. Summer

_____. *Spot Goes to the Circus.* Putnam, 1986. Also in Spanish: *Spot Va al Circo.* Putnam, 1986. Circus

_____. *Spot Goes to the Farm.* Putnam, 1987. Also in Spanish: *Spot Va a la Granja.* Putnam, 1987. Farms

_____. *Spot Goes to the Park.* Putnam, 1991. Also in Spanish: *Spot Va al Parque.* Putnam, 1993. Picnics

_____. *Spot in the Garden.* Putnam, 1991. (Board book) Gardens

_____. *Spot Looks at Colors.* Putnam, 1986. (Board book) Also in Spanish: *Spot Mira los Colores.* Putnam, 1995. Colors

_____. *Spot Looks at Shapes.* Putnam, 1986. (Board book) Sizes and Shapes

_____. *Spot Visits His Grandparents.* Putnam, 1996. Family

_____. *Spot's First Christmas.* Putnam, 1983. Also in Spanish: *La Primera Navidad de Spot.* Putnam, 1984. December

_____. *Spot's First Easter.* Putnam, 1988. Spring

_____. *Spot's First Picnic.* Putnam, 1987. Picnics

_____. *Spot's Friends.* Putnam, 1984. Friends

_____. *Spot's Walk in the Woods.* Putnam, 1993. Also in Spanish: *Spot Pasease por el Bosque.* Putnam, 1994. Walking

_____. *Sweet Dreams, Spot!* Putnam, 1984. Bedtime

_____. *Where's Spot?* Putnam, 1980. Also in Spanish: *Dónde Está Spot?* Putnam, 1983. Dogs

Hines, Anna Grossnickle. *Big Help.* Houghton, 1989. Helping

——. *Big Like Me.* Greenwillow, 1989. Growing Up Safe

——. *Gramma's Walk.* Greenwillow, 1993. Walking

Hoban, Julia. *Amy Loves the Rain.* Illus. by Lillian Hoban. Harper, 1988. Rain

——. *Amy Loves the Snow.* Illus. by Lillian Hoban. Harper, 1988. Winter

——. *Amy Loves the Sun.* Illus. by Lillian Hoban. Harper, 1988. Summer

——. *Amy Loves the Wind.* Illus. by Lillian Hoban. Harper, 1988. Wind

Hoban, Tana. *Dig, Drill, Dump, Fill.* Greenwillow, 1975. Trucks, Cars, and Buses

——. *I Walk and Read.* Greenwillow, 1984. Walking

——. *One Little Kitten.* Greenwillow, 1979. Cats

——. *Red, Blue, Yellow Shoe.* Greenwillow, 1986. Getting Dressed

——. *Shapes, Shapes, Shapes.* Greenwillow, 1986. Sizes and Shapes

——. *Where Is It?* Simon & Schuster, 1974. Rabbits

Holtzenthaler, Jean. *My Hands Can.* Illus. by Nancy Tafuri. Dutton, 1978. My Body

Hopkins, Margo. *Honey Rabbit.* Illus. by Cyndy Szekeres. Western, 1982. Spring

Hudson, Cheryl Willis. *AfroBets 1 2 3.* Just Us, 1988. Counting

——. *Bright Eyes, Brown Skin.* Illus. by George Ford. Just Us, 1990. My Body

——. *Good Morning, Baby.* Scholastic, 1992. (Board book) Morning

——. *Good Night, Baby.* Scholastic, 1992. (Board book) Babies

Hughes, Shirley. *All Shapes and Sizes.* Lothrop, 1986. Sizes and Shapes

——. *Two Shoes, New Shoes.* Lothrop, 1986. Getting Dressed

Hutchings, Tony. *Fluffy Little Duckling.* Sandvik, 1992. (Board book) Birds

Hutchins, Pat. *The Doorbell Rang.* Greenwillow, 1986. Also in Spanish: *Llaman a la Puerta.* Morrow, 1994. Friends

——. *Good-Night, Owl!* Simon & Schuster, 1972. Birds

——. *Happy Birthday, Sam.* Greenwillow, 1978. Birthdays

——. *Rosie's Walk.* Simon & Schuster, 1968. Also in big book format, Scholastic, 1987. Birds

——. *Tidy Titch.* Greenwillow, 1991. Helping

——. *Titch.* Simon & Schuster, 1971. Sizes and Shapes

——. *Titch & Daisy.* Greenwillow, 1996. Friends

——. *Where's the Baby?* Greenwillow, 1988. Babies

——. *The Wind Blew.* Simon & Schuster, 1974. Wind

——. *You'll Soon Grow into Them, Titch.* Greenwillow, 1983. Getting Dressed

Imai, Miko. *Sebastian's Trumpet.* Candlewick, 1995. Growing Up Safe

Inkpen, Mick. *Wibbly Pig Can Dance!* Western, 1995. Dancing

Isadora, Rachel. *I Hear.* Greenwillow, 1985. Sounds

——. *I See.* Greenwillow, 1985. My Body

Jackson, Ellen. *Brown Cow, Green Grass, Yellow Mellow Sun.* Illus. by Victoria Raymond. Hyperion, 1995. Colors

Jakob, Donna. *My New Sandbox.* Illus. by Julia Gorton. Hyperion, 1996. Playing

Janovitz, Marilyn. *Hickory Dickory Dock.* Hyperion, 1991. Read to Me

——. *Look Out, Bird!* North-South, 1994. Birds

Jensen, Virginia. *Catching: A Book for Blind and Sighted Children with Pictures to Feel as Well as to See.* Putnam, 1984. (Texture book) Sizes and Shapes

Johnson, Angela. *Joshua by the Sea.* Illus. by Rhonda Mitchell. Orchard, 1994. (Board book) Summer

——. *Joshua's Night Whispers.* Illus. by Rhonda Mitchell. Orchard, 1994. (Board book) Bedtime

——. *Mama Bird, Baby Bird.* Illus. by Rhonda Mitchell. Orchard, 1994. (Board book) Birds

——. *One of Three.* Illus. by David Soman. Orchard, 1991. Family

——. *Rain Feet.* Orchard, 1994. Rain

Johnson, Audean. *Soft as a Kitten.* Random, 1982. (Texture book) Cats

Jonas, Ann. *Color Dance.* Greenwillow, 1989. Dancing

——. *Holes and Peeks.* Greenwillow, 1984. Peek

——. *Splash!* Greenwillow, 1995. Counting

——. *Trek.* Greenwillow, 1985. Also in Spanish: *El Trayecto.* Lectorum, 1991. Walking

Kachenmeister, Cherryl. *On Monday When It Rained.* Photos by Tom Berthiaume. Houghton, 1989. Feelings

Kalan, Robert. *Blue Sea.* Illus. by Donald Crews. Greenwillow, 1979. Sizes and Shapes

——. *Jump, Frog, Jump.* Illus. by Byron Barton. Greenwillow, 1981. Also in Spanish: *Salta, Ranita, Salta.* Morrow, 1995. Frogs and Turtles

_____. *Moving Day.* Illus. by Yossi Abolafia. Greenwillow, 1996. Homes

_____. *Rain.* Illus. by Donald Crews. Greenwillow, 1978. Rain

Katz, Avner. *Tortoise Solves a Problem.* HarperCollins, 1993. Frogs and Turtles

Keats, Ezra Jack. *Jennie's Hat.* Harper, 1966. Hats

_____. *Kitten for a Day.* Simon & Schuster, 1984. Cats

_____. *Peter's Chair.* Harper & Row, 1967. Also in Spanish: *La Silla de Pedro.* Trans. by Maria Fiol. Harper Arco Iris, 1996; and in big book format, HarperCollins, 1993. Babies

_____. *Snowy Day.* Viking, 1962. Also in Spanish: *Un Dia de Nieve.* Viking, 1991. Winter

Keller, Holly. *Geraldine's Baby Brother.* Greenwillow, 1994. Babies

Kemp, Moira. *Baa, Baa, Black Sheep.* Dutton, 1991. (Board book) Read to Me

Kent, Jack. *Caterpillar & the Polliwog.* Simon & Schuster, 1982. Frogs and Turtles

_____. *Round Robin.* Simon & Schuster, 1989. Birds

Killingback, Julia. *Busy Bears' at the Fire Station.* Oxford Univ. Pr., 1988. Firefighters

Killion, Bette. *The Same Wind.* HarperCollins, 1992. Wind

Kitamura, Satoshi. *Lily Takes a Walk.* Puffin, 1991. Walking

Koch, Michelle. *Hoot, Howl, Hiss.* Greenwillow, 1991. Sounds

Kowalczyk, Carolyn. *Purple Is a Part of a Rainbow.* Illus. by Gene Sharp. Childrens, 1985. Also in Spanish: *El Morado es Parte del Arco Iris.* Childrens, 1988. Colors

Krasilovsky, Phyllis. *The Very Little Girl.* Scholastic, 1992. Growing Up Safe

Kraus, Robert. *Milton, the Early Riser.* Simon & Schuster, 1987. Morning

Krauss, Ruth. *The Carrot Seed.* Illus. by Crockett Johnson. Harper, 1945. Gardens

Kroll, Virginia. *Jaha & Jamil Went Down the Hill: An African Mother Goose.* Illus. by Katherine Roundtree. Charlesbridge, 1994. Read to Me

Kunhardt, Edith. *The Airplane Book.* Illus. by Carolyn Bracken. Western, 1987. Trains and Planes

_____. *Danny and the Easter Egg.* Greenwillow, 1989. Spring

_____. *Pat the Cat.* Western, 1984. (Texture book) Cats

_____. *Pat the Puppy.* Western, 1993. (Texture book) Dogs

Kuskin, Karla. *James and the Rain.* Childrens, 1995. Rain

Kvasnosky, Laura McGee. *Pink, Red, Blue, What Are You?* Dutton, 1994. (Board book) Colors

Lancome, Julie. *Walking through the Jungle.* Candlewick, 1993. Walking

Langstaff, John. *Over in the Meadow.* Illus. by Feodor Rojankovsky. Harcourt, 1957. Counting

Lapsley, Susan. *I Am Adopted.* Bradbury, 1977. Babies

Leemis, Ralph. *Mister Momboo's Hat.* Illus. by Jeni Bassett. Dutton, 1991. Hats

Leonard, Marcia. *Taking a Bath.* Bantam, 1988. Bath Time

Lester, Alison. *I'm Green and I'm Grumpy.* Puffin, 1993. Feelings

Levine, Abby. *You Push, I Ride.* Illus. by Margot Apple. Albert Whitman, 1989. Playing

Lewin, Hugh. *Jafta.* Illus. by Lisa Kopper. Carolrhoda, 1983. Feelings

_____. *Jafta's Father.* Illus. Lisa Kopper. Carolrhoda, 1983. Family

Lewison, Wendy Cheyette. *"Buzz" Said the Bee.* Illus. by Hans Wilhelm. Scholastic, 1992. Sounds

_____. *Christmas Cookies.* Illus. by Mary Morgan. Putnam, 1993. December

_____. *Don't Wake the Baby.* Illus. by Jerry Smath. Putnam, 1996. Babies

_____. *First Snow!* Illus. by Maryann Cocca-Leffler. Putnam, 1994. Winter

_____. *Going to Sleep on the Farm.* Illus. by Juan Wijngaard. Dial, 1992. Farms

_____. *Happy Thanksgiving!* Illus. by Mary Morgan. Putnam, 1993. Mealtimes

Lillegard, Dee. *Sitting in My Box.* Illus. by Jon Agee. Dutton, 1989. Friends

_____. *Where Is It?* Illus. by Gene Sharp. Childrens, 1984. Peek

Lillie, Patricia. *When the Rooster Crowed.* Illus. by Nancy Winslow Parker. Greenwillow, 1991. Morning

Lindgren, Barbro. *Sam's Ball.* Illus. by Eva Eriksson. Morrow, 1983. Playing

_____. *Sam's Bath.* Illus. by Eva Eriksson. Morrow, 1983. Bath Time

_____. *Sam's Car.* Illus. by Eva Eriksson. Morrow, 1982. Friends

_____. *Sam's Cookie.* Illus. by Eva Eriksson. Morrow, 1982. Mealtimes

_____. *Sam's Potty.* Illus. by Eva Eriksson. Morrow, 1986. Growing Up Safe

———. *Sam's Wagon.* Illus. by Eva Eriksson. Morrow, 1986. Dogs

Lionni, Leo. *Inch by Inch.* Astor-Honor, 1962. Bugs and Caterpillars

Lipson, Michael. *How the Wind Plays.* Hyperion, 1994. Wind

Little, Karen E. *Monkey Match.* Moonlight Pr., 1981. Monkeys

Little, Lessie Jones, and Eloise Greenfield. *I Can Do It by Myself.* Illus. by Carole Byard. Crowell, 1978. Birthdays

Little Robin Redbreast: A Mother Goose Rhyme. Illus. by Shari Halpern. North-South, 1994. Birds

Lodge, Jo. *If You're Happy and You Know It.* Barron, 1996. Feelings

———. *This Is the Way We Make a Face.* Random, 1996. Feelings

Lunn, Carolyn. *Bobby's Zoo.* Illus. by Tom Dunnington. Childrens, 1989. Zoos

Lynn, Sara. *Clothes.* Simon & Schuster, 1986. (Board book) Getting Dressed

Macauley, Craig. *Ten Men on a Ladder.* Firefly, 1996. Firefighters

McBratney, Sam. *Guess How Much I Love You.* Illus. by Anita Jeram. Candlewick, 1995. (Board book) Love

Maccarone, Grace. *Pizza Party.* Scholastic, 1994. Helping

MacCarthy, Patricia. *Ocean Parade: A Counting Book.* Dial, 1990. Parades

McCloskey, Robert. *Blueberries for Sal.* Viking, 1948. Bears

McCue, Lisa. *Bunnies Love.* Random, 1991. Rabbits

———. *Corduroy Goes to the Doctor.* Viking, 1987. Growing Up Safe

———. *Corduroy on the Go.* Viking, 1987. Trucks, Cars, and Buses

———. *Kittens Love.* Random, 1990. Cats

———. *Puppies Love.* Random, 1990. Dogs

McDonnell, Flora. *I Love Boats.* Candlewick, 1995. Boats

Mack, Stanley. *Ten Bears in My Bed: A Goodnight Countdown.* Pantheon, 1974. Bears

MacKinnon, Debbie. *Things to Wear.* Photos by Geoff Dann. Bantam, 1994. (Board book) Getting Dressed

McKissack, Patricia. *Little Red Hen.* Illus. by Dennis Hockerman. Childrens, 1985. Also in Spanish: *La Gallinita Roja.* Childrens, 1986. Read to Me

———. *Who Is Coming?* Illus. by Clovis Martin. Childrens, 1990. Monkeys

McKissack, Patricia, and Frederick McKissack. *Country Mouse and City Mouse.* Illus. by Anne Sikorski. Childrens, 1985. Read to Me

McMillan, Bruce. *Growing Colors.* Lothrop, 1988. Gardens

———. *Here a Chick, There a Chick.* Lothrop, 1983. Birds

———. *Step by Step.* Lothrop, 1987. Growing Up Safe

McMillan, Naomi. *Baby's Colors.* Western, 1995. (Board book) Colors

McNaughton, Colin, and Elizabeth Attenborough. *Walk Rabbit Walk.* Morrow, 1992. Rabbits

McPartland, Suzy. *Good Morning, Sun.* Illus. by William Neeper. Simon & Schuster, 1994. (Pop-up book) Morning

———. *Zoom, Car, Zoom.* Illus. by William Neeper. Simon & Schuster, 1994. (Board book) Trucks, Cars, and Buses

McPhail, David. *Farm Morning.* Harcourt, 1991. Farms

———. *Pig, Pig Grows Up.* Dutton, 1980. Growing Up Safe

———. *Pig, Pig Rides.* Dutton, 1985. Playing

Maestro, Betsy. *Big City Port.* Illus. by Giulio Maestro. Scholastic, 1984. Boats

———. *Ferryboat.* Illus. by Giulio Maestro. HarperCollins, 1986. Boats

Manushkin, Fran. *Be Brave Baby Rabbit.* Illus. by Diane de Groat. Crown, 1990. Autumn

———. *Peeping and Sleeping.* Illus. by Jennifer Plecas. Houghton, 1994. Frogs and Turtles

Maris, Ron. *Are You There, Bear?* Greenwillow, 1985. Bears

———. *Frogs Jump.* Candlewick, 1992. Frogs and Turtles

———. *Is Anyone Home?* Greenwillow, 1986. Homes

———. *My Book.* Puffin, 1986. Read to Me

Martin, Bill. *Brown Bear, Brown Bear, What Do You See?* Illus. by Eric Carle. Holt, 1992. Also in print-Braille edition, National Braille, 1992. Colors

———. *Polar Bear, Polar Bear, What Do You Hear?* Illus. by Eric Carle. Holt, 1991. Also in print-Braille edition, National Braille, 1991. Sounds

———. *Up & Down on the Merry-Go-Round.* Illus. by Ted Rand. Holt, 1988. Circus

Martin, Bill, and John Archambault. *Here Are My Hands.* Illus. by Ted Rand. Holt, 1985. My Body

———. *Listen to the Rain.* Illus. by James Endicott. Holt, 1988. Rain

Martin, David. *Little Chicken Chicken.* Candlewick, 1996. Circus

Marzollo, Jean. *I Am Water.* Illus. by Judith Moffatt. Scholastic, 1996. Bath Time

———. *Ten Cats Have Hats: A Counting Book.* Illus. by David McPhail. Scholastic, 1994. Hats

Masurel, Claire. *Good Night!* Illus. by Marie H. Henry. Chronicle, 1994. Bedtime

Matthias, Catherine. *Too Many Balloons.* Illus. by Gene Sharp. Childrens, 1982. Also in Spanish: *Demasiados Globos.* Childrens, 1990. Wind

Mayer, Mercer. *Just a Nap.* Western, 1989. Bedtime

_____. *Just a Rainy Day.* Western, 1990. Rain

_____. *Just a Snowy Day.* Western, 1983. (Texture book) Winter

_____. *Just for You.* Western, 1975. Love

_____. *The New Baby.* Western, 1985. Also in Spanish: *El Nuevo Bibi.* Western, 1994. Babies

Melmed, Laura Krauss. *I Love You as Much . . .* Illus. by Henri Sorensen. Lothrop, 1993. Love

Milios, Rita. *Bears, Bears Everywhere.* Illus. by Tom Dunnington. Childrens, 1988. Also in Spanish: *Osos, Osos, Aqui y Alli.* Childrens, 1989. Bears

Miller, J. P. *Good Night, Little Rabbit.* Random, 1986. (Board book) Rabbits

Miller, Margaret. *Where Does It Go?* Greenwillow, 1992. Parades

_____. *Whose Hat?* Greenwillow, 1988. Hats

_____. *Whose Shoe?* Greenwillow, 1991. Getting Dressed

Milne, A. A. *Pooh and Some Bees.* Illus. by Robert Cremins. Dutton, 1987. Bugs and Caterpillars

Min, Laura. *Mrs. Sato's Hens.* Goodyear, 1994. Spring

Moncure, Jane Belk. *Away Went the Farmer's Hat.* Illus. by Linda Hohag. Child's World, 1987. Wind

_____. *Happy Birthday, Word Bird.* Illus. by Linda Hohag. Child's World, 1983. Birthdays

_____. *Hi, Word Bird.* Illus. by Linda Hohag. Child's World, 1981. Friends

_____. *Hide and Seek Word Bird.* Illus. by Linda Hohag. Child's World, 1982. Peek

_____. *Stop! Go! Word Bird.* Illus. by Linda Hohag. Child's World, 1981. Trucks, Cars, and Buses

_____. *What Do You Say When a Monkey Acts This Way?* Illus. by Terri Super. Child's World, 1987. Monkeys

_____. *Word Bird's Christmas Words.* Illus. by Vera Gohman. Child's World, 1987. December

_____. *Word Bird's Circus Surprise.* Illus. by Linda Hohag. Child's World, 1981. Circus

_____. *Word Bird's Halloween Words.* Illus. by Vera Gohman. Child's World, 1987. Autumn

_____. *Word Bird's Hats.* Illus. by Vera Gohman. Child's World, 1982. Hats

_____. *Word Bird's Rainy-Day Dance.* Illus. by Linda Hohag. Child's World, 1990. Dancing

_____. *Word Bird's Shapes.* Illus. by Linda Hohag. Child's World, 1983. Sizes and Shapes

_____. *Word Bird's Spring Words.* Illus. by Vera Gohman. Child's World, 1985. Spring

_____. *Word Bird's Summer Words.* Illus. by Ric Miracle. Child's World, 1985. Summer

_____. *Word Bird's Thanksgiving Words.* Illus. by Linda Hohag. Child's World, 1987. Mealtimes

_____. *Word Bird's Valentine Day Words.* Illus. by Sue Fullam. Child's World, 1987. Love

_____. *Word Bird's Winter Words.* Illus. by Vera Gohman. Childs' World, 1985. Winter

Moore, Elaine. *Roly Poly Puppies.* Scholastic, 1996. Dogs

Moroney, Tracey. *Humpty Dumpty.* Wishing Well, 1994. (Board book) Read to Me

Morris, Ann. *Hats, Hats, Hats.* Illus. by Ken Heyman. Lothrop, 1989. Hats

_____. *Houses & Homes.* Illus. by Ken Heyman. Lothrop, 1992. Homes

_____. *Shoes, Shoes, Shoes.* Lothrop, 1995. Getting Dressed

Morris, Jackie. *Bears, Bears, and More Bears.* Barron, 1995. Bears

Moses, Amy. *I Am an Explorer.* Illus. by Richard Hackney. Childrens, 1990. Playing

Mother Goose Rhymes: Print-Braille Edition. Illus. by Lillian Obligado. Golden Press, 1991. Read to Me

My First Look at Home. Dorling Kindersley, 1990. (Board book) Homes

My First Look at Sizes. Photos by Steven Oliver. Random, 1990. Sizes and Shapes

My First Look at Sorting. Dorling Kindersley, 1990. (Board book) Helping

Neasi, Barbara J. *Just Like Me.* Illus. by Lois Axeman. Childrens, 1984. Also in Spanish: *Igual Que Yo.* Childrens, 1988. Friends

_____. *Listen to Me.* Illus. by Gene Sharp. Childrens, 1986. Also in Spanish: *Escúchame.* Childrens, 1988. Sounds

Newth, Philip. *Roly Goes Exploring: A Book for Blind and Sighted Children.* Philomel, 1977. Sizes and Shapes

Nicklaus, Carol. *Come Dance with Me.* Silver Burdett, 1991. Dancing

Nodset, Joan L. *Who Took the Farmer's Hat?* Illus. by Fritz Siebel. Harper, 1963. Hats

Noll, Sally. *Jiggle, Wiggle, Prance.* Greenwillow, 1987. Dancing

_____. *Lucky Morning.* Greenwillow, 1994. Morning

Numeroff, Laura. *If You Give a Mouse a Cookie.* Illus. by Felicia Bond. Harper & Row, 1985. Also in Spanish: *Si le Das Una Galletita a un Ratón.* Harper Arco Iris, 1995; and in big book format, Scholastic, 1989. Friends

Oppenheim, Joanne. *Do You Like Cats?* Illus. by Carol Newsom. Bantam, 1993. Cats

———. *Wake Up, Baby!* Illus. by Lynn Sweat. Bantam, 1990. Morning

Ormerod, Jan. *Messy Baby.* Lothrop, 1985. Bath Time

———. *Our Ollie.* Lothrop, 1986. My Body

———. *Reading.* Lothrop, 1985. Read to Me

———. *Sunshine.* Morrow, 1990. Summer

———. *To Baby with Love.* Lothrop, 1994. Love

———. *When We Went to the Zoo.* Lothrop, 1991. Zoos

Owen, Annie. *Wake Up, Frog!* Kingfisher, 1994. (Board book) Frogs and Turtles

Oxenbury, Helen. *All Fall Down!* Simon & Schuster, 1987. Playing

———. *Beach Day.* Dial, 1991. (Board book) Summer

———. *Birthday Party.* Puffin, 1993. Birthdays

———. *The Car Trip.* Dial, 1983. Trucks, Cars, and Buses

———. *The Checkup.* Puffin, 1994. Growing Up Safe

———. *Dancing Class.* Puffin, 1993. Dancing

———. *Dressing.* Simon & Schuster, 1981. (Board book) Getting Dressed

———. *Eating Out.* Puffin, 1994. Mealtimes

———. *Friends.* Simon & Schuster, 1981. Friends

———. *Grandma & Grandpa.* Puffin, 1993. Family

———. *I Hear.* 2d ed. Candlewick, 1995. My Body

———. *I Touch.* Candlewick, 1995. (Board book) My Body

———. *Mother's Helper.* Dial, 1991. Helping

———. *Our Dog.* Puffin, 1994. Dogs

———. *Playing.* Simon & Schuster, 1981. Playing

———. *Tom & Pippo and the Dog.* Simon & Schuster, 1989. (Board book) Picnics

———. *Tom & Pippo and the Washing Machine.* Simon & Schuster, 1988. Helping

———. *Tom & Pippo Go for a Walk.* Simon & Schuster, 1988. Walking

———. *Tom & Pippo in the Garden.* Simon & Schuster, 1989. (Board book) Gardens

———. *Tom & Pippo in the Snow.* Simon & Schuster, 1989. Winter

———. *Tom & Pippo Make a Friend.* Simon & Schuster, 1989. (Board book) Friends

———. *Tom & Pippo on the Beach.* Candlewick, 1993. Summer

———. *Tom & Pippo Read a Story.* Simon & Schuster, 1988. Read to Me

———. *Tom & Pippo's Day.* Simon & Schuster, 1989. (Board book) Monkeys

Packard, Mary. *I'm a Firefighter.* Illus. by Julie Durrell. Scholastic, 1995. Firefighters

———. *My Messy Room.* Scholastic, 1993. Helping

Parent, Nancy. *Oh, Bother! It's the Easter Bunny.* Illus. by Ed Murietta and Adam Devaney. Disney, 1997. (Board book) Spring

Paschkis, Julie. *So Happy, So Sad.* Holt, 1995. Feelings

Patrick, Denise Lewis. *No Diapers for Baby.* Western, 1995. (Board book) Growing Up Safe

———. *Peekaboo Baby!* Western, 1995. (Board book) Peek

———. *Red Dancing Shoes.* Illus. by James Ransome. Morrow, 1993. Dancing

———. *What Does Baby See?* Western, 1990. (Board book) Babies

Peek, Merle. *Mary Wore Her Red Dress and Henry Wore His Green Sneakers.* Houghton, 1985. Birthdays

Peek-a-Bug. Illus. by Jerry Smath. Random, 1990. (Board book) Bugs

Pegram, Laura. *Rainbow Is Our Face.* Black Butterfly, 1994. My Body

———. *Windy Day.* Black Butterfly, 1994. Wind

Peters, Sharon. *Stop That Rabbit.* Illus. by Don Silverstein. Troll, 1980. Rabbits

Petersham, Maud, and Miska Petersham. *Box with Red Wheels.* Simon & Schuster, 1986. Peek

———. *Circus Baby.* Simon & Schuster, 1968. Circus

Petrie, Catherine. *Joshua James Likes Trucks.* Illus. by Jerry Warshaw. Childrens, 1982. Also in Spanish: *A Pedro Perez le Gustan los Camiones.* Childrens, 1988. Trucks, Cars, and Buses

Pfloog, Jan. *The Kitten Book.* Western, 1968. Cats

———. *The Puppy Book.* Western, 1968. Dogs

———. *The Zoo Book.* Western, 1989. Zoos

Phillips, Joan. *My New Boy.* Illus. by Lynn Munsinger. Random, 1986. Dogs

Pienkowski, Jan. *Faces.* Simon & Schuster, 1991. (Board book) My Body

———. *Food.* Simon & Schuster, 1991. (Board book) Mealtimes

———. *Homes.* Simon & Schuster, 1990. (Board book) Homes

_____. *Oh My, a Fly!* Price Stern Sloan, 1989. (Pop-up book) Bugs and Caterpillars

_____. *Shapes.* Simon & Schuster, 1989. (Board book) Sizes and Shapes

_____. *Sizes.* Simon & Schuster, 1991. (Board book) Sizes and Shapes

_____. *Zoo.* Simon & Schuster, 1990. (Board book) Zoos

Piper, Watty. *The Little Engine That Could.* Illus. by George and Doris Hauman. Platt, 1961. Also: *Fast Rolling Little Engine That Could.* Putnam, 1985; Board book, Putnam, 1991; and Pop-up book, Putnam, 1984. Trains and Planes

Pocock, Rita. *Annabell and the Big Slide.* Harcourt, 1989. Picnics

Polushkin, Maria. *Who Said Meow?* Illus. by Ellen Weiss. Simon & Schuster, 1988. Dogs

Pomerantz, Charlotte. *How Many Trucks Can a Tow Truck Tow?* Illus. by R. W. Alley. Random, 1987. Trucks, Cars, and Buses

_____. *Where's the Bear?* Illus. by Byron Barton. Greenwillow, 1984. Bears

Porter-Gaylord, Laurel. *I Love My Mommy Because . . .* Illus. by Ashley Wolff. Dutton, 1991. Family

Potter, Beatrix. *Meet Peter Rabbit.* Warne, 1986. (Board book) Read to Me

Preller, James. *Wake Me in the Spring.* Illus. by Jeffrey Scherer. Scholastic, 1994. Spring

Preston, Edna Mitchell. *One Dark Night.* Illus. by Kurt Werth. Viking, 1969. Autumn

Price, Mathew. *Do You See What I See?* Illus. by Sue Porter. Harper, 1986. Circus

Radlauer, Ruth. *Molly.* Simon & Schuster, 1991. Growing Up Safe

_____. *Molly at the Library.* Simon & Schuster, 1991. Read to Me

_____. *Molly Goes Hiking.* Simon & Schuster, 1987. Walking

Raffi. *Like Me and You.* Crown, 1994. My Body

_____. *Shake My Sillies out.* Illus. by David Allender. Crown, 1988. Feelings

_____. *Spider on the Floor.* Illus. by True Kelley. Crown, 1993. Bugs and Caterpillars

Rathman, Peggy. *Goodnight Gorilla.* Putnam, 1994. Zoos

Reasoner, Charles. *Who Drives This?* Price Stern Sloan, 1996. (Slide-out board book) Trucks, Cars, and Buses

_____. *Who's Hatching?* Price Stern Sloan, 1994. (Slide-out board book) Spring

_____. *Who's There?* Price Stern Sloan, 1993. (Slide-out board book) Peek

_____. *Whose House Is This?* Price Stern Sloan, 1995. (Slide-out board book) Homes

_____. *Whose Mommy Is This?* Price Stern Sloan, 1994. (Slide-out board book) Family

Regan, Dian Curtis. *Daddies.* Scholastic, 1996. Family

Rey, H. A. *Curious George.* Houghton, 1941, 1994. Also in Spanish: *Jorge el Curioso,* Houghton, 1961; and in big book format, Houghton, 1994. Monkeys

_____. *Where's My Baby?* Houghton, 1943. (Lift-the-flap book) Babies

Rice, Eve. *Sam, Who Never Forgets.* Greenwillow, 1977. Zoos

_____. *Swim.* Greenwillow, 1996. Summer

_____. *What Sadie Sang.* Greenwillow, 1983. Feelings

Richardson, John. *Bedtime.* Simon & Schuster, 1994. (Board book) Bedtime

Roberts, Bethany. *Cat Parade!* Illus. by Diane Greenseid. Houghton, 1995. Parades

Rockwell, Anne F. *Apples and Pumpkins.* Simon & Schuster, 1989. Gardens

_____. *At the Beach.* Illus. by Harlow Rockwell. Simon & Schuster, 1987. Summer

_____. *Boats.* Puffin, 1993. Boats

_____. *Cars.* Dutton, 1984. Trucks, Cars, and Buses

_____. *Fire Engines.* Dutton, 1986. Firefighters

_____. *Hugo at the Park.* Simon & Schuster, 1990. Picnics

_____. *My Spring Robin.* Illus. by Harlow & Lizzy Rockwell. Simon & Schuster, 1989. Spring

_____. *No! No! No!* Simon & Schuster, 1995. Feelings

_____. *On Our Vacation.* Dutton, 1989. Summer

_____. *Our Garage Sale.* Illus. by Harlow Rockwell. Greenwillow, 1984. Homes

_____. *Our Yard Is Full of Birds.* Illus. by Lizzy Rockwell. Simon & Schuster, 1992. Birds

_____. *Planes.* Illus. by Harlow Rockwell. Dutton, 1985. Trains and Planes

_____. *Trains.* Dutton, 1988. Trains and Planes

_____. *Willie Can Count.* Arcade, 1989. Counting

Rockwell, Anne F., and Harlow Rockwell. *First Snowfall.* Simon & Schuster, 1987. Winter

_____. *Happy Birthday to Me.* Simon & Schuster, 1981. Birthdays

_____. *How My Garden Grew.* Simon & Schuster, 1982. Gardens

————. *I Play in My Room.* Simon & Schuster, 1981. Playing

————. *Nice and Clean.* Macmillan, 1984. Bath Time

Rockwell, Harlow. *My Dentist.* Greenwillow, 1975. Growing Up Safe

Roffey, Maureen. *Bathtime.* Simon & Schuster, 1990. Bath Time

————. *Look, There's My Hat!* Putnam, 1985. Hats

Rose, Dorothy. *Follow Me.* Simon & Schuster, 1994. (Board book) Parades

————. *Peek A Boo.* Simon & Schuster, 1994. (Board book) Peek

————. *What Do Lambs Say?* Simon & Schuster, 1994. (Board book) Farms

————. *Where's Your Nose?* Simon & Schuster, 1994. (Board book) My Body

Rosen, Michael. *We're Going on a Bear Hunt.* Illus. by Helen Oxenbury. Simon & Schuster, 1989. Bears

Ross, Anna. *Rock-a-Bye Babies.* Illus. by Carol Nicklaus. Random, 1994. Babies

————. *Say the Magic Word, Please.* Illus. by Norman Gorbaty. Random, 1990. Growing Up Safe

————. *Where, Oh, Where?* Random, 1994. (Board book) Peek

Rouss, Sylvia A. *Sammy Spider's First Hanukkah.* Illus. by Katherine Kahn. Kar-Ben, 1993. December

————. *Sammy Spider's First Passover.* Illus. by Katherine Kahn. Kar-Ben, 1995. Spring

Roy, Ronald. *Whose Hat Is That?* Photos by Rosmarie Hausherr. Houghton, 1990. Hats

Ruane, Joanna. *Boats, Boats, Boats.* Childrens, 1990. Boats

Rydell, Katy. *Wind Says Good Night.* Houghton, 1994. Wind

Ryder, Joanne. *My Father's Hands.* Illus. by Mark Graham. Morrow, 1994. Gardens

Sage, Angie. *In the House.* Random, 1995. Colors

Santoro, Christopher. *Lift a Rock: Find a Bug.* Random, 1993. (Board book) Bugs and Caterpillars

————. *Open the Barn Door: Find a Cow.* Random, 1993. (Board book) Farms

Sardegna, Jill. *K Is for Kiss Goodnight: A Bedtime Alphabet.* Illus. by Michael Hayes. Doubleday, 1994. Bedtime

Saul, Carol P. *Peter's Song.* Illus. by Diane de Groat. Simon & Schuster, 1992. Frogs and Turtles

Schneider, Rex. *The Wide-Mouthed Frog.* Stemmer, 1980. Frogs and Turtles

Schweninger, Ann. *Valentine Friends.* Puffin, 1990. Love

Scott, Ann Herbert. *On Mother's Lap.* Illus. by Glo Coalson. Houghton, 1992. Love

————. *One Good Horse: A Cowpuncher's Counting Book.* Greenwillow, 1990. Counting

Sendak, Maurice. *Where the Wild Things Are.* HarperCollins, 1988. Autumn

Serfozo, Mary. *Who Said Red?* Illus. by Keiko Narahashi. Simon & Schuster, 1989. Colors

Seuss, Dr. *Mr. Brown Can Moo! Can You? A Book of Wonderful Sounds.* Random, 1996. (Board book) Sounds

Shannon, George. *April Showers.* Illus. by Jose Aruego and Ariane Dewey. Greenwillow, 1995. Frogs and Turtles

————. *Dance Away.* Illus. by Jose Aruego and Ariane Dewey. Greenwillow, 1982. Dancing

————. *The Surprise!* Illus. by Jose Aruego and Ariane Dewey. Greenwillow, 1983. Peek

Shaw, Charles. *It Looked Like Spilt Milk.* Harper & Row, 1947. Also in board book format: HarperCollins, 1993. Rain

Shaw, Nancy. *Sheep Take a Hike.* Houghton, 1994. Walking

Showers, Paul. *Listening Walk.* HarperCollins, 1991. Sounds

Simon, Norma. *Fire Fighters.* Simon & Schuster, 1995. Firefighters

————. *What Do I Do?* (English and Spanish.) Illus. by Joe Lasker. Albert Whitman, 1969. Helping

Slater, Teddy. *All Aboard Fire Trucks.* Putnam, 1991. (Board book) Firefighters

————. *The Bunny Hop.* Illus. by Larry Difiori. Scholastic, 1992. Rabbits

Slier, Debby. *Brothers and Sisters.* Checkerboard, 1989. (Board book) Family

Slobodkina, Esphyr. *Caps for Sale.* HarperCollins, 1947. Also in Spanish: *Se Venden Gorras: La Historia de un Vendedor Ambulante, Unos Monos y Sus Travesuras.* Harper Arco Iris, 1995; and in big book format, Scholastic, 1989. Hats

————. *The Wonderful Feast.* Greenwillow, 1993. Farms

Smalls, Irene. *Jonathan and His Mommy.* Illus. by Michael Hayes. Little, Brown, 1992. Family

Smith, Mavis. *"Fred? Is That You?"* Little, Brown, 1992. (Lift-the-flap book) Peek

Smollin, Michael. *Ernie's Bath Book.* Random, 1982. Bath Time

Spier, Peter. *Crash! Bang! Boom!* Doubleday, 1990. Parades

————. *Firehouse.* Doubleday, 1981. Firefighters

_____. *Little Rabbits.* Doubleday, 1984. (Board book) Rabbits

_____. *Peter Spier's Circus.* Doubleday, 1992. Circus

Stott, Dorothy. *Up, Up in a Plane.* Grosset, 1995. (Board book) Trains and Planes

Sturges, Philemon. *Ten Flashing Fireflies.* Illus. by Anna Vojtech. North-South, 1995. Bugs and Caterpillars

_____. *What's That Sound, Woolly Bear?* Illus. by Joan Paley. Little, Brown, 1996. Bugs and Caterpillars

Suba, Suzanne. *The Monkeys and the Pedlar.* Viking, 1970. Monkeys

Szekeres, Cyndy. *Hugs.* Western, 1990. (Board book) Love

_____. *Thumpity Thump Gets Dressed.* Western, 1991. Getting Dressed

Tafuri, Nancy. *Early Morning in the Barn.* Greenwillow, 1983. Morning

_____. *In a Red House.* Greenwillow, 1987. (Board book) Homes

_____. *My Friends.* Greenwillow, 1987. (Board book) Friends

_____. *One Wet Jacket.* Greenwillow, 1988. (Board book) Counting

_____. *Rabbit's Morning.* Greenwillow, 1985. Morning

_____. *This Is the Farmer.* Greenwillow, 1994. Farms

_____. *Who's Counting?* Greenwillow, 1986. Dogs

Tagel, Peggy. *Pop-Up Baby Bunny.* Putnam, 1991. Rabbits

_____. *Pop-Up Little Duck.* Putnam, 1991. Birds

Taylor, Livingston, and Maggie Taylor. *Pajamas.* Illus. by Tim Bowers. Harcourt, 1995. Bedtime

Tolstoi, Aleksei Nikolaevich. *The Great Big Enormous Turnip.* Illus. by Helen Oxenbury. Watts, 1968. Gardens

Trapani, Iza. *The Itsy-Bitsy Spider.* Whispering Coyote, 1993. Bugs and Caterpillars

_____. *Twinkle, Twinkle Little Star.* Whispering Coyote, 1994. Bedtime

Tresselt, Alvin. *The Mitten.* Illus. by Yaroslava. Lothrop, 1964. Winter

Tryon, Leslie. *One Gaping Wide-Mouthed Hopping Frog.* Simon & Schuster, 1993. Frogs and Turtles

Tucker, Sian. *At Home.* Simon & Schuster, 1991. (Board book) Homes

_____. *Little Boat.* Simon & Schuster, 1993. (Board book) Boats

_____. *Rat a Tat Tat.* Simon & Schuster, 1994. Parades

Udry, Janice. *A Tree Is Nice.* Illus. by Marc Simont. HarperCollins, 1957. Picnics

VanFleet, Matthew. *Fuzzy Yellow Duckling: Fold-Out Fun with Textures.* Dial, 1995. (Texture book) Colors

_____. *One Yellow Lion: Fold-Out Fun with Numbers.* Dial, 1992. Counting

Van Laan, Nancy. *So Say the Little Monkeys.* Illus. by G. Brian Karas. Knopf, 1997. Monkeys

_____. *This Is the Hat.* Illus. by Holly Meade. Little, Brown, 1992. Hats

_____. *The Tiny, Tiny Boy and the Big, Big Cow.* Illus. by Marjorie Priceman. Knopf, 1993. Sizes and Shapes

Vaughan, Marcia. *The Dancing Dragon.* Illus. by Stanley Wong Hoo Foon. Mondo, 1996. Parades

Wabbes, Marie. *It's Snowing, Little Rabbit.* Little, Brown, 1987. Winter

Waddell, Martin. *Happy Hedgehog Band.* Illus. by Jill Barton. Candlewick, 1991. Parades

_____. *Let's Go Home, Little Bear.* Illus. by Barbara Firth. Candlewick, 1993. Walking

_____. *Little Mo.* Illus. by Jill Barton. Candlewick, 1992. Growing Up Safe

_____. *You and Me, Little Bear.* Illus. by Barbara Firth. Candlewick, 1996. Helping

Walsh, Ellen. *Hop Jump.* Harcourt, 1993. Dancing

_____. *Mouse Paint.* Harcourt, 1989. Also in big book format, Harcourt, 1989. Colors

Walter, Virginia. *"Hi, Pizza Man!"* Illus. by Ponder Goembel. Orchard, 1995. Sounds

Ward, Leila. *I Am Eyes: Ni Macho.* Illus. by Nonny Hogrogian. Scholastic, 1978. Morning

Watanabe, Shigeo. *How Do I Put It On?* Illus. by Yasuo Ohtomo. Putnam, 1979. Getting Dressed

_____. *I Can Take a Walk!* Illus. by Yasuo Ohtomo. Putnam, 1988. Walking

_____. *What a Good Lunch!* Illus. by Yasuo Ohtomo. Philomel, 1991. Mealtimes

Weiss, Nicki. *Sun, Sand, Sea, Sail.* Greenwillow, 1989. Summer

_____. *Where Does the Brown Bear Go?* Greenwillow, 1989. Bedtime

Welber, Robert. *Winter Picnic.* Illus. by Deborah K. Ray. Pantheon, 1973. Picnics

Wellington, Monica. *Baby in a Buggy.* Dutton, 1995. Babies

_____. *Season of the Swans.* Dutton, 1990. Birds

Wells, Rosemary. *Don't Spill It Again, James.* Dial, 1990. Trains and Planes

———. *Max's Bath.* Dial, 1985. (Board book) Bath Time

———. *Max's Birthday.* Dial, 1985. (Board book) Birthdays

———. *Max's Breakfast.* Dial, 1985. (Board book) Mealtimes

———. *Max's Chocolate Chicken.* Dial, 1989. Spring

———. *Max's Christmas.* Dial, 1986. Also in Spanish: *La Navidad de Max.* Santillana, 1994. December

———. *Max's Dragon Shirt.* Dial, 1991. Getting Dressed

———. *Max's Toys: A Counting Book.* Dial, 1979. Counting

———. *Noisy Nora.* Dial, 1973. Also in Spanish: *Julieta Está Quieta,* Santillana, 1995. Sounds

———. *Shy Charles.* Dial, 1988. Feelings

Wheeler, Cindy. *Marmalade's Yellow Leaf.* Knopf, 1982. Autumn

Williams, Garth. *The Chicken Book.* Dell, 1992. Birds

Williams, Sue. *I Went Walking.* Illus. by Julie Vivas. Harcourt, 1990. Also in Spanish: *Salí de Paseo.* Trans. by Alma F. Ada. Voyager, 1995. Walking

Williams, Vera. *"More, More, More," Said the Baby.* Greenwillow, 1990. Love

Winter, Susan. *A Baby Just Like Me.* Dorling Kindersley, 1994. Babies

Winton, Ian. *My First Book of Shapes and Colors.* Simon & Schuster, 1995. Sizes and Shapes

Wolde, Gunilla. *This Is Betsy.* Random, 1990. Feelings

Wolff, Ferida. *On Halloween Night.* Illus. by Dolores Avendano. Tambourine, 1994. Autumn

Wood, Audrey. *Napping House.* Illus. by Don Wood. Harcourt, 1984. Also in Spanish: *La Casa Adormecida.* Trans. by Alma F. Ada and F. Isabel Campoy. Voyager, 1995; and in big book format, Harcourt, 1984. Bedtime

Wood, Jacki. *Animal Parade.* Simon & Schuster, 1993. Parades

———. *Bumper to Bumper: A Traffic Jam.* Simon & Schuster, 1996. Trucks, Cars, and Buses

———. *Fiddle-I-Fee: A Noisy Nursery Rhyme.* Simon & Schuster, 1994. Sounds

Worth, Bonnie. *I Can Dress Myself.* Illus. by Tom Cooke. Western, 1993. Getting Dressed

———. *I Can Share.* Illus. by Tom Cooke. Western, 1993. (Board book) Friends

Wyndham, Robert. *Chinese Mother Goose Rhymes.* Illus. by Ed Young. Putnam, 1989. Read to Me

Yashima, Taro. *Umbrella.* Viking, 1958. Rain

Yee, Patrick. *Baby Bear.* Viking, 1994. (Board book) Bears

———. *Baby Monkey.* Viking, 1994. (Board book) Monkeys

———. *Let's Eat.* Viking, 1995. Mealtimes

———. *Playtime with Rosie Rabbit.* Simon & Schuster, 1996. (Lift-the-flap book) Rabbits

———. *Winter Rabbit.* Viking, 1994. Winter

Yektai, Niki. *Bears in Pairs.* Illus. by Diane de Groat. Simon & Schuster, 1987. Bears

Young, Ruth, and Mitchell Rose. *Spider Magic.* Schneider Educational, 1990. (Board book and fingerpuppet) Bugs and Caterpillars

———. *Turtle Magic.* Schneider Educational, 1990. (Board book and fingerpuppet) Frogs and Turtles

Younger, Jesse. *The Fire Engine Book.* Illus. by Aurelius Battaglia. Western, 1982. Firefighters

Zelinsky, Paul. *Wheels of the Bus, with Pictures that Move.* Dutton, 1990. Trucks, Cars, and Buses

Ziefert, Harriet. *Going on a Lion Hunt.* Illus. by Mavis Smith. Puffin, 1989. (Lift-the-flap book) Walking

———. *Happy Birthday, Little Bear.* Illus. by Susan Baum. Viking, 1995. Birthday

———. *Happy Easter, Grandma!* Illus. by Sidney Levitt. Harper, 1988. Spring

———. *Harry Goes to Fun Land.* Illus. by Mavis Smith. Puffin, 1994. Circus

———. *Let's Get Dressed!* Illus. by Lisa Campbell Ernst. Viking, 1988. Getting Dressed

———. *Nicky Upstairs and Down.* Illus. by Richard Brown. Puffin, 1987. Homes

———. *Nicky's Picnic.* Illus. by Richard Brown. Puffin, 1986. Picnics

———. *Parade.* Illus. by Saul Mandel. Bantam, 1990. Parades

———. *What Is Hannukah? A Lift-the-Flap Book.* Illus. by Rick Brown. HarperCollins, 1994. December

———. *What Is Thanksgiving? A Lift-the-Flap Book.* Illus. by Claire Schumacher. HarperCollins, 1992. Mealtimes

———. *What Is Valentine's Day? A Lift-the-Flap Book.* Illus. by Claire Schumacher. HarperCollins, 1993. Love

Zion, Gene. *Harry the Dirty Dog.* Illus. by Margaret Graham. Harper & Row, 1956. Also in Spanish: *Harry, el Perrito Sucio.* Trans. by Maria Fiol. Harper Arco Iris, 1996. Bath Time

Zolotow, Charlotte. *Mr. Rabbit and the Lovely Present.* Illus. by Maurice Sendak. Harper, 1977. Rabbits

———. *Not a Little Monkey.* Illus. by Michele Chessare. Harper, 1989. Monkeys

———. *When the Wind Stops.* HarperCollins, 1995. Wind

Discography

Following are sources for tunes used in songs. Wherever possible, sources of multiple applicable tunes have been cited.

"A'Hunting We Will Go." *Disney's Children's Favorites, Volume III.* Burbank, Calif.: The Walt Disney Company, 1986. Phonograph disc.

"A-Tisket, A-Tasket." Sharon, Lois, and Bram. *Stay Tuned.* Toronto, Ont.: Elephant Records, 1987. Audio cassette and lyrics.

"Baby Bumblebee." *Disney's Children's Favorite Silly Songs.* Burbank, Calif.: The Walt Disney Company, 1988. Audio cassette with lyrics.

"By the Beautiful Sea." *Coney Island Baby.* Roswell, Ga.: Intersound, 1991. Compact disc.

"Bye Baby Bunting." *Mother Goose Rhymes.* Buena Vista, Calif.: Walt Disney Studios, 1990. Audio cassette.

"Did You Ever See a Lassie?" *Singing Games.* Los Angeles: Tom Thumb Records, 1982. Audio cassette and lyrics.

"Down by the Station." *Buckle Up and Sing.* Racine, Wis.: Golden, 1992. Audio cassette.

"Eency Weency (Itsy-Bitsy) Spider." *Barney's Favorites. Volume 1.* New York: SBK Records, 1993. Audio cassette.

"Farmer in the Dell." *Disney Children's Favorites 2.* Burbank, Calif.: Walt Disney Records, 1979. Compact disc.

"Frere Jacques (Are You Sleeping?)." McGrath, Bob, and Katharine Smithrim. *Songs & Games for Toddlers.* Racine, Wis.: Golden, 1990. Audio cassette.

"Good Morning." Freed, Arthur, and Nacio Herb Brown. *Singin' in the Rain: Original Soundtrack.* New York: CBS Records, 1990. Audio cassette.

"Goodnight, Ladies." *Disney's Children's Favorites, Volume III.* Burbank, Calif.: The Walt Disney Company, 1986. Phonograph disc.

"Happy Birthday to You." *Birthday Songs: Games and Fun for Your Party!* Burbank, Calif.: Walt Disney Records, 1997. Compact disc and lyrics.

"Head & Shoulders, Knees & Toes." *Birthday Songs: Games and Fun for Your Party!* Burbank, Calif.: Walt Disney Records, 1997. Compact disc and lyrics.

"How Much Is That Doggie in the Window?" Sharon, Lois, and Bram. *Stay Tuned.* Toronto, Ont.: Elephant Records, 1987. Audio cassette and lyrics.

"Hush, Little Baby." Wilbur, Sandy. *All through the Night.* New York: Caedmon, 1989. Audio cassette.

"I Know an Old Lady." *Disney Children's Favorites 2.* Burbank, Calif.: Walt Disney Records, 1979. Compact disc.

"If You're Happy and You Know It." *Birthday Songs: Games and Fun for Your Party!* Burbank, Calif.: Walt Disney Records, 1997. Compact disc and lyrics.

"I'm a Little Teapot." Bradetich, Jeff. *Hear We Go! Traditional American Children's Songs Arranged and Acoustically Prepared for the Hearing Impaired.* Evanston, Ill.: Music for All to Hear, 1990. Audio cassette and song booklet.

"Little Drummer Boy." *Disney's Christmas Favorites.* Burbank, Calif.: Walt Disney Productions, 1981. Audio cassette.

"London Bridge Is Falling Down." *Birthday Songs: Games and Fun for Your Party!* Burbank, Calif.: Walt Disney Records, 1997. Compact disc and lyrics.

"Looby Loo (Here We Go)." *Barney's Favorites. Volume 1.* New York: SBK Records, 1993. Audio cassette.

"Mary Had a Little Lamb." Bradetich, Jeff. *Hear We Go! Traditional American Children's Songs Arranged and Acoustically Prepared for the Hearing Impaired.* Evanston, Ill.: Music for All to Hear, 1990. Audio cassette and song booklet.

"Me and My Shadow." Stewart, Georgiana Liccione. *My Teddy Bear and Me: Musical Play Activities for Infants and Toddlers.* Long Branch, N.J.: Kimbo Educational, 1984. Audio cassette.

"Muffin Man (Do You Know the)." Greenberg, Josh. *Rhythm and Rhymes.* Albany, N.Y.: A Gentle Wind, 1982. Audio cassette.

"Mulberry Bush." Bradetich, Jeff. *Hear We Go! Traditional American Children's Songs Arranged and Acoustically Prepared for the Hearing Impaired.* Evanston, Ill.: Music for All to Hear, 1990. Audio cassette and song booklet.

"Old MacDonald." Bradetich, Jeff. *Hear We Go! Traditional American Children's Songs Arranged and Acoustically Prepared for the Hearing Impaired.* Evanston, Ill.: Music for All to Hear, 1990. Audio cassette and song booklet.

"Paw-Paw Patch." Sharon, Lois, and Bram. *One Elephant.* Toronto, Ont.: Elephant Records, 1978. Audio cassette.

"Peter Cottontail." Scelsa, Greg, and Steve Millang. *Holidays and Special Times.* Los Angeles: Youngheart Records, 1989. Audio cassette and compact disc with lyrics.

"Pop Goes the Weasel." Bradetich, Jeff. *Hear We Go! Traditional American Children's Songs Arranged and Acoustically Prepared for the Hearing Impaired.* Evanston, Ill.: Music for All to Hear, 1990. Audio cassette and song booklet.

"Rig-a-Jig-Jig (As I Was Walking)." McGrath, Bob, and Katharine Smithrim. *Songs & Games for Toddlers.* Racine, Wis.: Golden, 1990. Audio cassette.

"Rock-a-Bye Baby." Wilbur, Sandy. *All Through the Night.* New York: Caedmon, 1989. Audio cassette.

"Row, Row, Row Your Boat." McGrath, Bob, and Katharine Smithrim. *Songs & Games for Toddlers.* Racine, Wis.: Golden, 1990. Audio cassette.

"Sailing, Sailing." *Disney Children's Favorites 2.* Burbank, Calif.: Walt Disney Records, 1979. Compact disc.

"Six Little Ducks." *Barney's Favorites. Volume 1.* New York: SBK Records, 1993. Audio cassette.

"Skinnamarink." Sharon, Lois, and Bram. *One Elephant.* Toronto, Ont.: Elephant Records, 1978. Audio cassette.

"Skip to My Lou." *Disney Children's Favorites 2.* Burbank, Calif.: Walt Disney Records, 1979. Compact disc.

"Ten Little Indians." Bertail, Inez. *Compete Nursery Song Book.* New York: Lothrop, 1947. (Print source)

"Ten in a Bed." *Count Me In: Number Songs for Children.* New York: Jim Henson Records, 1993. Audio cassette.

"Three Blind Mice." Bradetich, Jeff. *Hear We Go! Traditional American Children's Songs Arranged and Acoustically Prepared for the Hearing Impaired.* Evanston, Ill.: Music for All to Hear, 1990. Audio cassette and song booklet.

"Twinkle, Twinkle Little Star." Bradetich, Jeff. *Hear We Go! Traditional American Children's Songs Arranged and Acoustically Prepared for the Hearing Impaired.* Evanston, Ill.: Music for All to Hear, 1990. Audio cassette and song booklet.

"We Wish You a Merry Christmas." *Disney's Christmas Favorites.* Burbank, Calif.: Walt Disney Productions, 1981. Audio cassette.

"Wheels on the Bus." Bradetich, Jeff. *Hear We Go! Traditional American Children's Songs Arranged and Acoustically Prepared for the Hearing Impaired.* Evanston, Ill.: Music for All to Hear, 1990. Audio cassette and song booklet.

"Where Has My Little Dog Gone (Where, Oh Where . . .)." *Birthday Songs: Games and Fun for Your Party!* Burbank, Calif.: Walt Disney Records, 1997. Compact disc and lyrics.

"Who's That Knocking at My Door?" Winn, Marie. *What Shall We Do and Allee Galloo! Play Songs and Activities for Young Children.* New York: Harper and Row, 1970. (Print source)

Crafts, Giveaways, and Storytime Materials Index

Fingerplays, Songs, and Rhymes Index

Parents' Ideas Index

Sign Language Words Index

Judy Nichols resides in Wichita, Kansas, where she is a free-lance story-teller, puppeteer, and library consultant. She was previously the youth services coordinator for the Wichita (Kansas) Public Library and a children's librarian at the Decatur (Illinois) Public Library and the Elkhart (Indiana) Public Library. Nichols has also worked in school and academic libraries in Georgia and Texas. She is a member of the National Storytelling Association and the Puppeteers of America.